Jimmy Van Heusen

Swinging On A Star

Jimmy Van Heusen - Swinging On A Star

by Christopher Coppula

Twin Creek Books

2603 Elm Hill Pike Suite P

Nashville, TN 37214 USA

orders@twincreekbooks.com; http://twincreekbooks.com

Disclaimer: The views and opinions contained herein are strictly those of the author and do not necessarily represent those of the publisher. The author makes no claims, promises or guarantees about the accuracy, completeness, or adequacy of the information contained in any portion of the book.

ISBN: 978-0-9845345-1-7

Cover design by Hannah Babcock

Cover Layout by Vickie Harris

Published by Twin Creek Books, Nashville, Tennessee

Printed and bound in the United States of America

Library of Congress Control Number: 2013945833

DEDICATION

For my Dad, for making me listen to Sinatra at the Sands on our first trip to Notre Dame.

For my Mom, for not forcing us to turn it off after we had listened to it for the one hundredth time.

For my Wife and Children, for understanding why I will listen to it at least one hundred more times from today.

A NOTE ON SOURCES AND ACKNOWLEDGMENTS

One of the principal reasons I undertook to write this book was due to the dearth of resources regarding the life of Jimmy Van Heusen. Beyond brief biographical sketches in reference books or the odd (and often unattributed) anecdote in celebrity biographies, there was little to guide a more in-depth investigation into the complex character that was Jimmy Van Heusen. In this regard, Brook Babcock, Van Heusen's great-nephew, executor of his estate and head of Van Heusen Music, was invaluable. Brook opened the Van Heusen archives to me, which included two very important and unseen sources of material. The first was a never completed biography of Van Heusen by journalist Robert de Roos. This work included interviews with Van Heusen, his parents, friends and colleagues – all of whom, sadly, have passed on before work on this book began. The second, and most important, an incomplete autobiography. This is quoted liberally throughout the book as it provides the best example of Van Heusen in his own voice. The autobiography was Van Heusen uncensored on topics from Tin Pan Alley, airplanes, bathtub gin recipes and, of course, Frank Sinatra. Both the autobiography and de Roos' biography served as road maps for my work.

I wrote this book concurrently with the production of a documentary on the life of Van Heusen by the talented and generous Jim Burns. Jim had occasion to interview numerous celebrities for his documentary and was willing to share footage of those interviews with me.

Finally, I would be remiss in failing to thank the many people who took time from their busy lives to chat with me or respond to my emails. When I reached out to those people who had a personal connection to Van Heusen, I had no entree. I am a first time author and I have no connections in the music or entertainment industries. I simply introduced myself as the authorized biographer of Jimmy Van Heusen and inquired if they wanted to speak with me about the book I was writing. It is testimony to the high regard in which Van Heusen was held that so many notable people opened up to a complete unknown. And so, I offer my thanks to the following people: Brook Babcock, Don Babcock, Kit Babcock, Jim Burns, Carole Bayer Sager, Rise Stevens, Rosemary Riddle, Will Friedwald, Toni Tenille, Steve Lawrence, Kitty Kelley, Joan Collins, Pat

Boone, Rory Burke, Syracuse Department of Music, Phil Furia, Thomas Hampson, Nikki Hornsby, Stephanie DeLange, Earl Wentz, Bobbie Hampson, Peter Marshall, Ken Barnes.

Of the many discussions, there were two constants: 1) Jimmy Van Heusen was a true gentleman and genius; 2) The world needs to hear his story. I beg your indulgences as I bring to you this story from a first-time author who undertook this journey as a labor of love and a tribute to a musician whose story has gone untold for too long.

TABLE OF CONTENTS

ONE

Edward Chester Babcock at age 15

Photo Courtesy of Babcock Family Archives

Just My Luck

"Cock sounds like a dirty word, and you just can't keep saying it on the air," said Charles Kaleletsky, one of two operating heads of WSYR radio station in Syracuse, New York.

"But," I protested meekly, "it's part of my name, and it's no worse than Hancock, Glasscock, or just plain Cocke whether it's spelled with an 'E' at the end or not. Babcock is an old English name and the original version was Badcock, which in Old English meant fighting cock, that is, rooster ... it's on the family coat of arms."

"I don't care about what your name was or is. Every time you say that a program's announcer has been Edward Bab*cock*, I cringe, my wife cringes, and it sounds salacious. Either say something else or get out."

The year was 1928, and I was fifteen years of age, and my vocal chords, from a boy soprano

14

timbre, were now emitting a deep, round, bass baritone sound. I was working as an announcer, staff piano player, performing artist, record spinner, disc-jockey, janitor, news announcer and everything else they asked me to do for the glorious salary of $15.00 per week. Guzzling bathtub gin in between records, the alcoholic haze was cleared somewhat by the sudden realization that I was losing my job. Instant action was called for and I consulted a boyhood chum, Ralph Harris (Lena Horne's one time manager) who at the moment was looking out the window of the 11th floor of the Hotel Syracuse where the tiny radio station had padded cells for studios. His gaze fell on an ad for Van Heusen collars and absentmindedly repeated the words. I seized the solution and said, "Well, what's my first name?" After he mentioned that he had a favorite cousin named James, I appropriated that handle. From that moment on, Edward Chester Babcock was Jimmy Van Heusen.   — Robert de Roos

These were the first four paragraphs of the biography on Jimmy Van Heusen that was never completed. It is telling that Van Heusen chose to begin his life story with what is, essentially, his "second birth": when Edward Chester Babcock of Syracuse, New York, became James Van Heusen, court composer to the twin titans of American popular music, Bing Crosby and Frank Sinatra. By beginning his life story in such a manner (and devoting only three pages of his biography to his "pre-Van Heusen" days), Van Heusen appears to be subconsciously presupposing an unfortunate public perception — namely, that interest in his story (and, to a certain extent, his value) was commensurate with his affiliation with Crosby and Sinatra.

Far more than a Crosby/Rat Pack satellite, Van Heusen was a larger-than-life figure in his own right, one who succeeded in most of his endeavors. Through his hobbies, he developed into an accomplished aviator, military test pilot, horse breeder and classical music aficionado. He lived a lavish Hollywood lifestyle and deservedly so; his stature as a composer of popular music is beyond dispute. He is tied as the composer winning the most Academy Awards for Best Original Song[1] ("Swinging on a Star," "All the Way," "High Hopes," "Call Me Irresponsible"). He is the only composer to be honored with the Emmy Award for Best Music for an

---

[1] Jimmy Van Heusen is tied with Alan Menken for the number of Academy Awards for Best Original song, each having won four at the time of publication of this book.

original song[2] ("Love and Marriage"). His works formed the foundation of the canon of recordings made by Bing Crosby and Frank Sinatra. A brief listing reads like a greatest hits list of the 20th century; in addition to those mention above, there is "Moonlight Becomes You," "Here's That Rainy Day," "Come Fly with Me," and "But Beautiful," to name a few.

To be sure, the average listener of popular music is sure to know the melodies crafted by Jimmy Van Heusen. However, it is a stretch to claim that the average listener of popular music would know that Jimmy Van Heusen, in fact, composed those same melodies. There are no "Jimmy Van Heusen tunes" the way there are "Cole Porter tunes" or "George Gershwin tunes" or "Rodgers and Hammerstein tunes." "Climb Ev'ry Mountain" is the finale of *The Sound of Music* and is recognized as one of Rodgers and Hammerstein's greatest songs. However, Jimmy Van Heusen's "Come Fly with Me" is almost universally regarded as a "Sinatra tune."

Not that this apparent lack of recognition appeared to matter to Van Heusen. By all accounts, he was satisfied with his enviable position as the chosen tunesmith for Crosby and

---

[2]At the time of publication of this book

Sinatra. He understood, or accepted, that these men needed to be in the spotlight – and that he could do better than most by letting them take up most of it. Among Van Heusen's favorite stories is a battle of wits with Humphrey Bogart at a Sinatra party. As Van Heusen entertained at the piano, Bogart called, "Chester, you're nothing but a goddamned ass kisser, you know that? A stooge for the dago [Sinatra]. And fuck you."

Without missing a beat, Van Heusen, in mid-performance, responded, "Yeah. You're right you red-necked prick. And I'm the highest paid stooge in history. Last year, I made $300,000 ass kissing and that was only part time. That's more than you made working full time as a half-assed actor."

While at first blush, this might appear to be braggadocio, it, instead, reflects Van Heusen's acute awareness of the "Hollywood game": The celebrity elite paid well for a great talent who could supply their material without competing for their publicity. As a result, Van Heusen was free to share only in those parts of "the life" that interested him. This freedom had intangible benefits as well. Throughout his entire career, he remained firmly grounded and exuded uncommon generosity and self-awareness, remaining above the fray wrought by the gargantuan egos and unchecked vanities inhabiting and, in many cases, running the movie capital of the world. As Dorothy Manners, famed Hollywood columnist and *de facto* Hollywood historian wrote:

> Jim is something special because he's kept his feet on the ground. He has a peculiar nature for a man of rare talent. A lot of songwriters are very temperamental – you'd think they invented the word. They're stars in their own right and once you get to be a star you have your own little entourage sitting around listening to pearls of wisdom drop from your lips. Jim's never been that way. He's always made himself agreeable and pleasant to be with. Men in Jim's profession do not often like each other but come to think of it, I've never heard of anyone who didn't like Jim and most of them loved him.

While reminiscences such as these are amusing, they also are distracting. Read enough of them and you can come away with the idea that Van Heusen's success was the result of getting the right people to like him. In fact, there was one reason that "the right people" wanted him in their circle: his talent. Crosby's and Sinatra's position in the popular music world cannot be overestimated. Their incredible financial success emanated from their artistic accomplishments. Known across the world as the supreme interpreters of American popular song, their musicianship is legendary and was acknowledged by their musical contemporaries. Composers campaigned for Sinatra and Crosby to record their music, not only because they were stars but because their voices would give life and nuance to their creations unlike any other. As such, Crosby and Sinatra could have had their pick of Cole Porter, Harold Arlen, Irving Berlin, Richard Rodgers, Burton Lane or any of the major tunesmiths of the golden age of American popular music. They chose Jimmy Van Heusen. The import of this was not lost on Van Heusen, but he recalled it with his characteristic understatement, "The two singers I've always liked and most admired are Bing Crosby and Frank Sinatra, and I've spent a great deal of my life with those two guys. That's a bit of luck."

TWO

Edward Chester Babcock and Fritz April 30, 1925
His close friends and relatives would call him "Chet" or "Chester"

Courtesy of Babcock Family Photo Archives

Our Town

Syracuse, New York, is a mid-sized city in what is colloquially known as "upstate New York." Like the condescending moniker "flyover country" given to the vast swath of land from the western suburbs of Boston to the inland California, "Upstate New York" is a geographical denotation imposed on the area by those not living in it. It is somehow fitting that Van Heusen would be born in a major city in a state whose largest urban center is New York City — its charms and significance overwhelmed by the supernova 250 miles to the southeast. Yet, like Van Heusen, Syracusans bear no ill will toward their flashy neighbor. They are rightly proud of their city's heritage and history, which also includes mandated name changes and a unique bond with a famous Sicilian.

Nestled in the northeast corner of the picturesque Finger Lakes region of New York, Syracuse was first discovered by French missionaries in the 1600's. The Jesuit missionaries were guests of the original inhabitants of the area — the Onondaga

Nation, a member of the powerful Iroquois Confederacy —
and established a settlement known as "Saint Marie" among the
Iroquois. Perhaps with a keener sense of the deluge to come
over the Atlantic, the Mohawk Nation decided to take the land
back. Out of respect for their fellow confederacy members, the
Mohawk Nation suggested to the Onondaga that they choose
their friends a bit more carefully, lest they suffer the same fate
their Gallic guests were about to befall. The French
missionaries learned of the Mohawk Nation's plans and
departed the Syracuse region under cover of night. Their stay
was just under two years.

Following the conclusion of the Revolutionary War,
settlers moved north to the area to engage in trade with the
Onondaga Nation. During this time, salt was discovered in the
swamps surrounding Syracuse, thereby giving rise to the city's
first designation, "Salt City." Indeed, the original settlement
endured a frenzied identity crisis until finally settling on its
modern name: Salt Point (1780), Webster's Landing (1786),
Bogardus Corners (1796), Milan (1809), South Salina (1812),
Cossits' Corners (1814), and Corinth (1817). As a Corinth,
New York, already existed in 1817, the United States Postal
Service refused to permit a second adoption of the Greek city's

name in the state. A more suitable appellation was to be found approximately 400 miles to the west of Corinth. Syracuse, Sicily, was an important provider of salt to the Greco-Roman world and was founded, coincidentally, by the Corinthians. In 1825, the City of Syracuse was formally incorporated.

Syracuse was an important crossroads throughout its history due to the confluence of railroads in its town center, and, most significantly, the Erie Canal. The canal dramatically increased the sale of salt, and with it, the size of the city itself. By facilitating transport of the mineral, the canal enabled New York farms to switch from wheat to more lucrative pork. (To the everlasting chagrin of diet-conscious carnivores, pork farming requires copious amounts of salt to cure.) Rising pork sales heightened the demand for salt, causing an increase in production that eventually led to the wholesale mechanization of the salt production process. The new industry attracted many new families, and Syracuse grew to be the 12th largest city in the United States by 1850.

The end of the Civil War saw the manufacturing industry overtake salt production as the economic lifeblood of Syracuse. From the mid-1850 to the early 1900's, the modern identity of the city was being shaped. During that time, the

Franklin Automobile Company, Century Steam Car Company and Craftsman Workshops all set up shop and prospered. Most importantly, in 1870, Syracuse University was founded as a Methodist-Episcopal institution. Despite the many economic achievements of the region, Syracuse University would remain the face of "Upstate New York" to the remainder of the nation through today. The growth of industry and the advancements in transportation formed the melting pot of ethnicities that would shape Syracuse in the early 20th century. Poles, Italians, Jews, Greeks, English, Irish, Scott would all mingle, meet and intermarry to create the multicultural milieu in which Jimmy Van Heusen would spend his formative years.

Indeed, the Syracuse of the early 20th century was itself a microcosm of its more famous cousin to the south. Twenty-four separate trolley lines ran through Syracuse and its surrounding areas by 1928. The New York Central Railroad made Syracuse a "hub," docking its engines and cars at the posh New York Central Railroad Station in the city center between West Fayette and West Washington Street (later renamed "Railroad Street"). The Erie Canal, still the most important commercial thoroughfare in the state, cut through the middle of the city at Clinton Square. The square was lined with shops frequented by those people who gathered to watch the huge vessels dock and make their way north and south with commerce.

Knowing the company that Van Heusen kept in his later years, it seemed inevitable that he would be drawn to the flashy downtown center of Syracuse. The main artery here was South Salina Street. It boasted many of the landmarks dotting the Syracuse skyline of the 1900's. The McCarthy Building at the northeast corner of Salina and Fayette Streets and the Dey Brothers Building dominated the boulevard. Travelling southward, one would encounter the Onondaga County Savings Bank and the Kirk Fireproof Building. Then, at the 500 block of South Salina Street, the Chimes Building featured a wonderful carillon on its top floor.

The burgeoning city also provided its denizens with opportunities to purchase the newest wares. Stuyler's Candy Store, Park-Brannock Shoe Store and Shanahan's Women Clothing occupied the 300 block of South Salina Street. As a further testament to the status of this new metropolis, Syracuse even was home to a "chain restaurant" – Schrafft's. Offering an illuminating portrait of the restaurant, and of the era in general, the *New York Times* Magazine wrote, "'Schrafft's was ...

an institution of middle-class comfort.'" Its first "store" (as even the restaurants were called), offering candy and confections, opened in 1898 on Broadway in New York City, thanks to Frank G. Shattuck, who had been the top candy salesman for W.F. Schrafft & Sons. It lost money until his sister Jane was recruited from Syracuse to create a brief menu. "It was a much more genteel time then," his great-grandson Frank M. Shattuck said. "Everyone wore hats and hand-made suits. And if you were a lady, it was safe to sit at the soda fountain and drink gin from a teacup."

The downtown area was the cultural and entertainment center of the city. Among others, the Empire Theatre, the Strand Theatre and B.F. Keith's Vaudeville Theater lined Salina Street. Serving as the anchor of the entertainment district, the magnificent Hotel Syracuse hosted dignitaries from the business, political and entertainment worlds. Guests were treated to lunch on the Persian Terrace or cocktails in the splendid Rainbow Room. From its commanding height, one could survey the entire landscape of the bustling metropolis below. More important to our story, the roof of the Hotel Syracuse served as the antenna base for the second radio station to grace the Syracuse airwaves – WSYR. It was in the

Hotel Syracuse that the radio station housed its studios and quite likely where Jimmy Van Heusen was told Chester Babcock must go the way of all flesh. Alas, whether he contemplated his fate over gin at the Rainbow Room is a story lost to history.

Chester Edward Babcock was born on January 26, 1913, in Syracuse, New York, the second son of Arthur Edward Babcock and Ida Mae Williams. Arthur and Ida Mae were not native Syracusans. They each traced their lineage through Camden Village, New York — a small hamlet some 35 miles to the northwest of Syracuse. The town is quintessentially American with a mixture of light industry and agriculture. It could easily have served as the inspiration for Thornton Wilder's *Our Town*, and one wonders if Van Heusen was not inspired by his own history when composing his fine score for the television adaptation of the play. (To be sure, it was that production, not the Fox network sitcom, "Married with Children," wherein the immortal "Love and Marriage" was introduced.) Sammy Cahn's little-known lyric to the eponymously named title tune of "Our Town" provides an apt, if not slightly stereotypical travelogue of early 20th century life in the hamlet of Camden Village, which, in 1999, celebrated its second traffic light:

> We're mostly lower middle class
>> With a few professional men,
> We're mostly all quite literate,
>> Ten percent can't handle a pen.

> The men all vote at twenty-one
>> And the women vote indirect.
> We're mostly Protestants, plus some Catholics
>> The rest are all suspect!

Ida Mae Williams and Arthur Babcock were certainly not suspect. They were both devout Methodists and came from upright stock. Ida Mae's family lived in town and owned a grocery and bakery. Her ancestors were certainly well represented in Central New York. A family memorandum indicates that Ida Mae was descended from a line of Williamses which was, in turn, descended from a Vander Walker family and a line of Fosters. This gave rise to the family legend that Ida Mae (and, by extension, Van Heusen) was a distant relative of Stephen Foster — the father of American popular song. It might be impossible to verify, but there are certainly less shocking coincidences than Jimmy Van Heusen being the latter-day reincarnation of Stephen Foster.

Arthur's family lived in what he would later term "the sticks" outside of Camden Village where they owned a farm and ran a sawmill. The Babcocks' American lineage was at least as long as -- if not longer than -- that of Ida Mae's family. A Babcock genealogy records James Babcock (CQ) of Essex, England, settling in Rhode Island in 1642, and Arthur was the ninth generation of American Babcocks. Although Arthur's ancestry could not boast a musical pedigree on par with Stephen Foster, he certainly gave Van Heusen many of the personable traits that endeared him to Tin Pan Alley and Hollywood stars and producers — not to mention the business acumen to recognize good opportunities and the drive to seize them.

Ida Mae and Arthur met in the sixth grade of the local Camden public school, but it is likely they knew each other from membership in the Camden United Methodist Church where Arthur sang in the choir and Ida Mae played the organ. Neither Arthur nor Ida Mae graduated from high school. After the death of her brother's wife's, Ida Mae needed to leave school to help raise his child. Arthur left high school only to continue his education at the Albany Business College, perhaps believing that he could better serve his father's successful sawmill industry with those skills than those gleaned from the stuffy Camden Village schoolrooms. This rejection, subconscious or not, of the theoretical in favor of the practical, was a trait passed on to his son, who, never having received formal musical training, found himself at the top of the songwriting profession, having honed his skills in the parlors of Tin Pan Alley rather than the classrooms of Julliard or Curtis.

Arthur put his education to good use, earning a management-level position at the F.H. Conant & Sons chair factory, one of the largest businesses in Camden. He also proved himself to be quite the hale fellow well met, being elected Camden Village's Clerk in what local papers described as "a hot election." A successful businessman and well-respected citizen, Arthur wed Ida Mae Williams on June 10, 1907, in Syracuse at the First Methodist Church. It is not known why they did not wed in the local Camden church to which they both belonged. It can only be surmised that, even at that time, the Babcocks had their eyes on the larger city to the southwest. In particular, Seth Babcock, Arthur's father, might have seen the larger markets and opportunities provided by Syracuse as being particularly tempting and suited to his entrepreneurial spirit. The sawmill owned by Seth was very successful. It supplied most of the lumber used for the packing cases required by the numerous canning factories that sprang up in the Camden area in the early 20th century. So successful was Seth, he was able to loan $1,000 to a family member in 1890 (roughly $24,000.00 in 2009 value).

When Arthur and Ida Mae's first son, Wilbur, was born on April 11, 1908, any doubts about leaving for Syracuse vanished, as Arthur, Ida Mae, and young Wilbur joined Arthur's parents in a single family home at 417 Roberts Avenue in the Near Westside neighborhood of Syracuse in early 1909. Arthur went into business with his father, purchasing and building homes for the steadily growing population of Syracuse. No doubt most of the lumber for these new homes came from Seth's Camden saw mill — building homes for people proving more lucrative than building homes for cans. Arthur's business was successful. Seth and he built homes throughout the Syracuse area, and would always include a home for his family in the new housing developments. This would give the family a constant itinerant feel, but would provide steady income. Arthur would frequently take second mortgages on the homes he built, as well, staking his claim on the first true housing boom of the 20th century.

All of this meant that the home into which Chester was born was quite comfortable — not wealthy, but never lacking. In that home, there were two pillars: Methodism and music. Arthur Babcock recalled, "We are all fond of music. All of us. At that time, I played the cornet and she [Ida Mae] played the piano. We had a piano and we'd sing." But the cornerstone of the family life was the Methodist faith. Since their days at Camden Village, Arthur and Ida Mae always belonged to and participated in their local church. Ida Mae would play the organ, and Arthur would sing in the choir. It was no different in Syracuse, where Seth would regularly preach at the Syracuse Rescue Mission. Ida Mae and Arthur — with Wilbur and Chester in tow — frequented the Belleview Methodist Church every Sunday. Following services, the Babcocks would gather around the radio in the parlor and listen to several sermons, as well. If Chester did not ultimately end up a devout Methodist, it was surely through no lack of encouragement.

The Babcock home was a model of Methodist restraint. There was no card playing, no dancing, and of course, no drinking. Knowing what we know about Chester's later years, one might think that these years were horrible, stifling times, rife with conflict with his parents. Not so. Even at that young age, Chester was able to function without the hint of strife. As he later wrote:

> We were a happy family – there was always love and affection. The only unhappiness I remember, and that was nothing, was when [my brother] Wilbur and I would fight. I can't remember my Dad ever hitting me except once when he caught me stealing. And that was so minor I've forgotten what it was all about. He didn't hit me very hard.

Ida Mae introduced Chester to the piano at either the age six or seven. His talent was readily evident, but he was disinclined toward formal education and practice for him was drudgery. Nevertheless, Chester's love for music was clear. His father remembered, "Jim was very musical even when he was just a little kid. He'd always get up singing in the morning." He added that once his son heard a song, he was able to sing it perfectly or play it on the piano. By the age of eight, Van Heusen was composing songs, and a popular family quotes his prediction to his cousin Charlotte: "Someday there will be people who want to hear my songs."

Apparently, Van Heusen also knew that someone else would be singing those tunes — an idea that even at a young age held appeal. His early musical education included both piano and voice, and Ida Mae recalls that he was as gifted a singer as he was a pianist. "I don't know when I've seen anyone who could carry a tune as performed as Chet does, and I know music, too. He's got perfect tone," she said in an interview, adding support for her opinion. "His voice teacher, a Mr. Coulter, wrote us a note and said he thought Chet was making a mistake — not to keep up with the vocal."

No doubt Ida Mae's idea of a vocalist — one singing impassioned hymns at Sunday services — clashed with Chester's, and this led to his abandonment of his formal vocal studies. Recalling having to sing "Swing Low, Sweet Chariot" before the congregation, Chester described the experience with characteristic bluntness: "It was a pain in the ass. I hated to get up and sing before people because I wasn't sure of myself as that kind of singer. I could croon all right, after a fashion. I could sustain my notes a lot easier if I sang softly. When you sing full voice is when you get off-key."

Thankfully, Ida Mae was somewhat more successful keeping young Chester on the piano. Realizing that she was not the best person to teach him, she asked a friend of hers to step in. The association was brief. "I didn't think he made very good progress with her," she recalled. "I thought a man would do better, so we had him go to Syracuse University to a teacher up there who took him on as special pupil. His name was Dr. Howard Lyman."

Despite the matter-of-fact tone of this statement, being brought on as a "special pupil" of Dr. Lyman was no small accomplishment. Dr. Lyman was a long-time professor of music at Syracuse University and founded the Syracuse University chorus. Indeed, the music building at Syracuse University is named in his honor. Dr. Lyman was also choir director of University Methodist Church for 33 years. It is likely there that he met the Babcocks, fellow congregants enraptured by the energetic sermons of a young Norman Vincent Peale.

Although he continued to make progress with Dr. Lyman, Van Heusen's interest in music waned in his pre-teen years, the adulation of the Methodist congregation and family not suitable reward for practice. Fortunately for the musical world, Van Heusen's voice began to change and with that, his outlook on the opposite sex. Said Jimmy, "I fell in love with the whole idea of womanhood." It was a love affair that lasted a lifetime; sure, there were other suns in his firmament, but always women first. As Jimmy himself stated in the liner notes to his album *Jimmy Van Heusen Plays Jimmy Van Heusen,* "I dig chicks, booze, music, and Sinatra . . . in that order." Sinatra was still some 20 years away. The booze, frighteningly more imminent, and somewhat ironically more scandalous to today's society.

But, back to the dames.

Van Heusen learned at a very young age that a schmuck without a guitar was still a schmuck, but with a guitar he was a star. The girls would stop gazing at their dates when a piano was played. It was deceptively innocent but profoundly seductive. Coupled with Van Heusen's obvious talent and charisma, it was a lethal and devastatingly effective aphrodisiac. One need only look at the glamorous women later attracted to Van Heusen as proof: Angie Dickinson, Phyllis Maguire, etc. Well, you don't hit big league pitching without putting your time in American Legion ball, and the lovely ladies of Syracuse proved to be a fitting warm-up for his later conquests.

"I was crazy about those girls," Van Heusen said. "A guy had to do something to stick his head above the sea of idiots around him." His piano playing and composing proved to be just the ticket. Many decades later, Van Heusen was able to recall a waltz he wrote for a young lady named Harriet:

Moon shining above

    Thoughts of love – Harriet

Pining for love – Harriet

    For some, it's time for kissing.

But for me, I'm just reminiscing

    I need your charms, Harriet,

Right here in my arms, Harriet.

    Though you're far above me

And never could love me

    I'll still love you, Harriet.

"I can still remember that tune," Van Heusen recalled. "It was a waltz. I was about thirteen when I wrote that for a girl named Harriet Vaughn. I was crazy about her, out of my skull. I wrote a song with the name of every girl I was crazy about."

Women may have helped to rekindle young Chester's interest in music, but it is virtually certain that the thing which made music a way of life for him did not actually have legs. In 1922, WFBL began broadcasting from the Hotel Onondaga. Taking its call letters from its unique position in the area — First Broadcast License — its massive (for the time) 5,000 watt antenna was capable of broadcasting the latest dance band remote broadcasts from the dance halls and hotels of New York City. The recording industry was practically nonexistent at that time, so the success of a song was dictated largely by the willingness of bandleaders to perform the numbers and, ultimately, through sheet music sales. A particularly enterprising and quick-minded musician could earn quite a name for himself if he were able to recall what he heard and put those notes on paper. Van Heusen had that mind and put it to devious and exceptional use in his early adolescent years.

Girls, music, composing, romance. But wasn't there something missing? Something every 13 year old should do? Oh yes. School.

THREE

Young Edward Chester Babcock doing a handstand.
Courtesy Babcock Family Photo Archives

It's A Good Thing I Don't Care

"The boy was not suited for school," Van Heusen's father remarked. And, most certainly he was not. A selective learner, he ignored Latin and mathematics, while engrossing himself in literature, histories, classics, and biographies. He clearly heeded their lessons (how many 13 year olds do you know that can use "reminisce" in a sentence, much less a rhyming lyric?), demonstrating the same aptitude for independent learning that later would enable him to become a test pilot for Lockheed Martin and accomplished helicopter pilot without formal training.

If his draft autobiography is any indication, Chester did not recall much of those grammar school years, but from those stories told by his friends, it appeared that the roots of his unique persona of the Rat Pack years were sown in the salty soil of Onondaga County: Ralph Harris, one of Chester's schoolyard chums, tells the following story:

[Chester would arrive early at school and cover the blackboard with his cartoons.] He did some really fantastic cartoons and I laughed at them…Chester always seemed to go his own way and he was always doing outlandish things. He used to walk on his hands – all over the place. There was a stream which ran by the [grammar] school – Onondaga Creek – and there was a bridge with iron railings across it. I've seen Chester walk across the railing of that bridge – it couldn't have been more than four inches wide – on his hands, the whole way across the creek which must have been sixty feet. Or he'd climb a telephone pole and stand on his hands at the top – I guess thirty feet off the ground – or he'd stand and balance on the wires. Ridiculous stuff. He never hurt anybody – he just had the ability to do crazy things like that. He got into a lot of trouble that way. There was nothing in the rules against it – I don't think the rule makers ever thought such a thing would come up. But you can imagine his teacher's surprise when Chester was supposed to be in class and instead was standing on top of a telephone pole. I think he scared his teachers to death.

Van Heusen was enrolled at Nottingham High School, a new school constructed in 1921 and nestled on the corner of

Fellows Avenue and Harvard Place in the Westcott area of Syracuse. Although enrolled, it might be generous to say Van Heusen was an active student at Nottingham. He excelled at English and art, and eagerly read assigned texts in philosophy and archaeology. However, the only classrooms that he attended religiously were at Clark's Music Store, a pool hall, and the Five and Dime where Jimmy would pore over the latest sheet music. The real attraction, though, was the unused piano in the Hotel Onondaga roof garden where Jimmy would play for hours, honing his craft, learning the new songs and writing his own.

The Hotel Onondaga was a first class luxury hotel, and one of the tallest buildings in Syracuse. Within its walls, taking advantage of the commanding heights was WFBL, the premiere radio station in central New York. While Van Heusen certainly had his eyes on the studios at WFBL, he had to content himself with a part time gig on WSYR, referred to by Van Heusen as "the fourth rate, no power radio station, competing not at all with the fancy WFBL Syracuse."

WSYR was not able to afford the remote broadcasts from New York City hotels and ballrooms, like its CBS affiliated brother WFBL. So, it would have to be satisfied with remote broadcasts from the ballroom of the Hotel Syracuse or the junior and senior proms at Syracuse University. To make up the remainder of its broadcast day, WSYR would recruit local talent who "would be put on the air if they didn't faint at the sight of a microphone," as recalled by Van Heusen. Fortunately, he was one such stalwart, making his debut playing "Carolina Moon" and "My Kind of Love" in concert with a ukulele.

Jimmy spent many hours at WSYR — hours he should have been spending at Nottingham. The powers that were noticed his absence and finally expelled him. The news of expulsion, as might be expected, was not welcome news to Arthur and Ida Mae. Although indulgent people, both knew the value of education. Arthur's education at the Albany Business College was a prime factor in his success in business. And, at this time, Arthur was enjoying great success as a homebuilder, and Jimmy, though not wealthy, wanted for little. Ralph Harris recalled, "Chester was a rich man, as far as I was concerned. He always seemed to have a little money. And — the most enviable position of all — he used to have charge accounts. He could go into Wells & Coverly, a very good men's store, and buy a suit and say, 'Charge it!!!'"

So, expelled, and under some pressure from the parents to find a real job, Van Heusen found a temporary reprieve in a new program offered by the Central Business College to students of Syracuse University. These select students were to be instructed in Gregg shorthand and typing, with the hope the students would become proficient in both tools of the newly evolving business world. Although he was underage, Van Heusen was admitted to the program — something of a testament to his untapped intellectual abilities. Putting his mind to his studies at the business college, Jimmy excelled at the class. Based on this performance and some fast talking, he was permitted to return to school. This time, he would try his hand at Central High School. Central was an older institution than Nottingham, having been constructed in 1903 by Archimedes Russell for $340,000 ($7.5 million in 2012 dollars). The austere and serene surroundings proved to be no more inspiring to Van Heusen than Nottingham, and he was soon looking for a way out. Jimmy returned to his old habit of routinely skipping class in favor of his old gig at WSYR. This time, however, Arthur and Ida Mae were not about to let another opportunity go to waste. WSYR was strictly forbidden to Jimmy. His days as a broadcasting lothario were over. The only call sign in his future were the Three R's.

Temptation would soon present itself in the form of George Perkin, staff announcer at WSYR. Perkins saw Jimmy on the street and told him that he had just quit the station, and if Jimmy would hurry, he might be able to get the job. Two hours later, Van Heusen was a staff announcer making fifteen dollars a week – a full time job. It was a great deal, but Jimmy decided not to share the good news with mom and dad – for obvious reasons. He discovered something he loved and attacked it with characteristic intensity: In addition to reading the news, he was the staff piano player, sang, and even swept the place. Life was good. Until . . .

Central High School appeared to miss the presence of young Mr. Babcock, and inquired of his parents to his whereabouts. Confronted, in a burst of Methodist guilt, Jimmy confessed and faced the penance – WSYR was out . . . again. Already reeling from this blow, Jimmy was dealt another by the head of WSYR — Charles Kalefsky. Summoned to his boss' office, Jimmy was faced with a real problem, one that would take some ingenuity to fix: his name.

See, the denizens of Syracuse were not hearing Jimmy Van Heusen on the air, but Chester Babcock. It was, therefore, somewhat inevitable that Jimmy would be found out and his parents informed. For all of his bravado and faux-maturity, Van Heusen was still only fifteen years old, and his "plan" had all of the hallmarks of adolescent thought as its underpinnings. If one wishes to keep something from one's parents, radio broadcasting might not be the best profession in which to keep a low profile. That problem was about to present an opportunity.

The story of how Chester Babcock became Jimmy Van Heusen is one of those stories that varies from year to year, place to place and person to person. It's like the famous home run called by Babe Ruth — over 100,000 claimed they were there, in that 40,000 seat stadium. From a cold, analytical perspective, we know two things: Van Heusen had to change his name to stay on the radio, and second, he would have preferred not to. As Jimmy somewhat resentfully recalls, "Babcock's a perfectly good name. It's been in America for a long time — like way back in the 1600's." Adding with a tone of trademark stubbornness, he continued, "Anyway, I never changed my name legally. My passport and my pilot's license still read 'Edward Chester Babcock, also known as Jimmy Van Heusen.'" In his unfinished memoir, Jimmy gives full credit, though, to his pal Ralph Harris for his new moniker. Harris recalls telling Van Heusen:

> "Hell, it's simple. If you change your name, everything's solved: Kaletsky will be happy, the school won't know where you are and your Dad won't either." I lived close to a man I admired very much, William Van Deusen, who was a violinist with the Syracuse Symphony Orchestra – and I'd always admired his name. Then, I looked up and right in front of me (at the corner of South Salina and Onondaga Streets), I saw a posted for Van Heusen collars in the window of a store. "Perfect," I said. "We'll call you Van Heusen and no one will ever know who you are . . . We'll give you a catchy first name like, well, like Jimmy. Jimmy Van Heusen. How does that sound?" It was a ridiculous idea, but it worked. He kept his job and his Dad didn't know anything about it – for a long time, that is. He's been Jimmy Van Heusen ever since.

Smart guy, that Ralph Harris. It turned out he had a knack for helping out artists, becoming one of the top agents in show business. He is largely credited with facilitating Lena Horne's massive mainstream appeal, using his skills to bring Ms. Horne's immense talents to a broader (read here, whiter) audience. Jimmy Van Heusen and Lena Horne – not bad for a Syracuse kid who whiled away his teen years drinking bathtub gin with Chester Babcock.

With his name changed, and the cloak of anonymity restored, Van Heusen again resumed avoiding his scholastic duties, and had a twice daily show in WSYR called "Scribble and Sing," which Jimmy described as such:

> On every program, I'd play and sing a new song I
> had written and several I hadn't written. In those
> days, Guy Lombardo introduced a new song
> every week on his radio show and some of the
> other bands did, too. Whenever a new tune was
> announced, I was right there at the radio grabbing
> the lyrics with my Gregg shorthand – that was a
> cinch. I could remember the tunes. Popular songs
> then had an eight bar phrase which was repeated,
> a middle release and then the eight bar phrase

which was repeated. If I didn't get the middle part, I'd make it up. Next day I'd be on the air during my juvenile delinquent's hour with the newest music. Dozens of deluded citizens of Syracuse believed I begat these great gems and I began to get a kind of name for myself.

This story, recounted by Van Heusen, with characteristic matter-of-factness, demonstrates the true depth of his musical genius. Confronted with two distinct mental tasks (lyrics and music), he was able to record the lyrics, shorthand, and recall the melody in such detail that it could be accurately transcribed. No pause button. No recording equipment. No playback. And without formal musical theoretical transcription education. Paper and ink in short supply. Sound easy?

While daunting for those of us with less innate ability, the task proved less than challenging – or profitable – enough for the young upstart, who "got cute and asked my listeners to send in a lyric or a tune or just a title and I guaranteed to make a song out of the stuff." Having actively composed since the age of 7, Van Heusen had plenty of material, in case the contribution did not properly inspire him. With titles like

"Let's Fill in the Swamps and Build a Boulevard around Onondaga Lake," it could prove to be no small task. Sadly, the aforementioned tune and lyrics have been lost to history. It can only be assumed the Syracuse city fathers did not deem it to be a suitable theme song for the ever-growing city.

Van Heusen's new found "semi-celebrity" status afforded him the opportunity to create a tidy little side business, in some way demonstrating the business savvy that served him so well in his Hollywood future. When Van Heusen would receive efforts from the listeners for "Scribble and Sing," he would write back to the budding tunesmith/lyric-writer and given them a dose of self-styled "Methodist malarkey," and convince the author that the song showed promise and could really be something with his touch. So, through correspondence on official "JAMES VAN HEUSEN/WSYR" letterhead, he would offer to prepare a piano part and perform the song on the air for ten dollars. For another ten dollars, he would supply the author with the newly minted song on genuine manuscript paper. To paraphrase one of Sinatra's monologues from the Sands live shows, the business was supposed to be completely legitimate – but it wasn't. For, if the number of "hit song writers" according to the Van Heusen/WSYR boondoggle was even remotely accurate, the library of research on American popular song would include the title "Poets of Onondaga Street" rather than "Tin Pan Alley."

To think that Van Heusen treated music in a trivial manner, based on these dalliances, would be a grave mistake. By the age of 15, he knew he wanted to be a songwriter and did all he could to make that dream come true. He insured that he was impeccably groomed, shopping at many of Syracuse's finest men's shops, and, so groomed, would take his growing manuscript catalogue with him to the right places. He pressed his songs on Leon Royky, the leader of the orchestra at the Terrace Room at the Hotel Syracuse and Irv Orton, bandleader at another local haunt – Snell's Ballroom.

Van Heusen also continued his formal musical education, but not with the same zeal. He maintained his thrice weekly piano lessons, but the stern aegis of Bach, Beethoven and Liszt could not compare with the new sounds from the radio and ballrooms of New York City. Like most musicians of the day, Van Heusen had limited formal musical education. Of his training, Van Heusen said:

I studied other songwriters and I learned every song I could get my hands on. If I didn't have the money to buy the sheet music, I'd copy it. They had the new songs at the Five and Dime and the girl who played the piano there, Mildred McGonigle, gave me some lessons. Actually, I taught myself more than my teachers taught me just by playing the piano all the time. But it wasn't until I was exposed to the pianistics of Teddy Wilson and Fats Waller that I discovered what the piano was all about.

This is not to say he found the world of classical music uninteresting or uninspiring – quite the opposite. Throughout his life, he collected rare manuscripts of the masters and maintained a sophisticated library of classical recordings showcasing not only the traditional masters but also more modern experimental composers. Despite this lifelong fascination with classical music, Van Heusen produced no serious compositions like Jerome Kern, Richard Rodgers or Victor Young. Moreover, given the complexity of his work and symphonic scope of his songs like "To Love and Be Loved" or "Where Love Has Gone," there is no denying his talent was on par with other "serious" American composers. Such a contradiction makes it interesting to contemplate whether Van Heusen was intimidated by the masters or whether he simply felt more at ease with the new style.

Perhaps the reason behind his failure to expand into more serious music had more to do with Benjamin Franklin than Sigmund Freud – i.e., there was little money to be made in serious music. Aaron Copland and Samuel Barber might have been studied at Harvard, but they most assuredly did not live in mountaintop, ultramodern bachelor pads or own airplanes. In this regard, one is reminded of the famous (perhaps apocryphal) exchange between Igor Stravinsky and George Gershwin, when Gershwin sought lessons from the Russian master. Stravinsky asked Gershwin his yearly income. When Gershwin replied $100,000, Stravinsky immediately rejoined that perhaps it was Gershwin who should be giving him lessons.

Maybe the story was a figment of Gershwin's imagination or public relations machine, but it reflects a front in the cultural music wars – that of the "serious" musician's resentment at lack of popular success (and subtle disdain for the popular composers who do reap financial success) and the "popular" composer desirous of critical acclaim, only to content himself by telling others the serious composer is out of touch. Again, it is not clear whether Van Heusen fell into this stereotype, but if any person would be an exception to the rule, it would be Van Heusen.

FOUR

Jimmy Van Heusen June 1931
Courtesy of Babcock Family Photo Archives

He Was A Perfect Gentleman

Van Heusen was not the only kid Central High was having difficulty engaging. A fellow dweller at the Onondaga Hotel was Murray Wolfe. Murray should have been studying science and math, but instead studied poker and booze. Murray had two uncles: Meyer Berman who ran a speakeasy, and Ben Wolfe, a tailor, whose principal source of income was the making of gin.

Like cigarettes, alcohol was a critical component of image and, to some degree, virility. Alcohol certainly did not carry with it the taboo of modern day. In many ways, alcohol represents an interesting irony of the times. The 30s, 40s and 50s are somewhat unfairly criticized as staid, stale social times. Still, it was nothing for business lunches to be washed down by three martinis, housewives to sip cocktails during the afternoon and every evening concluding with the innocuously titled "nightcap." Such behavior would be considered scandalous and deviant by today's supposedly ultramodern, hip society.

Van Heusen was no different from any other youth of his time when it came to alcohol. It became a part of his life at a relatively young age, and it stayed with him so long as his body could endure it. But, like everything else, Van Heusen was no blind pack follower; he drank because he liked it:

> I just loved to drink. I loved the effect. Because Murray was his (Meyer's) nephew, we could always get into Berman's speakeasy, and Uncle Meyer made a wonderful drink he called the Iceberg. I don't know what it was made of but I suspect gin and lime juice or something. Those drinks kept us polarized a good part of the time. I went around with Uncle Ben's daughter, Rosalie Wolfe, a beautiful girl who had a good voice and used to sing on my show. Whenever I'd pick up Rosalie, I'd go to the Wolfe bathroom, roll up my sleeve and dunk a square-faced bottle into the gin in the tub. When the bottle gurgled itself full, I'd moisten a Gordon's label and slap it on the bottle. I'd leave two dollars on the wash stand and off with Rosalie to WSYR or some place and kiss and hug and drink. The best thing you could get in those days was medicinal alcohol. We mixed it

with a soft drink called Mission Orange. With this
stuff, you wouldn't get falling down drunk as you
did with gin — you'd just get anesthetized. The
stuff must have been 150 proof. It made for one
hell of a party.

Van Heusen and his cohorts seemed to care little that his

partying ran afoul of federal law. Prohibition, at least in

upstate New York, was treated as a mere annoyance — another

impediment to a good time. Van Heusen was somewhat

fearless in this regard — having already spent an evening in

the infamous Tombs of New York City at age 14 following an

aborted effort to sample the pleasures of the big city.

"Anything for a good time" seemed to be the motto for teenage

Jimmy, as it would be later for the other members of the Rat

Pack. Unlike many others of the era, Jimmy found it easy to

maintain the insouciance of youth and build up his

constitution. In addition to having friends with connections,

Jimmy also had the good fortune of being insulated from the

full effects of the Great Depression, since the home-building

industry in Syracuse did not feel the pain of other industries in

the area.

Central High simply could not compete with WSYR, bathtub gin and Rosalie. Van Heusen's attendance was spotty and his enthusiasm waning, but the public school system kept its patience. However, even those souls had their limits. And, true to form, the last straw was reminiscent of a Summit routine at the Sands. One of Van Heusen's posse was a fellow named Harry Mattison, who worked at Clark's Music Store — a frequent haunt. Mattison ran a concession for a Speak-O-Phone, which was a recording machine that produces a rudimentary record album. In the hopes of giving the students a pedagogical experience, the staff of Central High invited Mr. Mattison to give a demonstration to the student body. Mattison asked Jimmy to play the piano and sing a song which Mattison would then record with the gizmo. Van Heusen sat down and began to play a song he wrote that adorned the WSYR airwaves earlier. Of course, you recognize it, "My Canary Has Circles under His Eyes":

> Since making whoopee became all the rage
>> It's gotten around to the old bird cage.
>> And my canary has got circles under his eyes.

The student body erupted. While innocuous by our standards, shouting/singing "making whoopee" would be the equivalent of reciting the lyrics to a rap number, with its attendant sexual innuendo. Before the grown-ups could give Jimmy the hook, he continued:

His only pals are a yellow lark
And just a tiny sparrow
But I'm afraid when he's in the dark,
He leaves the straight and narrow.

The song ended to thunderous applause. Once the crowd was stilled, Mattison went on to explain the rather mundane scientific workings of the Speak-O-Phone. Jimmy smirked to himself, knowing what was to come next. The recording was replayed, and the student body erupted again. Like any other idiot teenager, Jimmy thought this was the ideal outcome to the day.

All that could be said is that Van Heusen ended his career at Central High with a bang and not with a whimper. Three days after this exhibition, he was expelled from a second high school, because, in Jimmy's recollection, "I was pointed in the wrong direction, and the other innocents should not be exposed to my licentiousness."

Whatever adolescent bravado Jimmy felt after his Speak-O-Phone triumph vanished when his parents informed him that he must finish high school. The choices were grim: Manlius Military Academy or Cazenovia Seminary. There was really no choice — the thought of the military regimen drove him to the Methodists at Cazenovia Seminary. There would be no more WSYR or bathtub gin, but there would be no reveille or drill instructors. There would also be girls.

Cazenovia was a quiet, idyllic town that Jimmy described as having "about twenty churches and one pool hall." As expected, Jimmy frequented the pool hall. He also continued to write songs, continually honing his craft as he wiled away the time in the quite quasi-suburbia of Cazenovia. The strictures of Methodism did little to quell his taste for the fairer sex, as he used his compositions for the alternate purpose of pitching the woo to his coeds, hoping he could convince them to join him for a tryst in the local cemetery — a sort of bizarre Lovers' Lane for Cazenovia students.

Indeed, it was his lust for the ladies that ostensibly ultimately doomed Jimmy at Cazenovia (and ended his formal education). Reverend Charles Hamilton expelled Jimmy twice before for improper relations with coed students, until February, 1930, Reverend Hamilton removed Jimmy from Cazenovia for the third and final time, personally driving him the twenty miles to Syracuse to convey the message to Jimmy' parents.

In later retellings of the tale, Van Heusen claimed that he was asked to leave Cazenovia because of too many late night visits to the cemetery. Whether that is actually the case is a question lost to history and the Cazenovia records — both of which have faded considerably since 1930. Throughout several periods of his life, Van Heusen sketched parts of his never completed autobiography. The work recounts his life from age 8 to about the late 1960s. It did not appear to be a work that Van Heusen sat down for any extended period of time to complete but rather a work that was produced in fits and starts. There is little discussion of his childhood and early adolescent years, even less on his time at Cazenovia.

However, of the many institutions of learning through which Van Heusen attempted to matriculate, it was Cazenovia that he held in highest regard. At least, if one measures such things by donations of time and money. In 1961, Van Heusen was the recipient of Cazenovia College's first Distinguished Alumni Award. In 1963, Van Heusen generously permitted Cazenovia College to use his song "High Hopes" as a means of attracting alumni donations by having none other than Bing Crosby record a special 45 rpm record for alumni with lyrics specially written by another Cazenovia College alumnus, Ralph Larsen. Mr. Larsen claimed that the recording was responsible for more alumni donations than any alumni mailing in school history. Finally, in 1967, Van Heusen made an exceptional donation of music manuscripts and awards. Included in this collection were Van Heusen's four Academy Awards, his Emmy Award, his Christopher Award and music autographed by Igor Stravinsky, Frederic Chopin, Giacomo Puccini, Edvard Grieg, Maurice Ravel, Johannes Brahms, Peter Illyich Tchaikovsky, Claude Debussy, Irving Berlin, Darius Milhaud and Eric Delius (the only signed manuscript by Delius).

Quite the gift.

They must have done something right.

FIVE

Jimmy Van Heusen and admirers.
Courtesy of Van Heusen Photo Archives

Love Is The Darndest Thing

Of uniform recollection was Van Heusen's respect for women that is he would treat them very well. Ralph Harris recalled:

> One time I was staying with him at his place in Palm Springs and I went out with a girl I liked very much. We stayed in a bar until it closed and then we drove around the desert - we had a marvelous time — and I didn't get home until about seven in the morning. Chester was outraged. "Where have you been?" he said. I told him and he said, more in sorrow than in anger, "I don't see how you could do that - stay out all night with a nice girl." Here was a guy who stayed up all night, every night of his life, but with me, he couldn't see it. Part of it stemmed from his real respect for women . . . I have never, never heard him make a derogatory remark about any woman he has ever been with — and I've known him almost fifty years."

No less an aficionado of courtly behavior, Bing Crosby, observed Van Heusen's treatment of women: "Jimmy was very much a gentleman and very gallant with the ladies. He'd send flowers and all kinds of things — the ladies got cavalier treatment from Jimmy. . . He was really gallant to all the ladies — my wife, all the ladies at any party. That was noticeable in Jimmy, and he meant it. It can't be faked."

At the same time, though, there was a noticeable reluctance on the part of Van Heusen to commit to any woman for any period of time. Ralph Harris recalled, "He didn't like to have girls around." By that, he meant hanging around for extended periods of time, as his romantic exploits testify to his ready acceptance of evening-long engagements. It was the entanglement, the interference. Furthermore, Van Heusen would not be embarrassed for people to know of his frequenting houses of ill-repute and engaging the services of prostitutes. It was well known among friends and, again, an unabashed revelation in the notes of his autobiography.

Adding to the contradiction of Van Heusen's romantic life was his treatment of children. He loved kids. Crosby's children and Sinatra's children were all treated like his own sons and daughters might be. He bestowed fatherly and professional advice on them all throughout his life, and his door was always open to them. Frank Sinatra, Jr., tells the story of his first album with Nelson Riddle, and his inability to come up with a suitable title track for the album. Sinatra decided he would compose the title track, and the end product was a nice tune called, "Spice." As he was performing at a small club in Los Angeles, Van Heusen entered the club, sat down and had some drinks. Sinatra immediately told his mates to fetch the Van Heusen tunes, and he performed them to the composer's satisfaction. After the conclusion of the show, Sinatra sat with Van Heusen and told him about his project. Van Heusen immediately wanted to know if the masters were available. Not wanting to waste this opportunity, Sinatra took Van Heusen to his apartment and played the demos. When it came time to listen to Sinatra's creation, Van Heusen insisted upon hearing no fewer than three reprises of the tune, each one keeping Van Heusen's full attention. At the end, he smiled, telling Sinatra, "It looks like Sammy (Cahn) and I taught you pretty well."

Van Heusen's largesse to children was not reserved only for those of the fabulously wealthy or famous. Although the granddaughter of legendary bluesman Dan Hornsby, Nikki Hornsby first met Van Heusen when he became acquainted with her father during his test flight days at Lockheed Martin. Her family became fast friends with Van Heusen, and throughout his life Van Heusen maintained close contact with the Hornsby's. Nikki was a frequent visitor to Van Heusen's home in Palm Springs, and whenever Jimmy and friends (including Frank Sinatra, Dean Martin and the group) were in northern Virginia, they would pay visits to Nikki and her family. Van Heusen treated Nikki as a daughter, bestowing on her countless gifts that would make memorabilia enthusiast green with envy. When her friends did not believe she was friends with Sinatra and Van Heusen, Jimmy forwarded the problem to Sinatra who presented Nikki with an autographed album which boldly proclaimed, "Maybe they'll believe you now. Frank Sinatra." In her later years, when Nikki was pursuing her own musical career, Jimmy's door was always open to her and she would regularly visit Van Heusen in Palm Springs where she would receive advice that Jimmy was more than willing to dispense. The door was always open to friends, and his love of their children was great.

Perhaps the legendary pianist and close Van Heusen friend, Joe Bushkin, said it best, "He's said to me, dead sober, that he'd be willing to trade his whole catalogue for mine — meaning his catalogue of songs for my kids."

Van Heusen never had children. If he did, though, it is a likely wager that he would have insisted they complete their formal education. While many successful people achieved great things without the benefits of formal education, they uniformly agree many more doors are opened with a diploma. Also, it needs be said that for every Van Heusen or Sinatra, there are countless other uneducated people who failed. Still, when Van Heusen returned ignominiously from Cazenovia, he and his parents knew the prospects for formal education were bleak, at best. He went to work with his father at this construction business and resumed lessons with Dr. Lyman. For whatever reason, even the thought of this formality proved too much and the lessons came to an end. Jimmy looked back on this with some degree of regret, "I should have continued with my music. I should have gone to college and if I had I would have been a serious musician."

There's that phrase again: serious musician. It weaves through Van Heusen's life like a leitmotif through a Wagner opera. It is the one phrase he would never use to describe himself. This, even after four Oscars, an Emmy, election to The Songwriter's Hall of Fame (inaugural class) and numerous other accolades. In many ways, he suffers from the same cultural inferiority complex that affects all Americans. We may rule the world economically and militarily, but in our minds, we still take a back seat to our European cousins, perpetually banished to the folding card table at dinner with regards to things cultural. Serious musicians write operas and symphonies, not songs. Even the great composers of lieder — Brahms, Schumann and Schubert — all wrote larger, grander works, as well. For all of our advances as Americans, the aesthetic criteria for music remain firmly European.

This was the cultural world in which Van Heusen found himself. And, despite his apparent aversion to formal education, Van Heusen was quite well-educated, knowledgeable and well-read on many topics — most importantly, music. Among his prized possessions were rare manuscripts from the great masters, many of them donated to Cazenovia College in the late 1960s. It was, therefore, quite unlikely Van Heusen was unaware of these cultural mores.

It was in the person of Aaron Copland that American serious music first found voice amid the Europeans. Ironically, though, it was the jazz idiom that brought America acclaim in the serious world. European composers such as Milhaud, Ravel, Debussy and Stravinsky all experimented with the new jazz form, and it was perhaps time for Americans to reap the benefits of their own labor.

In their outstanding biography of Oscar Levant, *A Talent for Genius*, Sam Kashner and Nancy Schoenberger described the American serious musical scene thusly:

> Since Copland's return to America [from study in Europe] in 1924, one thing had not changed in the musical world: the critical establishment and its chilly response to new American composers. Oscar Levant agreed with Copland that the audience for serious American music was coolly apathetic. "A new generation of composers was emerging which inevitably would be subjected to the same cycle of mild patronizing interest and essential indifference as that which preceded them." Levant further observed, "There was on the horizon no critic of sufficient influence to occupy the position of Edwin Evans in England . . . Jean Coucteau in France, Einstein in Germany — all of whom had a profound effect on the

emerging new talents in their countries. The interested critics were not influential and the influential critics were not interested."

Such was the situation facing Van Heusen: even if he were a "serious musician," he would not be a serious musician. Van Heusen was not much of a serious anything. Unemployed and with little prospect for finishing school, Van Heusen was once again rescued from mundanity by the air waves. This time Van Heusen was ready for the big time, as Bill Shannon, the chief radio personality for WFBL, hired Van Heusen to reprise his style of show he produced at WSYR. It was during this time that Van Heusen heard music that would change his life.

SIX

Edward Chester Babcock as a teenager
Photo credit to E.W. Edwards

Shake Down The Stars

The Rhythm Boys were a singing group associated with the Paul Whiteman Orchestra. The group consisted of Harry Barris, Al Rinker and Bing Crosby. The 1930 film, *The King of Jazz*, featured Whiteman's orchestra and the Rhythm Boys singing five numbers: "Mississippi Mud," "I'm a Fisherman," "Bench in the Park," "Happy Feet," and "So the Bluebirds and the Blackbirds Got Together." Old friend Ralph Harris brought Van Heusen a record of "So the Bluebirds and the Blackbirds Got Together." The effect on Jimmy was immediate:

> Bing had a chorus all by himself on that record, and it was a revelation to me as it was to millions of others who ultimately heard it. It was the age of high-singing tenors and the sound of someone with balls was exhilarating. I made up my mind then and there that I'd get Crosby to sing my

songs. That was a farfetched dream for a truant teenager and I knew it, but I dreamed it anyway.

Through the miracle of modern technology, we are able to view again the Rhythm Boys' performance in the *King of Jazz*, and the effect experienced by Van Heusen is still evident. Harry Barris, uncle of Chuck, tells a silly tale about frolicking avians, whose sounds are captured by his squeaky, high-pitched voice and frenetic keyboard. Then, in the middle of the whole selection, Crosby stops the productions, slows the tempo and croons a chorus. Rhythm Boy Al Rinker noted that the delivery of the group marked a dramatic departure from the style of the day of "putting over songs with much more emotion and broad showmanship." Instead, the Rhythm Boys and Crosby, in particular, "were more intimate and sang [their] songs in a more modern way."

During his time at WFBL, Van Heusen divided his time between his work with his father, his show duties and the occasional visit to the local theaters and ballrooms to hear new music and peddle his own works. 1930 was, in many ways, a seminal year in American popular song. The following is but a sampling: "A Cottage for Sale," "Love for Sale," "Georgia on

My Mind," "Get Happy," "Dancing on the Ceiling," and, of course, the Gershwins' classic *Girl Crazy*, which contained masterworks, such as "Embraceable You," "I Got Rhythm," "But Not For Me," and "Bidin' My Time."

One of the great innovators of the time was young Harold Arlen. The Buffalo born son of a Jewish cantor was making his mark as a popular composer of some note with such standards as the aforementioned "Get Happy" and "Between the Devil and the Deep Blue Sea." These two numbers made him one of the stars of the famed Cotton Club in New York City. Music ran in Arlen's family, and his younger brother, Jerry, also tried his hand at the music game. While attending Syracuse University, Jerry Arlen was a member of the stage orchestra at Loew's State Theater on Salina Street — only a couple of blocks away from WFBL's studios at the Hotel Syracuse. It would have been one of the venues where Van Heusen plugged his songs to the local bandleaders.

There is little account of how Arlen and Van Heusen met — a story that Arlen ran into Van Heusen on the street, introduced himself and said, "Let's write songs together," while nice for an RKO movie, seems largely mythical. It is more likely that the two met either at the Lowe's State Theater or through Van Heusen's radio program. No matter the circumstances, the two got together and summoned the courage to make the first of many charges of New York City. It was a great benefit, to be sure, that Harold Arlen had entry to the music world, could listen to their tunes, and more important, had an apartment. "I'd stay in New York until my money ran out and then it was back to Syracuse," Van Heusen later remarked. "I hated Syracuse but mostly because I was trying to be a songwriter in a city where they didn't have songwriters. I had to get out."

Van Heusen was nothing if not driven, as an unnamed friend described: "Chester wanted desperately to be successful. I think part of it was that he wanted to prove himself to his father and I know he wanted to get into a position where he wouldn't have to depend on his family for money. There was a bit of star-gazing mixed in, too. Chester always had a tremendous drive toward success. He drove himself to it."

In 1932, Van Heusen and Jerry Arlen packed their things and made the commitment to stay in New York City and become songwriters. Jimmy's decision was met with cautious resignation by his parents: Ida Mae offered prayer and Arthur offered money. Armed with both, Van Heusen took up residence at Harold Arlen's apartment at the Corwin Hotel at Madison and 86th Street. For a songwriter, there was no place better than Arlen's apartment. In 1932, Arlen wrote, with Ted Koehler, the wonderful "I've Got the World on a String" for the Cotton Club Parade of 1932. Also in 1932, the same team wrote the classic "Stormy Weather" for the 1933 edition of the revue. Arlen was named "Most Prolific Songwriter" in 1933 by Billboard Magazine; that same year, Shakespeare was also named "Most Prolific Playwright."

Arlen represented a new generation in American music. The groundwork was laid by Jerome Kern, George Gershwin and Irving Berlin, all of whom advanced American popular song beyond the ragtime rhythms of Ben Harney or the simplistic craftsmanship of the late 19th century or early 20th century. Those writers (Gershwin, Kern, Berlin, etc.) offered, in the words of Alec Wilder, "More sophistication, more complex melody writing, much more involved harmonic patterns, shifting song form, greater elegance and infinitely superior theater song writing." Arlen, however, was different in one very important element: his distinctive American-ness. As

Wilder explained, "He never drew upon or was influenced by European music of any kind. He is wholly a product of American jazz, big band music and American popular song." Wilder further posits that he needed "the enriched and color-drenched sounds which had developed by the late twenties in order for him to be a writer."

Van Heusen would stand on the shoulders of these songwriters as well, including Arlen. He would, in his own way, expand the craft and place his own indelible mark on the art form. At this point, though, he just needed a first step. In a classic instance of foreshadowing, it was Hollywood that proved to be the impetus for advancement. Attempting to capitalize on the success of the Arlen/Koehler partnership, Columbia studios signed the team to provide the music for the new film, *Let's Fall in Love*. The film yielded the title song, which more than justifies its existence. More important for Van Heusen at least, Arlen and Koehler left their spot at the Cotton Club. New composers would be needed; brother Jerry and his pal Jimmy hoped to fill the void.

Harold used his influence with the Cotton Club management to persuade them to, at least, listen to Jimmy and Jerry's songs. It must have worked, and for Van Heusen, the break could not have come too soon – his appetite, social or otherwise, in desperate need of funding:

> There I was with these big, good-looking dames who made a thousand a week – in those days – and I was getting around in the music business trying to get my songs heard and well, like it wasn't Syracuse. When Harold Arlen got the call to go to Hollywood for his first picture, he had enough muscle to get Jerry, his brother, and me a chance to write for the new Cotton Club show. Three of our songs were accepted. Cab Calloway recorded one of them, "Harlem Hospitality." That was my first published song. When I saw my name on a printed song copy, I was then and there a song writer forever.

"Harlem Hospitality" was somewhat indistinguishable from the parade of songs composed for the Cotton Club by other tunesmiths. While the song lists Jimmy Van Heusen as the lyricist, it is clear Van Heusen had a significant hand in writing the melody. Its effective use of chromatic passages is a Van Heusen trademark (most notably in "Call Me Irresponsible" and "But Beautiful"), and it is used particularly well in this tune. It was not a remarkable start but it showed promise of things to come.

A couple of notes about the Cotton Club. It was, without a doubt, the jewel of Harlem. All the great stars of music performed there: Duke Ellington, George Gershwin, Irving Berlin, Cab Calloway, and Bill Robinson. As the place for jazz in New York City, it was every bit as colorful and dynamic as portrayed in popular culture. Founded in 1920 by boxing champion Jack Johnson, the Cotton Club was originally called Club De Luxe. In a tragic and ironic twist, the club was excluded to blacks, despite the almost exclusive African-American talent contributing to the club's success.

In 1923, the club caught the attention of notorious gang member Owney Madden, who purchased the club with his partner, "Big Frenchy" DeMange. That same year, Madden was serving time at Sing Sing for the murder of gang rival Little Patsy Doyle in 1914. Madden was a larger than life figure catching the public imagination in the early days of the romantic era of American gangsters such as John Dillinger, Bonnie & Clyde, and others. His purchase of the Club De Luxe was one in a series of nightclub/speakeasy acquisitions in New York City, including the exclusive Stork Club.

After Madden's acquisition, the club changed its name to the Cotton Club. Fletcher Henderson was the first band to play at the rebranded venue, and his stellar career was launched. However, the Cotton Club reached its zenith from 1927-1931 when Duke Ellington's Orchestra was the house band, electrifying audiences with its innovative rhythms, arrangements and melodies. It was, in fact, at Ellington's request, that the club relaxed its "whites only policy." It would be unfair, though, to ascribe this policy shift to either a sense of justice or Ellington's power. It was a matter of color: green. The Harlem Renaissance brought an influx of income into the African-American community, and club owners were more than willing to permit them to spend money to see their favorite performers.

So, the long and short of it was that Van Heusen was working for a well-known criminal – a fact not lost on Arthur and Ida Mae. When Van Heusen proudly sent a copy of the sheet music and recording of "Harlem Hospitality" back home, he received a note from a concerned Ida Mae: "Chester, do you realize you're working for that awful man Owen Madden that everyone says is Public Enemy Number One?" Although the reaction surprised Van Heusen, he did little to assuage his concerned parent:

It hadn't occurred to me that the owner of the
Cotton Club had made the headlines in Syracuse.
I wasn't real chummy with Madden. I'd heard he
carried around six or eight bullets which someone
had shot at him in a fit of pique and he had quite a
reputation as a lover boy-gangster-racketeer
hoodlum . . . but he was nice to me the few times I
saw him. I dealt with Big Frenchy De Mange and
Mike Best and Herman Stack – when anybody
spoke to me at all. Madden . . . was a big shot but
I thought it would be a waste of time explaining to
Ida Mae what a nice man he was.

In fact, there would turn out to be no reason to argue.
As quickly as the Cotton Club opportunity appeared, it
vanished. In 1934, Harold Arlen and Koehler returned from
Hollywood to write for one of the Cotton Club's final
productions, contributing the wonderful "Ill Wind" and "As
Long as I Live." Jerry Arlen and Van Heusen returned to the
streets, so to speak:

I was broke. I don't suppose we made more than
$25/week at the Cotton Club. I could always get
money from my folks – and Ida Mae sent cookies
and things like that – but I hated to do that. They
didn't want me to be 19 years old and drunk in

New York City and not getting educated and that's just what I was. I wanted to make enough money so I wouldn't have to ask them for anything. All the time I'd been in New York City, I'd sent my laundry home to be washed and ironed. I wanted to get my laundry done on my own and all the rest.

SEVEN

Young Van Heusen
Courtesy of Babcock family photo archives

Busy Doing Nothing

After the Cotton Club gig ended, a friend from Syracuse helped Van Heusen land a job running the service elevator at the Park Central Hotel at West 56th Street and 7th Avenue. He earned \$15/week and lived across the street at the Wellington Hotel for \$14/week. A pretty lean profit margin, but, as usual, Van Heusen had an angle: he would take from the trays of food being delivered and stash them at various places in the elevator shaft. He ate very well, and, as he, himself might say, gave management the shaft.

He paid for the meals in other ways, though, specifically with a lingering apprehension about room service:

> Once, on an afternoon shift, a waiter got on my elevator with a whole platter of caviar, and he dumped it right on the floor, spilled it all over the place. Now, a platter of caviar, which was

obviously going to some multi-zillionaire's party, was impossible for the poor guy to pay for. Holy Jesus, he'd have to work nine years to pay for that much caviar. So, he got it off the floor and back on the platter and we went on up to the zillionaire's party. I've always been a little leery of room service since that day.

The Park Central provided a job. It provided food. It provided income. It also provided something seeming invaluable to a young songwriter: encouragement. At the top of the hotel was a famous supper club, the Coconut Grove. Charlie Barnet's Orchestra played at the club, and every once in a while Barnet would play Van Heusen's "Harlem Hospitality." Van Heusen would "gun [his] elevator up there to listen to the melody filtering through the kitchen doors."

The music business was in its infancy when Van Heusen started his career. It was dramatically different from the music business of today. Most significant, the recording element of the business was practically nonexistent. Bandleaders controlled, for the most part, the performance element of the industry. In Van Heusen's world, the real powerhouses were the publishing houses. Aspiring songwriters would sell their songs to publishing houses in the hopes the publishing houses would peddle the songs to bandleaders. There were many players in the universe of the music house. There were songwriters, of course. There were rehearsal pianists. There were song pluggers, those people whose job was to peddle the songs to bandleaders and other performers. Then, there were counter boys whose principal task, outside of reception, was to guard the free professional copies of the publisher's songs from small time singers and bandleaders.

The most difficult introduction is the first. Van Heusen had his first success with "Harlem Hospitality" because of Arlen and Koehler's departure for Hollywood. His second published song, "There's a House in Harlem for Sale," was also due to Arlen's intervention. Arlen requested the people at Santly Brothers Music to listen to some of his brother, Jerry's, and Jimmy's tunes. Jimmy and Jerry performed their numbers for Lester Santly and Herb Reis (brother of Les Reis of the singing duo Reis and Dunn) — one of the top song pluggers of the day. Reis was impressed with Jerry's rendition of "There's a House in Harlem for Sale" and convinced Santly to publish it. At this time, Van Heusen also convinced Santly to take him on as counterboy, song plugger, rehearsal pianist or anything else he might need. He ended his career as an elevator operator and moved out of the Wellington Hotel to live with Herb Reis in Tin Pan Alley.

In 1935, Van Heusen moved from Santly Brothers to the more prestigious Irving Berlin Music Company where he was fourth rehearsal pianist and song plugger. He still composed but found no audience for his works at Berlin. They needed piano players and song pluggers, not composers. As the new hire, he was assigned the less than desirable numbers:

> As the new man, they laid the dogs on me. For a long time they hadn't been able to get any action out of the Cotton Club's orchestra led by Claude Hopkins, and they sent me to Harlem with ten songs from a picture called "Hooray for Love." I knew I'd have to get some action or I'd be fired.

> [At the Cotton Club,] A warm welcome was given me by Big Frenchy, and even Herman Stark, and when I explained that Hopkins was not playing the songs of the company I worked for, he said, "Follow me." I tagged along behind Big Frenchy to Claude's dressing room. [He] burst through the door, and after asking Claude if he remembered "the kid, Jimmy," he demanded, "Well, why aren't you playing the kid's songs?"

Hopkins turned white, and stuttered that they would be on the air immediately and Big Frenchy departed. Claude, petrified with fright, said, "Jeez, you didn't have to go to Big Frenchy did you? After this you come straight to me, hear?" I made some excuse and left the score of professional copies and stock orchestrations and returned to the Berlin offices. There was disbelief when I declared that the songs would be on the Hopkins program tonight or tomorrow night.

Despite the success of this Damon Runyan-style escapade, Van Heusen was soon fired, following a major shakeup at Berlin.

Van Heusen was looking for work again. There was little choice for him but to pound the pavement with his own music. "Harlem Hospitality" was a modest success but not a breakout hit that would open publishers' doors. Van Heusen later recounted how Herb Reis "made the amazing deduction that I should be collaborating with bandleaders and let them share whatever royalties I might collect. This was called a 'cut-in,' which made them songwriters and eligible for royalties and for ASCAP and for performing rights." This was not particularly uncommon, with Irving Mills, Billy Rose and Al

Jolson being the principal perpetrators of this overt money grab. Van Heusen would have an angry reaction to Billy Rose's insistence on credit sharing later in his career, but during these lean years he had no problem with the practice.

Soon, Van Heusen had published songs with Willie Bryant, Benny Meroff, Hugh Barrett, Al Donohoe — and performed by the likes of Red Norvo, Charlie Barnet, and Jimmy Dorsey. The songs were less than noteworthy, but they did serve to keep Van Heusen in the public eye and established him as something of a "regular" in the New York music scene. Additionally, Van Heusen's association with Norvo and Barnet introduced him to a young pianist named Bill Miller, who left an impression that would last nearly two decades. In 1951, while Miller was performing at the Desert Inn, Van Heusen recommended to his friend, Frank Sinatra, that he listen to Miller and use him as his accompanist. Sinatra also obviously liked what he heard, as a four-decade collaboration ensued.

EIGHT

Jimmy Van Heusen in the early years
Courtesy of Van Heusen Photo Archives

It's a Darn Good Thing

The winds of fortune blew Van Heusen to the offices of James V. Monaco, or "Rag Time Jimmy" Monaco, as he was known. James Vincent Monaco was born in 1885 in Fiorina, Italy. In 1891, his family emigrated to Albany, New York. After playing ragtime piano in Chicago for a time, Monaco had his first big hits "Oh, You Circus Day" from *Hanky Panky* – and "Row, Row, Row" from the *Ziegfeld Follies of 1912*. The next year, Monaco composed his most enduring hit, "You Made Me Love You (I Didn't Want to Do It)" with lyrics by Joseph McCarthy from *The Honeymoon Express*. That song, of course, would be catapulted to fame in 1938 when Judy Garland performed it in the film *Broadway Melody of 1937* (with altered lyrics, "Dear Mr. Gable...").

Monaco was a talented composer, no doubt, but his lack of formal music training made it difficult to prepare his songs for public consumption. He composed all of his music using only the black keys of the piano, in the style of Irving Berlin. The result would be songs written in very difficult keys to play (F#: key signature with 6 sharps; C#: key signature with 7 sharps; Gb: key signature with 6 flats; Cb: key signature with 7 flats). Monaco needed someone to transcribe his melodies, then transpose them to more accessible keys to play and sing, and finally, assist him in playing his tunes to producers and performers. Van Heusen was well-suited to these tasks.

Van Heusen's association with Monaco was fortunate. Monaco was a founding member of ASCAP in 1914 and one of the major players in the music game. Van Heusen recalled, "Monaco was a slight sort of man, dapper and ASCAP Double A, which meant he received 25 or 30 thousand a year, whether he wrote or not. He would lay a buck for dinner on me, and I was allowed to bunk in an adjacent room next to his suite in the flea bag hotel known as the Forrest." However, not everything about the living arrangement was easy. Van Heusen noted that Monaco "had many idiosyncrasies. He would open and close the window of his suite a hundred times a day. It was either too drafty or too stuffy." Like a future companion of Van Heusen's, Monaco hated to be alone. Constantly occupying Monaco's apartment were "out of work vaudevillians, a poet named Walter Hannan, some track touts, elderly jockeys, and an occasional Italian tough guy or racketeer from downtown. He laid loot on them all if they needed it..."

Tolerance ran both ways. Monaco, who drank nothing stronger than wine, was amazed at Van Heusen's ability to consume hard booze and still function. He also did not complain about Van Heusen's occasional indulgence in smoking marijuana, which was prevalent in the music industry and looked upon with only slight disfavor.[3] All in all, Van Heusen's descriptions of Monaco reveal him to be a generous man who "was widely loved. I loved him too."

Unconventional living arrangements aside, Van Heusen was principally employed to assist Monaco and McCarthy in promoting a potential Broadway show. The show went nowhere, and Monaco could no longer afford to keep Van Heusen around. However, true to his generous nature,

---

[3]   Indeed, during this time marijuana was not illegal, its illegality having been established by the Marijuana Tax Act of 1937. Still, the matter was largely academic as Van Heusen and pals dismissed marijuana as an ineffective mood altering substance. "Marijuana's the longest stage wait in history. I'd stand around waiting to get high and nothing even happened. Usually, it made us sleepy or hungry."

Monaco introduced Van Heusen to Rocco Vocco — the head of Music Publishers Holding Corporation and the premiere music man of his time. He was also the boss of all of the professional managers of the Warner Brothers music companies — Witmark, Harms, Remick, and New World Music. As a favor to Monaco, Vocco introduced Van Heusen to Charles "Mousie" Warren, brother of famed songwriter Harry Warren and professional manager at Remick, the music company where George Gershwin was once a song plugger. Jimmy described the meeting thusly: "I played for him, and he grunted what I hoped was approval, and then handed me twelve professional copies of songs they were working at the time. He instructed me to come back only when I could play each one of those songs in every key on the piano."

Van Heusen went to the appointed task with gusto. For twenty hours per day, for a week, Van Heusen practiced at the piano in the basement of the Hotel Knickerbocker and in the Southern Music Company offices in the Brill Building. He returned to Warren and nervously played through the songs in whatever key Warren requested. Duly impressed, Warren hired Van Heusen to be a rehearsal pianist for Remick.

Warren would prove to be another larger-than-life figure who would leave an enduring impression on the young musician, and one certainly can see the similarities between "Mousie" and Van Heusen's later, more famous associates: a wandering eye, brave heart, and active funny bone:

> Like a lot of little guys – Mousie was only five foot tall – he liked big broads, and he called all girls "mice" as in, "Hey, lookit that great looking mouse with the big knockers." That's the way he got the tag. You see him around with some broad that he doesn't even come up to her navel, but he didn't pal around with the guys at all.

His size was certainly no impediment to striking fear in the hearts of his underlings: "The Mouse took on men twice his size, and worked them over with insults until it would seem that he'd get killed . . . he was fearless." When he wasn't chasing ladies or taking on the world, Warren loved practical jokes:

> Tin Pan Alley guffawed at the gullible singer Mousie persuaded to sing into a grilled wall thermometer — to make a demonstration record. Mousie's secretary kept popping in from the other

room to say to sing louder. The poor guy never could understand why Mousie'd never play the record back to him.

In addition to being fascinated by the persona of his new boss, Van Heusen shared his admiration for the piano style of Teddy Wilson, the dynamic star of Benny Goodman's Orchestra. Van Heusen made a conscious effort to imitate Wilson's style while rehearsing songs for those singers running through Remick songs or introducing them to aspiring artists. By all accounts, Van Heusen was exceptional, "Mousie'd hear someone like Glenn Miller or Tommy Dorsey or Red Norvo praise my playing and that raised my stock with him — especially when some of them wanted to hire me. Mousie'd always say he couldn't spare me."

Van Heusen was not a mere song plugger. He demonstrated a high regard for the works he was demonstrating. He felt the new music was dynamic and exciting, and it thrilled him to be a part of it. As part of what Alec Wilder dubbed the first generation of American popular composers raised exclusively on American popular songs, Van Heusen had enormous enthusiasm and respect for his craft, and this was not lost on those musicians to whom he demonstrated songs. Jazz great Joe Bushkin recalls:

> I first met Jimmy when I was playing with Bunny Berigan at the Famous Door, a little saloon where the musicians sometime outnumbered the customers. Jimmy was a musician's musician — a songwriter's songwriter kind of thing. He always had a high regard for the instrumentalists in the bands who were never catered to in any sense. The publisher obviously catered to the arrangers and bandleaders to get their material played, but Jimmy always had a feeling for the guys. That's how he and I became friends. He'd come around to hear us and he had a solid regard for my playing, and I always had a great leaning toward his melodies.

His experience at Remick gave Van Heusen the opportunity to mingle with the stars of the musical world, once and future. It was at Remick that Van Heusen first met Sammy Cahn. Cahn, at that time, already had two major hits to his name, "Bei Mir Bist Du Schoen" and "Please Be Kind." In his autobiography, *I Should Care*, Cahn recalls being quite impressed with various aspects of Van Heusen. "In addition to playing the piano as prettily as anyone can play piano, he was reputed to be an incredible swordsman with the ladies." For his part, Van Heusen was slightly more modest in recalling, "I made a pass or two at some of the girl singers but mostly I struck out. If anyone took notice of the skinny, six foot piano player, it was because of my playing and not because of any visible physical charm."

The song plugging industry put Van Heusen in contact with other popular figures in music as well. To Van Heusen, at least, it appeared this group of talented men all had their eyes on the brass ring, uniting them in the common goal:

> There was a wonderful camaraderie in the business in those days. I got to know and associate with all the music guys. I'd go to the Hotel New Yorker where Jimmy Dorsey was working, or I'd check in for dinner at the Manhattan Room at the Pennsylvania. I knew all of them — Kay Kyser, Duke Ellington, Tommy Dorsey, Guy Lombardo, Charlie Barnet, Artie Shaw, and all the arrangers and singers. Nan Wynn, who was a very big singer, took a liking to me, and I went around with her for a while. And Lee Wiley, another great girl singer. Later on, when I was plugging my own songs, it was even better — to get my songs played by the top people.

Of course, not everyone Van Heusen encountered at Remick was a star. Part of Van Heusen's job at Remick, like at Berlin, was to ensure that so called "kolos," Warren's pet name for unemployed singers, would not steal the arrangements of the newest songs. A frequent visitor to Remick was the featured singer at the Rustic Cabin, a less than first class New Jersey roadhouse above the Jersey Palisades. He went by the name Frankie Trent, until his mother found out. He promptly changed the billing to his given name: Frank Sinatra. Sinatra would stop by Remick when he would visit his good friend and future business partner Hank Sanicola, who was a counter boy at Witmark Music. Despite being against policy, Van Heusen took mercy on the struggling crooner and would ordinarily give Sinatra the precious arrangements.

NINE

Eddie DeLange on the cover of Billboard Magazine in 1939.
Courtesy of DeLange Family Photo Archives

Darn That Dream

Van Heusen knew his musical future would never be realized as a song plugger, even if he was employed by one of the best in the business. He needed to compose. Warren did not oblige him. "Stick to the piano," he was told. And so he did, composing at night, sometimes playing a tune or two for his bosses. One day in 1938, Jimmy Dorsey came to Van Heusen with a tune, and needed lyrics. Van Heusen was more than happy to oblige. Ironically, to date, Van Heusen's limited successes had all been through his lyric writing. Still, with Warren blocking his songwriting progress, this Dorsey/Van Heusen collaboration would have to be taken to another publishing company. The resulting song, "It's the Dreamer in Me," was published by Leo Feist, Inc., and it was a hit.

"It's the Dreamer in Me" was the first Van Heusen tune recorded by Bing Crosby, and in Van Heusen's estimation, at least, it was not one of Crosby's best efforts, "Bing recorded it –

the first song of mine he ever did – and he was more than slightly sour. He hadn't taken the trouble to learn the odd intervals in the melody – really a saxophone solo – and the notes he sang had little to do with the chords the orchestra played. It seemed a shame that he should make such a mess out of my brain child." This evaluation seems a bit harsh, and was almost certainly delivered with tongue firmly in cheek. However, it certainly did not affect Mousie Warren's evaluation of the song. After some initial disappointment that the song was not offered to Remick, Warren recognized the talent and offered Van Heusen a songwriting contract: $75 a week against future royalties.

The first songs written by Van Heusen under this new contract were unremarkable. Of the group, the bouncy tune written with Jimmy Dorsey, "I Love You in Technicolor" stands out. It has a charming melody and uses syncopation to good effect, but like Van Heusen's other efforts at this time, it did not make a real dent in the charts. Then, one day, Van Heusen was summoned to Warren's office to meet "an oversized, red haired guy in a sweat shirt and sandals named Eddie DeLange." Warren brought DeLange and Van Heusen together for the sole purpose of writing hits — a three way split of the royalties would follow.

At the time of this meeting, Eddie DeLange was an established musical personality, having written the lyrics to Duke Ellington's "Solitude" and Will Hudson's "Moonglow." He was a successful bandleader, teaming with Hudson to create the Hudson-DeLange Orchestra. And, like so many other Van Heusen partners, he was a character.

A typical description of DeLange is found in the December 1936, publication, *The Metronome*: "Eddie DeLange – an excitable New York, red-top bundle of nerves...likes ascot scarfs; to wear tails and his nine-year old battered raccoon coat...all without a hat...but his biggest passion of all is singing in four languages: English (1), Brooklyn (2), and Double Talk (3 and 4)." A typical story of DeLange's antics from Louis Sobol's April 25, 1939 column, "New York Cavalcade" in the *New York, NY Journal American*: "DeLange once walked into the Stork Club in tails — and a red flannel sweatshirt. He stood up boldly and defiantly in the 18 Club and revealed for all to see a neat dinner jacket — and brown suede shoes, also a red tie on a green shirt." This no doubt endeared DeLange to Van Heusen from the start.

Like Van Heusen, DeLange's roguish appearance was deceiving. DeLange was no ill-bred lout. He was born in 1904 in Long Island, New York, the son of a theatrical family — lyricist/playwright father and Broadway actress mother. He graduated from the prestigious McBurney School, a preparatory school in New York City whose alumni include J.D. Salinger and Ted Koppel. DeLange then attended the University of Pennsylvania, graduating in 1926 with a degree in business. The lure of the movies brought DeLange to Hollywood where he labored as an extra for six years. However, during that time, DeLange cultivated his interest in lyric writing, drafting more than 100 songs before he returned to New York City in 1932.

DeLange found it difficult to find a willing publisher for his songs, so, in an attempt to bring his music to a broader audience, he formed the Eddie DeLange Orchestra. The gambit proved successful, as one of his lyrics, "What Are Little Girls Made Of?" brought him to the attention of the powerful Irving Mills Music Corp. At Mills, DeLange penned the lyrics to the Ellington classic "Solitude." It was Mills who gave DeLange a tune crafted by Will Hudson that was serving as the theme song to Hudson's own orchestra. The result was

"Moonglow." This was the impetus for the union of Hudson and DeLange to create the Hudson-DeLange Orchestra in 1935.

The collaboration between the two was rocky. DeLange was outgoing, mercurial, devil-may-care. Hudson was fastidious, punctual and concerned with mundane details like keeping the bank operating. Each had their realm of expertise: DeLange was the front man, dancing with the girls, singing the tunes and ostensibly conducting the orchestra. Hudson rehearsed the men and wrote the arrangements, and was primarily responsible for the band's signature "hard swinging" sound. He was not generally comfortable in front of the orchestra and sometimes did not even travel with the orchestra.

These types of "yin and yang" collaborations can often yield great results, and the Hudson-DeLange Orchestra was popular. They had hit recordings of "Organ Grinder's Swing" in 1936 and "Yours and Mine" and "Sunday in the Park" in 1938. However, the strain of competing personalities was too great, and the Hudson-DeLange Orchestra dissolved in 1938. Apparently more comfortable with Hudson, the lion's share of the musicians remained with him to create the new Will Hudson Orchestra. DeLange was left to this own devices, and by sheer force of personality and fame, was able to raise a new orchestra shortly. The Eddie DeLange Orchestra was soon featured on the CBS Dole Pineapple Show starring Phil Baker, a popular comedian of the day. DeLange's hard swinging sound was too overpowering for the show, sometimes drowning out Baker's skits, and so DeLange was replaced by the softer sounds of Harry Salter. Salter remained a mainstay in studio orchestras, working for Milton Berle and serving as producer and orchestra leader for the popular "Name That Tune."[4]

Despite the success of the orchestra, DeLange considered himself primarily to be a songwriter. His inability to write songs from 1935-1938 must have frustrated him, making the deal to work with Van Heusen and Warren that much sweeter. Van Heusen explained the allure of the arrangement, which was not lost on DeLange, who was a veteran of the Mills machine:

> That [the compelled pairing] was highly unusual but Eddie and I didn't quibble. It meant the chance to have Remick exploit our songs —

---

[4]　Of further interest regarding Salter, he once led a radio orchestra in the 1920s with these members: Jimmy and Tommy Dorsey, Artie Shaw, Gene Krupa and Jack Teagarden.

tantamount to guaranteed hits if the material we wrote was any good at all. In the song business in those days, the publisher would take your song and print it and then try to get it on the air. But unless they made it their number one plugged song, it never went anywhere. Your contract called for a cent and a half royalty on the sheet music and a third of what the publisher got for the mechanicals — the records and player-piano rolls. The only way for you to make any money was for the publisher to make your song the number one plug song. Before the deal with Mousie, I must've had twenty song published without making any money. All I would up with was a printed copy of the song. But, if a publisher chose your song, you had a good chance of getting a hit because they got it played — good, bad, or indifferent — and it would get on the air and be recorded.

TEN

Young Jimmy Van Heusen at work.
Courtesy of Van Heusen Photo Archives

Welcome to My Dream

Despite the success of the Van Heusen/Dorsey tune, "It's the Dreamer in Me," Van Heusen did not truly come into his own as a songwriter until his collaboration with Eddie DeLange. Whether it was a matter of timing or inspiration, or both, it is uncertain. However, an examination of Van Heusen's earlier works provides something of a roadmap to these future successes. Van Heusen was unique among songwriters in that he started writing lyrics, then ultimately exclusively wrote music. This sense of the importance and more significant, the difficulty of writing lyrics, certainly made Van Heusen a superior collaborator in the future.

Van Heusen's lyrics were pedestrian, but effective. The lilting, yet tragically dated words to "Harlem Hospitality" fit the bouncy rhythm of the Jerry Arlen tune to a "T." They roll off the tongue, and Calloway's spirited performance is testament to Van Heusen's ability to capture the spirit of a time:

You don't need to eat an apple every day
   Hi de ho will keep the doctor far away
Cause you can't get ill
   When you feel that thrill
of Harlem Hospitality.

Van Heusen's next lyric, "There's a House in Harlem for Sale"
sees him falling into a familiar trap for the novice lyricist —
derivation and over-sentimentality. All things being equal, as
a middle class Syracusan, Van Heusen does a decent job of
capturing the lament of an African-American in Harlem, and
the lyric succeeds in communicating the overall message of the
song, which, for the time was powerful — the city failing to
live up to expectations and a return to the simpler life of the
country. The sentiment would have been better served with a
master economist of words, like Johnny Burke, as, indeed, less
truly would have been more. The lyric does manage to
incorporate an inside reference, that it is doubtful many, aside
from Van Heusen or Arlen might have known: "I won't miss
Harlem's 'Hi-De-Ho'/When I start singing 'Old Black Joe.'"
The preference of the music of Stephen Foster (from whom Van
Heusen could trace his lineage) to the current popular music

projects the understated – but rock solid – confidence Van Heusen always had in his own vision and work.

The first song where Van Heusen received a composing credit was "Unforgettable," written with Jerry Arlen. It is unclear how the division of labor was calculated between lyrics and music, but the disjointed nature of the song suggests an uncomfortable collaboration. (As an aside, whoever is responsible for the lyric: "Your charms might be harmless/Had I been armless/And wouldn't hold you near me", should have been man enough to take responsibility.)

The music of "Unforgettable" is largely good. However, any momentum the tune musters is completely dashed by a two measure figure that opens the song and serves as an amateurish leitmotif: starting and ending on the dominant "D," it makes an awkward leap of a major 6th to "B." From this "B," though, the tune progresses delightfully for several measures until it hits this roadblock again. The bridge is pleasant, but again gives way to the offending passage, this time made worse with the lyric "upsettable." There were promising nuggets in the tune, though, and one wonders how this song would have been different had Van Heusen assumed sole songwriting responsibilities.

"If I Look How I Feel" and "You Can Read Me Like a Book" were collaborations with bandleader Benny Meroff. They were basic, upbeat numbers but were complete songs, to be sure. "You Can Read Me Like a Book" opens with a triplet figure that evokes Burton Lane's "Don't Let It Get You Down," which would be written three years later in 1940. The first iteration of the title is phrased with Van Heusen standard figure: the dominant "C," moving up a minor third to "Eb," to the augmented fifth "Db" to the dominant "C." The second iteration of the title before the bridge and in the final cadence make much better use of the major sixth interval C to A, resolving to the tonic "F." For the more casual listener, this tune is catchy and hummable, but with many Van Heusen songs, underneath the melody is a more complex stream of chords and intervals.

"If I Look How I Feel" is another rhythm driven song for Meroff, with its principal figure being a series of chromatic passages introducing the title of the song. It is a fitting complement to "Book," as both capture the prevailing "sweet swing" sound of the day, employed by Meroff. Also like "Book," it has rather ordinary lyrics, which is somewhat remarkable given the sheer number of notes in the song —

almost always a dead giveaway that the tune was written first. Given this starting point, the songs are relatively free from painfully forced rhymes, something of a commendable achievement for two amateur lyricists.

"If You're Ever in My Arms Again" was a collaboration with Herman Mahr, a longtime contributor to the Irving Mills Music House. Like "Unforgettable," it is impossible to know how much each contributed to music and lyrics. There is little surprise, but nothing as jarring as the opening figure of "Unforgettable."

"Argentina Skies" and "It's the Dreamer in Me" represent Van Heusen's best lyrical efforts.[5] And, perhaps, more important, Van Heusen's last efforts as a "contract-less" songwriter. For after the success of "It's the Dreamer in Me," Van Heusen was signed by Remick, through the intercession of Mousie Warren, as a songwriter.

The "post-Remick" songs by Van Heusen represent a growth in this skill as a songwriter. "When a Prince of a Fella Meets a Cinderella" and "I Love You in Technicolor" are

---

[5] From "It's the Dreamer in Me" - "Please be sympathetic/When I grow poetic concerning your charms/If they seem to melt in my arms/It's the dreamer in me." A much better way to apologize for over-sentimentality than the plea for amputation expressed in "Unforgettable."

among the best swing numbers Van Heusen wrote before his collaboration with Eddie DeLange. "Anytime at All," written with Jimmy Dorsey marks an improvement over "Unforgettable" and "If You're Ever in My Arms Again" as a ballad. Written in question/answer echo format, the song is well-crafted and has a charming hook in the penultimate measures: "I've built my dreams around you/And if you ever fall."

However, one tune from this period deserves a better fate than to be forgotten: "Say Something Sentimental," written with Nat Burton and Jack Milford. The tune is without pretense, devoid of cliché and serves as the perfect transition from Van Heusen's early work to his more mature songs with DeLange such as "Darn That Dream" and "Deep in a Dream." Van Heusen's use of the augmented seventh in the bridge is a precursor to innovations to come, and serves to remind us that we have not yet panned all of the gold from the works of the great songwriters.

In an interview with the BBC, Van Heusen remarked that Eddie DeLange was the first "top drawer" lyricist with whom he worked. This is true vis-á-vis Van Heusen as a composer, but it does disregard Van Heusen's 1938 collaboration with the great Mitchell Parrish, redoing an older tune, "Shadow Sweetheart." The song was not noteworthy for any other reason but the union of two great songwriters and a testament to the fecundity of talent during the Golden Age of American Popular Song.

Van Heusen wrote about his time with DeLange:

> Almost invariably, he (DeLange) would write out his lyrics before I did a melody. If I wrote a melody first, he simply couldn't put a lyric to it. I'd take his lyric which was almost always too long and edit it down to size and put it to music. Sometimes, we'd collaborate by phone or by mail, but mostly we worked after hours, on the bandstand after the people had gone home or at my place - wherever there was a piano. It was nip and tuck.

This estimation of DeLange's inability to compose lyrics for a tune already written is seemingly undercut by DeLange's two biggest hits to date: "Solitude" and "Moonglow", both written for melodies already composed. Still, it is possible with DeLange's attention divided with his orchestra and performing, the process was simpler for Van Heusen to construct melodies around DeLange's completed lyrics than vice versa. This should not be taken, though, as the totality of Van Heusen's opinion of DeLange as a lyricist. All indications were that Van Heusen had immense respect for DeLange's talents. As Van Heusen stated in a 1939 article in *Syracuse, N.Y. Journal*: "The subject matter [of the song] depends on the cleverness of the lyric writer. DeLange is clever in his presentation of old things in a new way."

Whatever the arrangement, it worked. All told, Van Heusen and DeLange wrote only 20 songs from 1938-1940. However, of those 20 songs, one half of them charted either on the Hit Parade or other music popularity services.

ELEVEN

Eddie DeLange
Photo Courtesy of DeLange Family Photo Archives.

Can I Help It?

The first Van Heusen/DeLange collaboration was "A Cigarette and a Silhouette," for which bandleader Red Norvo also received a writing credit. The tune bears some mark of vibraphone solo, such that Norvo's influence was actual. Naturally, it also helped that Norvo and Mildred Bailey recorded the song in May, 1938. It did not chart, but it laid the foundation for their next effort, "So Help Me." Recorded again by Norvo and Bailey, the song reached number 2 on the Hit Parade and was Van Heusen's first, unadulterated hit. Norvo and Bailey's recording remained on the Hit Parade for 12 weeks. From a musical perspective, "So Help Me" does not represent a significant step forward from his previous tunes, such that it merited, by fiat, the popular success it enjoyed. It is a nice, catchy tune, but it is not at all certain that without Warren's pull, would have been on the charts. Still, Van

Heusen always spoke of the tune fondly, as one might a first child, even seeming somewhat disappointed that it no longer is in the public perception. The song does bear the distinction of being the first Van Heusen song to be heard in a motion picture: the 1938 James Cagney/Pat O'Brien Dead End Kids film *Angels with Dirty Faces*.

"So Help Me" also gave Van Heusen his first taste of real financial success and served as a portent for business adventures yet to come:

> When the first royalty period came around, and I received a check for $17,000 for my half of the first hit "So Help Me", I asked the accountant who gave it to me to call the bank so I could go over and cash it. The Mouse wanted his third in cash, and I didn't have a bank account anyways. I ran back to Remick and counted off the bills and gave them to the Mouse. He was delighted. However, now a friend of one of my fellow song pluggers who worked in the Internal Revenue Service offices, was standing by and warned me to declare that income. I had never made out an income tax statement. He said he would do it for $100.00 and I would be in the clear. Naturally, he deducted, the third I gave to the Mouse, and all sorts of

imaginary expenses, and I gave him a very small sum for the tax. Some months later a notice for examination arrived in the mail and when our friend from the IRS walked in the office he said, "I'll handle that for another $100.00." Good deal. Good deal that is, until the Mouse yelled for me to come to his office. What the hell had I done? He had not declared the third of the royalties I gave him and Uncle Sam had seen it on my report as a deduction. Though I volunteered to pay his tax on it, he said it was too late, and called me ungrateful for getting him into that jackpot.

My income tax continued to be made out by the same IRS employee, a former musician, a drummer. I later learned that when the notices of examination were given to him he simply went to the file, located my papers and tore them up. A few years later in Hollywood, when Edward Traubner, who took over my laughable books and the tax chores, and was striving to keep me from a jail term for fraud, it was learned that the IRS fellow back in New York had jumped out of a high window. Penalties and apologies and pleadings and promises and the wartime atmosphere probably helped make a settlement with Uncle Sam. I never was so foolish again. Although many of Traubner's clients were not examined for years by the IRS, my returns were microscopically examined within days after filing. There's probably a little tab on my file in the IRS that says in red ink: "CHEAT-ROBBER-WATCH HIM." All the result of that very helpful ex-drummer back in New York.

Van Heusen's next song with DeLange, "This Is Madness," also recorded by Norvo and Bailey, was more musically adventurous and less popular. Its unique intervals gave it something of the distinctive Van Heusen chromatic sound, but it was not polished. The abrupt cadence — "This is the madness of love" — seems more of a cop out, such that a couple more drafts might have yielded a more complete product.

The year 1938 closed for Van Heusen with the composition of his first standard —"Deep in a Dream." It did not chart as highly as "So Help Me" (Artie Shaw and Helen Forrest's recording only reached number three), but its legacy was certainly greater. A thoroughly unscientific survey of recordings plainly demonstrates this was the earliest work of Van Heusen to be widely recorded. Artists essaying this work include Chet Baker, Frank Sinatra, Ella Fitzgerald, Barbara Lea,

Connie Boswell and Cab Calloway, among others. "Deep in a Dream" follows a simple chromatic structure, its melody building with the emotion of DeLange's lyric, each verse reaching its emotional apex with the realization that the singer is only "deep in a dream," and the melody then fades back to the melancholy mood of the opening measures.

It is the bridge that is truly memorable. Moving in an artful arc from the tonic, the bridge changes keys 14 times in 8 measures. However, at no time does the melody seem lost or rambling, despite its difficulty or complexity, in fact, its resolution seems almost inevitable such that, at the end of the release, it is impossible to imagine it being written any other way.

Van Heusen and DeLange also were impacted by another of the pains of success: litigation. Following the success of "Deep in a Dream," coming so closely on the heels of "So Help Me," made them easy marks for frivolous claims of infringement by lesser talents. In a 1939 interview with the *Syracuse, N.Y. Journal*, Van Heusen remarked, "Nearly every time a writer scores with a popular tune, somebody is there to claim that the tune was stolen from him. Why after we wrote 'Deep in a Dream,' three suits, cropping up in different sections of the country, claimed that the song had been lifted." The suits, predictably, went nowhere, and based on the future successes of both Van Heusen and DeLange, were proven to be similarly baseless.

The adage "the professional can do it twice" was certainly borne out with the new songwriting team. And the string of hits continued with their next effort: "Good for Nothin' But Love." Fats Waller's recording of the tune went to number seven on the Hit Parade and marked the third of the first five DeLange/Van Heusen to chart in the top ten. It is a bluesy, boozy tune that can in some ways be considered a more naïve version of "Empty Tables."

If there was any doubt about Van Heusen and DeLange's status as "hit-makers," it was immediately dispelled by their next chart-topper, "Heaven Can Wait." The title of the tune was suggested by a friend of DeLange who was hoping to write a Broadway show with the same name. The show went nowhere, but the tune was the first Van Heusen song to reach number one on the Hit Parade — courtesy of Glen Gray's 1939 recording. The first stratospheric hit the team had, "Heaven Can Wait" is an interesting lyric in that the title serves as both the opening phrase of the tune and the cadence of each verse.

It is also the first Van Heusen tune where lyricist and composer could be said to be in synch — the benefits of a long-term collaboration, albeit long-distance at times.

However, its fame was also seasoned with a bit of notoriety. A parson in Boston branded Van Heusen and De Lange as heretics. The lyrics suggested the scandalous belief that people could experience some degree of happiness, some measure of heaven on earth through love. The "heretical" lyrics follow:

> Heaven can wait,
> This is paradise,
> Just being here with you,
> And breathing the air you do,
> Heaven can wait.
> Darling it's true
> This is paradise
> Gazing at all your charms,
> It's heavenly in your arms,
> Heaven can wait.
> You must be an angel on a visit from the skies
> Now I look at heaven when I look in your eyes
> Heaven can wait
> This is paradise
> Loving the way you do
> Until I go there with you.
> Heaven can wait.

Events conspired to make matters worse, as news of a tragedy broke through otherwise glowing reviews: "Heaven can wait — and thousands of boys hold thousands of girls a little tighter, a little more certain that love is after all, the finest thing in the world . . . . Heaven can wait — and thousands of married couples clasp hands, a surer, finder understanding binding them together . . . Heaven can wait — and a boy and girl seek death together in a closed automobile, the words scrawled on a bit of paper clutched in her hand."

That last phrase was, unfortunately, not hyperbole. Page one of the *Syracuse Journal*, for all of his hometown family and friends to see, showed a gruesome photo of two teenage lovers (from Syracuse, no less) who had committed suicide by carbon monoxide consumption in their vehicle; between them: a copy of the sheet music to "Heaven Can Wait."

"It just sickened me," Van Heusen recalled, "and the next thing I knew, Ida Mae was on the phone, 'Chester, are you sure you're in the right business?' First, Owney Madden and then this. I tore up the clipping and drank it away from my thoughts."

Public and private adversity did not have a serious effect on Van Heusen's continued production of hit songs. Following the success of "Heaven Can Wait," Van Heusen and DeLange wrote their wonderful ballad "All This and Heaven Too" to promote (but was not featured in) the 1940 Bette Davis/Charles Boyer film of the same name. The "hook" in Van Heusen's melody is the nearly octave difference in the first four measures of the chorus: "You gave me your lips/And your lips are so heavenly." It was tailor-made for crooning, as evidenced by the wildly popular competing recordings made by the warring Dorsey brothers, Jimmy's featuring vocalist Bob Eberly and Tommy's showcasing Frank Sinatra. (Jimmy won this particular round.)

The lyrics of DeLange also merit attention. DeLange, consciously or not, employed a rather sophisticated lyrical trick in the last measures of the song. Throughout the tune, DeLange would rhyme the phrase "And heaven too." However, in the last phrase, DeLange uses the following rhyme: "You gave a love so divine/All this is mine." The last iteration of "And heaven too" has no rhyme, giving further emphasis to the strength of the love being given. It is pure speculation, to be sure, but given the mischievous personalities of both DeLange and Van Heusen (and his significant irritation with overly judgmental folks), it would not be beyond the pale for them to tweak the sector of the public that condemned "Heaven Can Wait" by not only writing a lyric that is nearly identical in theme (i.e., the ability of earthly love to bring heaven), but also hammering the point home by employing the aforementioned lyrical technique. Certainly the great popular success the song enjoyed was doubly sweet to the team.

"All I Remember Was You" was the final song written under the exclusive DeLange/Van Heusen contract negotiated by Mouse Warren. It also is another tune that suffers, unjustly, from neglect. Tommy Dorsey had a popular recording of the song in 1939, but there has not been a definitive recording since that approximate time.[6] The song, as published, lacks a bridge. There is no obvious reason for this omission, and it certainly is not typical of the time period. In fact, it would be perilous to publish such a brief song, as it might impact whether performers would want to pay for two-thirds of a song. That the song was, in fact, published speaks volumes as to the level

---

[6] Through the courtesies of Stephanie DeLange, the daughter of Eddie, the author was provided with a 1939 recording of the tune sung by Lee Wiley accompanied by Van Heusen.

of popularity the team enjoyed at the time. The melody marked a departure from previous Van Heusen efforts, and demonstrated the first significant emergence of the unique Van Heusen style. In fact, it is not unfair to claim that "All I Remember Was You" is a first, working draft of "But Beautiful."

In an internal reorganization at Remick, Warren left to join Irving Berlin Music. Edwin H. Morris, the head of Music Publishers Holding Company (Warren's superior), left to start his own music publishing company. There was some reporting in local New York entertainment columns that Van Heusen, DeLange and Morris were going to establish their own publishing company with the backing of a "Park Avenue dowager." Obviously, the idea never came to fruition, and it is unlikely that this item was anything more than a gossip columnist's fantasy. DeLange and Van Heusen, though popular composers, were hardly in the financial or professional position to anchor a publishing company. Nor were they particularly well-suited temperamentally to embark on such a journey at this time. DeLange and Hudson split professionally, in part, because of DeLange's difficulty in keeping his non-performing commitments. Similarly, Van Heusen was much too involved in writing music and generally being a man about town to run a publishing company. Moreover, his earlier recounted income tax escapades also cast some relevant doubt as to whether Van Heusen would be the best choice to lead the business side of the songwriting game.

In an attempt to shore up assets, Remick required Van Heusen to re-sign his exclusive contract. When Van Heusen refused, Remick released him. This was not greeted by Van Heusen with great dismay, as it enabled him to work with other lyricists. This is not to imply that Van Heusen was dissatisfied with DeLange, but Van Heusen realized he was on the cusp of superstardom, and limiting himself to one lyricist risked his being pigeon-holed commercially and creatively. Nevertheless, he knew a good thing when he saw it, and until new opportunities arose, Van Heusen happily continued collaborating with DeLange on three more songs and a "can't miss" Broadway hit.

TWELVE

Jimmy Dorsey and his orchestra
Courtesy of Van Heusen Photo Archives

Turn It into a Musical

Alec Wilder described theater songs as "undoubtedly the finest examples of popular song writing." Wilder further elaborated:

> It is true that there is a greater tendency to play safe in pop (non-theater) writing, and undoubtedly those who never moved out of it . . . knew that they weren't competent to handle the larger horizon of show tunes. They did, however, often manage to write better songs for films, which bolsters my conviction that film songs are generally one degree less polished than theater songs.

Wilder wrote this passage to conclude the portion of *American Popular Song* entitled "The Great Craftsmen," which included Hoagy Carmichael, Walter Donaldson, Harry Warren, Isham Jones, Jimmy McHugh, Duke Ellington, Fred Ahlert, Richard Whiting, Ray Noble, John Green, Rube Bloom and Jimmy Van Heusen.

It is not the intention of this book to controvert Wilder's thesis. However, Wilder's conclusion is not beyond reproach. For instance, can it fairly be said that Gershwin's "They Can't Take That Away from Me," written for the film *Shall We Dance?*, or "A Foggy Day," written for the film *Damsel in Distress*, is less polished than his theater works? Jerome Kern's score for the movie *Swing Time* ("A Fine Romance" and "The Way You Look Tonight") is masterful. Harold Arlen's finest works were written for films. Many of Irving Berlin's great songs were either written for revues (which, it is assumed, are not the same as "theater writing") or films. Perhaps Wilder believed that merely essaying musical theater was redemptive or indicative of talent. Indeed, of the composers listed as "the great craftsmen," none, save Van Heusen, had any significant Broadway musical theater experience.

Wilder himself acknowledges some difficulties with his argument. In his subsequent analyses of the aforementioned "great craftsmen," he notes that Rube Bloom did go beyond his comfort zone to make larger contributions to music. Although not as openhanded in his assessment of Van Heusen, Wilder does admit that the composer presents a problem with his seemingly irrational banishment of film writers to permanent second class status to theater writers:

> The difficulty is simply this: there is no film writer category. Also those who have been written about as theater writers spent the major part of their creative life writing shows. This, Van Heusen hasn't done. And many of his film songs, it must be admitted, are not on a par with great theater music. Some of them are, but that truly doesn't make him a theater writer either. He is a great writer, but he refuses to make life simpler for me by staying put like Carmichael. I can only apologize for finding no proper niche for him."

Van Heusen's journeys on the Great White Way were interesting, to say the least, and it would be unfair to judge him solely on the accomplishments of those endeavors. Certainly to the extent they were not his most successful outcomes, it cannot be blamed on some inability to write polished songs or otherwise expand outside of some mythical "comfort zone." To the contrary, despite being in great demand by Hollywood and popular singers, Van Heusen wrote five stage musicals, working with each of his significant lyricists — DeLange,

Burke and Cahn. Each failed to measure up to expectations. Many were outright financial disasters.

In 1939, Van Heusen and DeLange were called upon by publisher Jack Bregman to contribute the music and lyrics to an adaptation of William Shakespeare's *A Midsummer Night's Dream*, set in turn of the century Louisiana entitled *Swingin' the Dream*. This musical was the brainchild of producer Erik Charell, who had prior success adapting a German operetta, *White Horse Inn*, for Broadway in 1936. Bregman also served as Charell's publisher for that musical.

Van Heusen felt that *Swingin' the Dream* "was a show that simply couldn't miss." And, he had good reason for this optimism. The previous year, Rodgers and Hart scored a big hit with their adaptation of *The Comedy of Errors* — *The Boys from Syracuse*. So, there was no reason to fear the subject matter being too "highbrow." The choreography was by Agnes De Mille, her first effort in her illustrious Broadway career that would include *Oklahoma!*, *Carousel* and *Brigadoon*.

The cast was nothing short of amazing. Often adjectives such as "amazing" are overused, diluting their significance, but the description is assuredly apt. The following is a sampling of the talent one would have seen if he would have been fortunate enough to be present at the Center Theatre on November 11, 1939:

Louis Armstrong

Bill Bailey

Troy Brown

Dorothy, Etta and Vivian Dandridge

The Deep River Boys

Juan Hernandez

Moms Mabley

Dorothy McGuire

Butterfly McQueen

Nicodemus

The Rhythmettes

Maxine Sullivan

The production also featured the latest in "special effects," as Samuel Leitner in his *Encyclopedia of the New York Stage, 1939-1940* writes:

> The huge Center Theatre's stage was exploited for various trick and interesting effects, with sets and costumes modeled after Walt Disney's cartoons. Titania made an entrance in a World's Fair "World of Tomorrow" electric wheelchair, a Murphy bed emerged from a tree in the forest; microphones (to

help audibility in the cavernous playhouse)
sprang up in the shape of caterpillars and snails.

Then, there was the music. The music was to be performed by Benny Goodman and his Sextet (consisting of Goodman, Fletcher Henderson, Lionel Hampton, Charlie Christian, Nick Fatool, and Arthur Bernstein), as well as Bud Freeman and the Summa Cum Laude. Goodman served as musical supervisor, along with Don Voorhees. Goodman and Freeman, of course, were personally well known to Van Heusen from his song plugging days.

In his unfinished autobiography, Van Heusen claimed that the team had already written the show's biggest hit, "Darn That Dream" at the time they were requested to provide the music for the show. Van Heusen played the song for Goodman, and it was immediately inserted into the show. Including "Darn That Dream," Van Heusen and DeLange wrote seven excellent songs for the show. There were also jazz arrangements of the music of Felix Mendelssohn, including "Spring Song" and "Wedding March" — the latter of which was from Mendelssohn's *Incidental Music to A Midsummer's Night Dream*. Count Basie's popular number "Jumpin' at the

Woodside" was also featured prominently. However, the showcase musical number in the show was the staging of an "opera" entitled "Pyramus and Thisbe," a sendup of the play within a play in Shakespeare's work. The "opera" was a massive medley of popular songs of the day played by Armstrong, Goodman and Freeman, involving the singing and dancing talents of the entire cast. Some noteworthy songs included in this operatic setting were: "Jeepers Creepers," "Oh! You Crazy Moon," "St. Louis Blues," "Ain't Misbehavin'," "I Can't Give You Anything But Love," "Moonglow," "My Melancholy Baby," "Christopher Columbus," "Way Down Yonder in New Orleans," "Down by the Old Mill Stream," and "Flying Home."

With all of this going for it, why is this musical known only among Van Heusen enthusiasts, Harlem Renaissance scholars and Broadway trivia buffs? Why, with all of this talent, did this musical lose $100,000 (1939 value) and close after 13 performances? There may be no satisfactory or logical answer to this question. However, it can fairly be said it had nothing to do with the music or the performances. The cast was predominantly African-American, but it is unlikely the racial component was responsible for its commercial failure.

Indeed, the one element of society where African-Americans were "tolerated" was in the field of entertainment. It is not the province of this book to address the propriety *vel non* of that societal phenomenon, nor the internal hypocrisy of the same (Nat Cole entering through the service entrance of the Sands Hotel.) The fact remains that African American performers were quite popular, and that popularity transcended racial barriers. Recall that the famous Cotton Club, the home of jazz in New York City, was originally a whites-only club. Following its desegregation, it did not suffer in attendance. Moreover, producer/developer Erik Charell would not have invested substantial sums into a project that would have faced an insurmountable obstacle from the start. This failure cannot be blamed on race.

Was the subject matter too high brow? Was the theater going audience or swing audience not ready for Shakespeare? Rodgers and Hart had a major success with *The Boys from Syracuse* in 1938. Their librettist, George Abbott, did not change the location or time period of the play, making it somewhat less accessible than Charell's 1890's Louisiana locale of *Swingin' the Dream*. Of course, any score that contains "This

Can't Be Love" and "Falling in Love with Love" would be difficult to ruin.

Perhaps the problem is construing *Swingin' the Dream* as a traditional musical. There are precious few resources discussing the show. Van Heusen speaks only rarely about it, and when he did, it was only to mention that it was a "can't miss" musical. Goodman's many biographies either omit it completely or pass it quickly. James Collier's treatment of Louis Armstrong is similarly silent. It may be that no one likes to dwell on the losses, and that is certainly understandable, but the fact remains that there seems to be no good reason why this show failed. Those resources that do exist are almost exclusively concerned with the trappings of the show — the talent of the cast, special effects, and musicians. There is nothing about the show itself. Is this where it failed? Is this the classic example of the whole being less than the sum of its parts?

It is more likely that the show served merely as a pretext for presenting the extraordinary cast to the public, a modified revue of sorts. In this regard, the show was destined for failure. Broadway in the late 1930s was in a transitional phase. The old stand-by revues (*Broadway Melody, George White*

Scandals) were being replaced by more traditional book musicals, such as *Babes in Arms, Strike Up the Band,* and *Boys from Syracuse.* The avant garde of musical theater was experimenting with sophisticated librettos and integration of music and plot – fully achieved for the first time with Rodgers and Hammerstein's *Oklahoma!* in 1942. It was nothing short of ironic that the ultramodern music of *Swingin' the Dream* was presented in an archaic and dying format.

Those attracted by the cast were more than likely frustrated by the format. Why endure the half-baked idea of a Shakespeare play set in 1890 Louisiana to hear the cast sing jazz standards? While immensely musically talented, the cast was not known principally for stage acting. The adaptation was not sophisticated enough to qualify as a full-blown musical, but there was just enough distraction of a plot to place this outside the definition of a revue.

In the end, the audience was doubly thwarted: no engaging plot/play and not enough emphasis on the music. By way of example, Louis Armstrong reportedly played trumpet only near the end of the show, despite carrying it with him for nearly the entirety of the production. *The New York Times* reviewer Brooks Atkinson wrote, "Although Louis Armstrong carried his golden horn whenever he appears, he hardly has a chance to warm it up until the show is well over." Like so many other endeavors, the producers needed to make a commitment to one form or the other. They "messed with Mr. In-between," to coin a phrase, and disaster ensued. The *Theatre Arts'* review put it aptly when it said, "The show which was meant to be a mammoth orgy of swing missed its objective...A dreadful distance...separated the audience from dancers and music alike (and did not) reach out to the spectator and make him take part, even vicariously, in the festivities."

Although it is an interesting exercise to ascertain why this production failed, in the end, Alan Corrigan, may have the best answer in his essay: "Jazz, Shakespeare and Hybridity: A Script Excerpt from *Swingin' the Dream*": "Despite the potential that one might see...it is entirely possible that *Swingin' the Dream* was a travesty not only in the sense of being a burlesque, but also in the sense of simply being bad." In any event, it was an unfair and unfortunate result given the extraordinary opportunity presented by having the stars gathered as they did in the Center Theatre in late 1939.

Van Heusen's role in the production is not well documented. In interviews, he only found time to mention the lone shining spot from the endeavor — "Darn That Dream." It is somewhat ironic that the only extant copy of a portion of the script was found among Van Heusen's papers at UCLA. Given the structure of the show, it is unlikely Van Heusen or DeLange had any intimate role in the production. After all, they were not the composers of the show in the same sense as Rodgers and Hart were with *Boys from Syracuse.* At the most, Van Heusen and DeLange contributed original songs to a swing revue.

According to Alec Wilder, he was originally slated to compose the songs for *Swingin' the Dream* — a fact that he ruefully recalls in *American Popular Song,* and which might have subconsciously affected his critical evaluation of Van Heusen therein: "I was inclined, without having more than met him, to dislike him at this point, since I had written an entire score for this show and had to take it back due to the duplicitous character of the producer." Wilder did contribute one song to the show: the rather pedestrian "Love's a Riddle." Written in the style of a madrigal, the song was an ironic attempt to write an Elizabethan madrigal for a Shakespearean tale set in turn of the century Louisiana. There is no record of how it fared during the production, but it seemed to be the weakest of the original songs written for the show. The publisher credits Van Heusen and DeLange with the lyric, but if that were, in fact, the case, it is doubtful that Wilder would have permitted any meaningful partnership. This credit appears to be a bow more to the formality of royalty sharing than anything else.

The music that Van Heusen wrote for *Swingin' the Dream* demonstrated a unique understanding of the effect that the show was attempting to portray. He wrote hard swinging numbers —"There's Gotta Be a Weddin'," "Swingin' the Dream," and "Peace, Brother." He also composed beautiful, but understated mood music such as "Moonland (A Fantasy)" and one of his finest ballads, "Darn That Dream." Of the songs, only "Darn That Dream" enjoys current popular appeal. However, "Peace, Brother" was something of a minor hit in the early 1940s, presumably fueled by its message in the time of war.

The composition of "Darn That Dream" more than justified the entire *Swingin' the Dream* endeavor. Recorded by countless artists, it remains a mainstay of both jazz vocalists and instrumentalists. Alec Wilder describes the song as having "a very interesting and difficult melody in that its chromatic character makes the notes hard to find ... I've never heard a song quite like it." K.J. McElrath, a jazz musicologist for *JazzStandards.com,* aptly depicts the tune when he said, "At his most sophisticated, Van Heusen presents an angelic melody that is devilishly difficult for the novice jazz performer." In the song, Van Heusen employs a neat harmonic trick, with the key changes working inversely with the bass to give the impression of simultaneous ascent and descent.

No doubt Benny Goodman found Van Heusen's music engaging and intriguing. His 1940 record of "Darn That Dream" with Mildred Bailey was yet another number one hit for Van Heusen and DeLange.

THIRTEEN

Jimmy Van Heusen and Johnny Mercer
Courtesy of Georgia Tech University Photo Archives

I Thought About You

Swingin' the Dream was a commercial and critical failure. However, the main exponents of the show – Goodman, Armstrong, Sullivan, Van Heusen and DeLange – emerged with reputations unscathed. Van Heusen and DeLange would write only three more songs together after *Swingin' the Dream*: "Looking for Yesterday," "Shake Down the Stars," and "Sympathy."

"Shake Down the Stars" bears the distinction of being the first Van Heusen song recorded by Frank Sinatra. In New York City on February 26, 1940, at his second recording session with Tommy Dorsey, Sinatra produced the first of his 85 recordings of Van Heusen songs – the most of any composer. "Shake Down the Stars" is a typically complex Van Heusen song, with harmonies that befuddle and can leave the careless artist hopelessly lost. The song starts in a minor key, but not the relative nor parallel minor of the tonic, rather it is the parallel minor of the dominant. Indeed, it does not make its way to the tonic until six measures into the tune. The bridge offers no relief to the performer, as it, too, challenges with odd intervals and unique harmonics. Like all such Van Heusen songs, despite this complexity and ostensible meandering, one cannot conceive of the song being written in any other way.

DeLange suffers in comparison with Mercer and Burke, but he nevertheless is vastly underrated as a lyricist. While some of his verses might seem saccharine in the cynical light of post modernity, he was able to convey, in a manner appropriate for the time, some "darker" motifs. To wit, the bridge lyrics, "I gave you my arms, my lips, my heart, my life, my all/But the best that I had to offer you I found was all too small." A tone of bitterness or ingratitude is expressed, a more subtle incarnation of the "she done him wrong" line of blues songs. The rejecting lover is cast as the villain — unique among Van Heusen/DeLange collaborations, but in many ways, an appropriate song to start the Sinatra/Van Heusen relationship. Crosby, though, was no fan of this lyric, calling it "the most violently wasteful song I've ever heard. . . A guy rips down the whole firmament because some flutter-brained dame doesn't love him. He sounds like an H-bomb scientist gone nuts."

"Looking for Yesterday" is another forgotten Van Heusen/DeLange gem. It is similar thematically to "Shake Down the Stars," and again Sinatra and Dorsey provide the authoritative interpretation. The critical hook in the melody is another Van Heusen daring leap — from the seventh to an augmented tonic — a hellish interval, but in the hands of a skilled technician, tailor-made for crooning. DeLange has a graceful turn of phrase in the tune: "My heart lives in misery/Always a stone in its shoe/Looking for yesterday/And you." There are only so many ways to communicate sadness, and DeLange had a talent for creativity in that regard.

The final Van Heusen/De Lange collaboration was the awkward "Sympathy," a rather inauspicious conclusion to a very commercially and critically profitable partnership. The end of the DeLange/Van Heusen partnership was amicable. Both men were drawn in different directions and by different impulses. Eddie DeLange continued to write hit songs with other writers following the break with Van Heusen in 1940. In particular, he wrote the wonderful ballad "Just As Though You Were Here" — containing some of his most thoughtful and warm lyrics: "Velvet Moon" (a major hit for Harry James Orchestra), "String of Pearls," "So You Know What It Means to Miss New Orleans?," and "Along the Navajo Trail." DeLange would later follow Van Heusen to Hollywood in 1944 where he contributed songs to *The Bishop's Wife* with Cary Grant, David Niven, and Loretta Young; *If I'm Lucky* with Perry Como, Harry James, Carmen Miranda, and Vivian Blaine; and *New Orleans* with Billie Holiday and Louis Armstrong.

Van Heusen was a frequent guest at the DeLange household when both men were in Hollywood. By all accounts, the men remained friends, and in interviews and recollections, Van Heusen spoke of DeLange with heartfelt and sincere admiration. DeLange died in 1949 at the too young age of 45. His legacy is now preserved by his daughter, Stephanie, and his son, Warren. They are rediscovering their father's unique contribution to American popular music, and are engaged in the noble pursuit on ensuring these contributions are not forgotten.

In spite of this auspicious first effort, the early Van Heusen/Burke partnership was sporadic due primarily to Johnny's tight connection to Bing Crosby and the demands of his resulting Hollywood obligations. Never one to wait around, Van Heusen rounded out 1939 with yet another collaborator who also had worked extensively in Hollywood, and also owed his current fame to Bing Crosby.

In 1932, Johnny Mercer had won a national contest sponsored by Paul Whiteman to find singing talent to fill the void left by the Rhythm Boys, following Crosby's departure from the Whiteman organization. At the time, Mercer was concentrating on songwriting and acting, but his wife, Ginger, entreated him to enter the New York portion of the contest. Upon hearing him sing, Whiteman declared Mercer the winner of not only the New York but also the national contest.

Unfortunately for Mercer, the victory netted him no additional popularity as a singer and did nothing to propel his songwriting career; Whiteman abandoned him. Only in 1932, with the hit "Lazybones," did Mercer attract Whiteman's attention again, and Whiteman asked Mercer to assemble a trio to become the new Rhythm Boys. The new Rhythm Boys were a disaster, but Whiteman recognized, at last, Mercer's talent and signed him to a singing contract.

Mercer was making good money in the mid-1930s and, like many other New Yorkers, was attracted by the lure of Hollywood. In 1935, he made the journey west and labored as a singer and role player in various motion pictures. On a 1936 journey back to his home in Savannah, Georgia, Mercer wrote the tune "I'm an Old Cowhand." Upon his return to Hollywood, the song came to the attention of Bing Crosby who had it featured in his film, *Rhythm on the Range*. The song was a hit, and it led to many others: "Goody Goody," "Too Marvelous for Words," "Hooray for Hollywood," "Jeepers Creepers," and "You Must Have Been a Beautiful Baby."

However, in 1938, the hits stopped for Mercer. He returned to performing, and, again, it was Crosby who provided for his return to prominence. Courtesy of a vaudeville number written by Mercer called "Mr. Crosby and Mr. Mercer" and performed by the same, Mercer was again in demand as a performer. He followed the work to New York City, and it was there that he established the Mercer-Morris publishing company with Edwin H. Morris, the former head of Warner Brothers Music Company in 1939.

One of the first actions Mercer took for his own company was to work with Van Heusen. Mercer knew that Van Heusen was working already with Johnny Burke, but that did not faze him. If anything, it may have been sauce for the goose. Van Heusen was an immensely talented composer to be sure, but the budding rivalry with Burke might have made him even more attractive. The roots of this stormy relationship can be traced to the lyrics to "What's New?" The tune was written by Bob Haggart, an arranger for the Bob Crosby Orchestra. Crosby loved the soulful melody, which at that time had the moniker, "I'm Free," and asked Mercer to supply a lyric. However, Mercer was unable to complete the task. He worked at it for two months, and all Mercer could write was "I'm free, free as the birds in the trees, dad da da da."

The tune was given to Burke, who supplied his ingenious conversational lyric, and a standard was born. This failure was doubly painful to Mercer, as it not only represented a professional/creative failing, but Mercer felt that Burke's lyric cemented him as the chosen lyricist of Bing Crosby. Philip Furia, in his masterful biography of Johnny Mercer, *Skylark: The Life and Times of Johnny Mercer*, advances the theory that Mercer harbored a jealousy, bordering on resentment of Crosby. He was unable to emulate Crosby's success as a performer (which, perhaps, was Mercer's first love), and with the favor now enjoyed by Burke, Mercer could not even aspire to be Crosby's wordsmith. Furia writes, "Mercer would ever after carry a chip on his shoulder about Johnny Burke. In the 1960s, his son-in-law, a jazz pianist, was trying to write songs. When Bob Corwin showed Mercer one of his lyrics, Johnny scoffed at it: 'Sounds like Johnny Burke.'"

The first tune written by Van Heusen and Mercer was "I Thought About You." There are conflicting stories as to how this tune was borne. Furia writes that the lyric was already written by Mercer and given to Van Heusen as a way of starting the collaboration and finding songs for Mercer's new publishing company. Gene Lees' biography, *Portrait of Johnny: The Life of John Herndon Mercer*, quotes Mercer as saying the following, "I can remember the afternoon that we wrote it. He (Van Heusen) played me the melody. I didn't have any idea, but I had to go to Chicago that night. I think I was on the Benny Goodman program. And I got to thinking about it on the train. I was awake, I couldn't sleep. The tune was running through my mind, and that's when I wrote the song. On the train, really going to Chicago."

Both stories could be true. By 1939, Van Heusen had a vast backlog of songs, such that he could have provided Mercer (as he did with Burke) an already-completed song. Also, from working with DeLange, Van Heusen was equally capable of writing songs around a finished lyric. In the end, it did not matter, the Mercer/Van Heusen team yielded a standard at their first at bat.

"I Thought About You" provides an excellent example of this marriage of words and music: Mercer's opening line: "I took a trip on a train" is accompanied by an ascending melodic figure implying hopefulness. The next line: "And I thought about you" is accompanied by a descending musical figure, demonstrating a mood of sadness. The listener is immediately drawn in: why is the singer sad? Is he pining for a lost love or missing a lover waiting for him. The successive lines add to the suspense, while offering glimpses into Mercer's unique ability to paint scenes with words:

> I passed a shadowy lane
> And I thought about you.
> Two or three cars parked under the stars
> A winding stream
> Moon shining down on some little town
> And with each beam
> Same old dream.

This last couplet is notable for several reasons. Mercer's omission of the article "the" before "same old dream" is masterful. It subtly conveys an intimacy with the listener after a recitation of sight and sounds that perhaps only the singer has seen. The melody also builds to its highest dramatic point, theretofore, with "and with each beam" only to resolve with a complex melodic descending figure, that uniquely reintroduces the "A" section of the song.

In an attempt to avoid these thought-provoking scenes, Mercer's traveler draws the shade of the window. However, even that does not help:

> I peeked through the crack
> And looked at the track
> The one going back to you
> And what did I do?
> I thought about you!

Van Heusen's melody is similarly creative. The song has a false cadence of sorts. The highest melodic point of the song is the phrase: "The one going back to you." However, the next phrase does not resolve the tension, as might be expected. Instead, Van Heusen creates additional melodic suspense to complement Mercer's question: "And what did I do?" He even adds to the effect by starting the last measure of the song with a quarter (one beat) rest.

"I Thought About You" was a hit for Mercer and Van Heusen, with its most popular recording that of Mildred Bailey with the Benny Goodman Orchestra. Bailey had an affinity for the music of Van Heusen, having recorded Van Heusen's earliest hits with Red Norvo, and Benny Goodman, an old acquaintance of Jimmy's from his song plugging days, was also working with him on *Swingin' the Dream*. With Benny Goodman's Orchestra, she would record the balance of the Van Heusen/Mercer collaborations - "Blue Rain" and "Make with the Kisses." To be sure, the appeal of Mildred Bailey had an important role in establishing the young Van Heusen as a popular songwriter. Van Heusen never forgot Bailey, and when the chronically unwell Bailey took seriously ill in the late 1940s, he, along with Frank Sinatra and Bing Crosby, arranged to pay her medical bills.

It was a promising beginning to what amounted to a great tease. In 1939, Van Heusen and Johnny Mercer wrote three songs, "I Thought About You," "Blue Rain," and "Make With the Kisses." They would not collaborate again until 1974 when Frank Sinatra asked his two old friends to write him another saloon song, the apt "Empty Tables." The collaboration did not continue due to any personal animus between the two. Mercer spoke well of Van Heusen, saying he was "easy to write with …he seems to have a series of chords waiting at his command to which he can fashion a melody the moment his lyricist springs any idea on him." In looking at the songs they composed, it is obvious the two developed a rapport that belied the brief time the men knew each other.

FOURTEEN

Celeste Holm, actress from the movie The Tender Trap,
and Jimmy Van Heusen studying his composition.
Courtesy of Van Heusen Photo archives

It Could Happen To You

Van Heusen was at his most popular and most marketable at this time. No longer signed to an exclusive deal with Remick (or any publisher) and demonstrating a marked ability to write hits, he was courted by many different people. As he recalled, "For a while I was working with five lyric writers (DeLange, Mercer, Burke, Mack Gordon, and Joseph McCarthy). I had an apartment at 400 East 52nd Street and I'd work all night every night. I had hammers on my piano muffled so the neighbors could get their sleep."

The true path to financial success as a songwriter, though, was through membership in the American Society of Composers, Artists and Publishers (ASCAP).

ASCAP was founded in New York City on February 13, 1914, by composer Victor Herbert. It is, in brief, an organization created to protect and encourage the composition of copyrighted music. ASCAP collects license fees from those who perform or utilize the music of ASCAP members in any manner, then redistributes those fees to its members in the form of royalty payments. At the time Van Heusen was writing his earliest hit songs with DeLange, Mercer, and Burke, ASCAP distributed royalty payments according to a classification committee, based principally on past revenue rather than recognition of the actual popularity of the song for which royalties were being paid. As a result, a member of the highest class, though never having written a hit in over 10 years, might collect more revenue than a hit songwriter.

Van Heusen's experience with ASCAP is revealing. Upon entering ASCAP, it is likely that Van Heusen was unaware of the non-egalitarian nature of the royalty distribution. In fact, in spite of his earlier association with Monaco, one of its founding members, Van Heusen did not even know the process of gaining entry to ASCAP, believing that membership was bestowed by invitation. When he learned it was via sponsorship, he reached out to Harold Arlen and Yip Harburg. However, once he learned of the royalty structure, it rankled him to the core. First, the Depression was still very much a reality, and Van Heusen, like most of his generation, fiercely sought financial security. More important, Van Heusen felt it to be unfair. Unfairness to Van Heusen was a mortal sin. Adversity he would encounter and face stoically. Unfairness, in any sense, he would rail against, whether it be racial or religious intolerance or more personal matters such as contract terms or royalty payments:

> I was the hottest new writer in the very closed shop that was the music business. One old timer asked me why I wasn't a member of ASCAP. . . . [Upon obtaining membership], the membership committee assigned me to Class 4, the lowest. After 4, came 3, 2, 1, then D, Double D, C, Double C, B, Double B, Permanent A, Class A, and Double A. My income from ASCAP was something like $300 per year, and by this time with a dozen smash hits, my songs were being performed more than 3/4ths of the writers in the top class Double A. I never understood this disparity, even though it was explained that the classification committee would promote me as I continued to have hits, and when I got to the top, I'd stay there, forever. Other writers, jealous as hell of this new upstart, formed the classification committee and handled promotions. As a result my classification was still way at the bottom with less than 800 dollars a year

income, long after I invaded Hollywood and amassed a string of hit song credits. A few years later, after permanently partnering with Johnny Burke, who was suing the ASCAP for not putting him at the top, I joined up with the same lawyer and same lawsuit. When the performance figures were tabulated by the attorneys' accountants, the necessity for court action was removed when both Burke and myself were jumped to the top classes. We stayed there for over thirty years, and even though Burke passed on and nothing new has been added to his catalogue, ASCAP pays his estate, based on the performances of old songs, in excess of 100,000 per year, [1973]. We had to yell like hell to get the right count however.

For the time being, though, Van Heusen did not need to "yell like hell" to attract the attention of the music business. He was wooed by many different music publishers, chief among them Jack Robbins, sometimes called "Mr. Music." Robbins would eventually found the music publishing company of Robbins Feist & Miller, notable for being the first music publisher to strike a deal with MGM. Robbins' company would handle the entirety of MGM's music publishing during the heyday of the MGM musicals. But, in 1939, he was, in Van

Heusen's words, "dapper, debonair, a stylish rhumba dancer and lover of Latin music. A great friend of music writers and would never insult or abuse one until he had him under contract."

Robbins introduced Van Heusen to a new style of nightlife. Van Heusen was certainly no stranger to the after-hours life, and, in fact, craved it, spending countless hours in clubs and hotels long after closing to pitch songs to musicians. Robbins went strictly first class, in the heart of the evening, through the front door. It was under Robbins' aegis that Van Heusen cultivated the bon vivant lifestyle that so endeared him to Sinatra and others in the Hollywood set. He dressed Van Heusen in tuxedos, the best suits, ties, shoes and shirts.

Of course, it was all on Robbins. "Everyone goes first class with me," he told Van Heusen. To him, it was an investment. Every music publisher was looking for the next Irving Berlin, Richard Rodgers or Cole Porter. As Van Heusen learned, Robbins' "generosity" was not all that it seemed: "It wasn't until I'd written a few songs for him that the few thousand bucks he spent that day appeared on my royalty statement as a debit — as an 'unearned advance'. It took me awhile to earn enough to pay off for that wardrobe, which I didn't much need in the first place."

Robbins took Jimmy to Havana (or rather, vice versa), which would be Van Heusen's first time outside of the United States. Per custom, the entire affair was first rate: the best hotels, casinos and restaurants. Robbins sprung for a sumptuous suite at the Hotel Nacional de La Habana. The hotel and casino were both operated by the legendary Ben Marden, of New Jersey Riviera fame. Robbins was interested primarily in making Jimmy happy, and casing the local songwriting talent. Latin American-inspired music was just starting to enter the American mainstream, and Robbins wanted to be ahead of the curve. In a short while, Americans would flock to theaters to see Carmen Miranda and dance to Latin rhythms.

Jimmy was interested primarily in having a good time. He found that and more. While taking in a show at the Nacional, Jimmy was smitten by Tamara Drasin, the casino's featured singing star. Drasin was known principally as having introduced the songs "Smoke Gets in Your Eyes" and "The Touch of Your Hand" from the 1933 Jerome Kern/Otto Harbach musical, *Roberta*. Drasin was billed only as "Tamara," in a transparent attempt to capitalize on the exoticism of the dark Ukrainian beauty. By the time Van Heusen saw her in Havana, Tamara had appeared in no fewer than seven musicals, including *Right This Way* — the 1938 Irving Kahal/Sammy Fain flop that yielded "I Can Dream, Can't I?" and "I'll Be Seeing You."

Jimmy romanced her, and, as usual, succeeded: "She was a beautiful girl, slightly Russian, and a good artist. She treated me like a little boy [she was 8 years his senior] and I was enchanted. I bathed in her beauty and attention. We were sweethearts for a long time after we got back to Manhattan where she had a penthouse." Van Heusen left New York in 1940, and it is unclear whether he maintained a relationship after his departure. It is unlikely, though. Drasin married Edwin D. Swann, a vice president of a powerful advertising firm. On February 22, 1943, while travelling on a USO tour, Drasin was killed in an airplane crash in Portugal, along with 24 others. She might have survived the crash had she not exchanged seats with singer Jane Froman, who survived the crash after sustaining several lifelong injuries. According to Froman's biographer, Ilene Stone, the event bothered Froman for the remainder of her life.

There is no contemporary record of Van Heusen's thoughts about Drasin's death. It is likely that in 1943, with the world in the midst of war, and Van Heusen consumed with both his test piloting and musical responsibilities with Paramount, the event, to him, did not merit public comment. The fact that Drasin was then married might also have been a factor. However, his own autobiography only contains a passing reference: "A very nice girl. I enjoyed her." Van Heusen obviously had difficulty expressing personal emotion, outside of music. Van Heusen appears to be worried about shedding his alpha male persona, even for a moment, to express grief (albeit some 20 years later) over the untimely death of someone he loved. Men of that era were permitted to express emotion in only certain ways — Van Heusen composed, Sinatra sang, Gable acted.

Robbins also introduced another woman who would play an important, if not interesting, role in Van Heusen's life — the legendary madam Polly Adler. Van Heusen unabashedly kept companionship with prostitutes and madams throughout his life. But, Van Heusen did not treat prostitutes in the common manner. He would take them to dinner, clubs and social functions. As one of his former companions said, "Jimmy was never ashamed of hookers. He was never hypocritical or moralistic. The average guy can't get away fast enough after being with a hooker, but not Chester. He'd take them to dinner and treat them as nicely as he treated any of his other girls and he always was very thoughtful and gracious – gallant – to every lady he knew."

Van Heusen may have been gallant, but it does not change the fact that in personal reminiscences, he considered hookers to be a means to an end: "As a bachelor, I made a point of taking every good looking girl I could to bed – I thought I was ordained to grab every girl I could to bed – I thought I was to grab every girl if she was good-looking at all. Plus, when I got stuck I knew a lot of hookers."

Ralph Harris recalls, "I don't gainsay there were a great many women in (Van Heusen's) life but he was always prone to call in hookers. He had a very special reason for that. 'Look,' he said, 'I call a broad and she comes and I give her money and she's gone. You get a girl in here and she's always hanging around. I can't stand that.'"

Van Heusen was even more direct when he discussed his use of the prostitutes he knew as an "incentive" to potential purchasers of the songs he plugged: "I was good friends of three or four other madams in New York. I used to know all the swinging guys in those days. Remember that as a song plugger, I was entertaining people, constantly entertaining some band leaders and some singers or somebody that would be doing some good for the songs, and sometimes that meant getting them laid. Somebody would say, 'Say, let's go get laid,' and that would be it."

Van Heusen's morality regarding prostitutes is revealing. In one sense, prostitutes were the worst kept secret in the world. Businessmen, politicians, entertainers, sports figures and celebrities of every stripe frequented houses of prostitution or engaged the services of "escorts." Van Heusen, as was his wont, simply did not see the need to engage in hypocrisy. Whatever sin or crime prostitution was, it was to Van Heusen a lesser transgression than hypocrisy.

Van Heusen's sexual morality was complicated, to say the least. He obviously had no problem with engaging the services of prostitutes. He had no problem with one night stands or other limited sexual dalliances. He also had no problem with relations with younger – sometimes much younger – women. Van Heusen stated the following about his relationship with a woman known only as "Gail," one of Polly

172

Adler's "girls": "Gail used to come out to the field with me when I was flying around. Then she started to take lessons on her own. I saw her learner's permit one day and noticed her age – she was 14. She was like me. She started her business early." At the time of this revelation, Van Heusen was most likely 27.

Business aside, not long after Robbins made the introduction to Adler, Van Heusen made her place a second home and had a genuine affection for her:

> I used to hang around Polly's a lot. I'd go up and have a drink or play backgammon with her. I didn't pay to jump on any of her broads. Polly taught me to play backgammon and she was good – that cost me money. I had a great time, drinking and playing with Polly and trying to nail all the girls in sight.
> . . .Polly Adler was one of the most fascinating females I ever knew. How the hell do you explain why you like someone? Polly was warm and funny, smart and gutsy and fun to be around. We liked each other and didn't take the time to think about it much.

One reason for the friendship could be that Van Heusen admired competency in any field, and Adler was quite good at what she did. He recalled:

> Polly would proposition any good-looking girl she met, no matter where. "Wouldn't you like to make two hundred dollars in about a half hour without any effort?" she'd ask. As a result, she had dozens of legitimate girls who never were anywhere near her place available via telephone for some well-paid dates with well-heeled swingers. Many a girl turned a trick or two every week or so for years and no one knew about it. Polly was a discreet dame.

Van Heusen's way with the ladies of the night would serve him well in his travels, but at this point, the fun had to end, at least for a time. There was work to do.

FIFTEEN

Lyricist Johnny Burke and Jimmy Van Heusen
collaborating on a piece of music.
Courtesy of Van Heusen Photo Archives

Polka Dots and Moonbeams

In the midst of winding down his partnership with DeLange, Van Heusen, newly freed from Remick, found the time to collaborate with a man that would define his career for the next thirteen years – Johnny Burke. The Irishman from Antioch, California, had already developed a reputation as an adept lyricist, most notably creating hits for Bing Crosby movies writing with Arthur Johnston and Jimmy Monaco. In particular, Burke had already written the lyrics for "Pennies from Heaven," "The Moon Got in My Eyes," "An Apple for the Teacher," "Pocketful of Dreams," and the remarkable "What's New."

Van Heusen has told the story of his introduction to Burke with typical understatement, furthering the belief that he lived a sort of charmed musical existence, just happening upon people who could – and did – influence his life. Van Heusen recalled Burke walking into Remick in 1940 just "to shoot the breeze." Burke then asked Van Heusen if he had any tunes, to which Van Heusen replied, "Sure." The result was "Oh, You Crazy Moon." Completely true or purposely understated, there could be no more appropriate way for the two to begin their long and fertile collaboration, as the moon would prove to be the most enduring topic of their songs. Burke's lyric is from the point of view of either the unrequited or rejected lover, watching the object of his affection, apparently entranced by the moon, go with another. It is an interesting lyric in that the singer's dismay is directed not at the new lovers, but at the moon. It is the modern equivalent of an Irish ballad, the singer lamenting forces beyond his control causing heartache. However, the song never even approaches the maudlin, as Burke tells the story with a twinkle in his eye, carefully balancing the wistful with the witty. For his part, Van Heusen's music had a new edge to it; it was sharper, and the melody had bite. This song, for lack of a better word, was new.

Maybe it was the financial success, maybe it was the freedom to collaborate with other artists, maybe it was the lure of working with someone who had the ear of the great Crosby. But, whatever it was, "Oh, You Crazy Moon" marked a musical turning point for Van Heusen. One cannot look back at his previous songs and find a true analog. It seemed, at last, Van Heusen was stepping out of the shadow of hit songwriters and finding his own voice. The previous songs were unassuming, warm, charming. The future Van Heusen songs were edgy and, to a certain extent, dangerous. They started to embody the personality of the composer.

To be sure, 1940 was an exciting time in the musical world. The Big Bands still dominated the music scene, but their time in the sun was coming to a close. The exciting vocals of Frank Sinatra, the emergence of Hollywood as a rival source of music to New York, and the financial and administrative obstacles to maintaining a large orchestra spelled doom for the popularity of the swing orchestras. Richard Rodgers was nearing the end of his collaboration with Lorenz Hart, preparing to alter the Broadway musical scene in 1943 with

Oklahoma!. Cole Porter and Irving Berlin had written the lion's share of their great songs. A new generation in American songwriters was emerging, and Van Heusen knew he wanted to be in the vanguard.

With *Swingin' the Dream* and his last songs with DeLange and Mercer completed, Van Heusen composed two landmark ballads with Johnny Burke: "Polka Dots and Moonbeams" and "Imagination." "Polka Dots" was notable as being the first chart hit Frank Sinatra had with Tommy Dorsey. It remains a standard, having been recorded by numerous instrumentalists and vocalists — all in spite of Van Heusen's treacherously difficult bridge, and Burke's rather "corny" lyrics. Burke had proven himself infinitely more adroit than "a house built of lilacs and laughter," and he would continue to do so in the future.

Of infinitely more importance to the Jimmy Van Heusen story was "Imagination." This was another ballad that Van Heusen claimed to have written when he was 15-years-old, using the title "I Had Delusions of Love"; however neither he nor anyone else has credibly denied that "Imagination" was a vast improvement. Burke liked the tune and crafted his masterful lyrics to it. The result was another in a series of hits.

Glenn Miller and Ray Eberle had a chart-topping recording, and Tommy Dorsey and Frank Sinatra also had a top ten hit. Van Heusen had hits before, but this one had transcontinental ramifications. The story is best told in Van Heusen's voice:

> "Imagination" was now a smash hit and unbeknownst to me had caught the ear of the great director/producer in Hollywood, Mark Sandrich. He had a song in one of his movies (*Buck Benny Rides Again*) by Jimmy McHugh called "Say It" that could not nudge "Imagination" out of first place, and he gave orders to "get me that guy."
>
> This directive to the extensive Paramount organization would have been easily carried out had I not been a bordello habitue. I'd been out of circulation for two weeks when I was tracked down and visited at Rose Stewart's satin-y apartment. An executive of the New York (Paramount) office knocked on the door and was arguing with the madam until I woke up and listened. I invited him in. He was Sidney Kornheiser, the manager of the music companies owned by Paramount. After he bowed to my insistence that he partake of at least one girl, we

talked business. Sandrich wanted to see me and he was making tests in the Long Island studios.

Having been on an extended bender, I asked for a few days in which to quit shaking, but no, it had to be that afternoon. So, off I went to Long Island, being somewhat supported by my companion. I reeked of whiskey and had road maps for eyes, and though I had managed to don clean garb, there was no hiding some evidence of delirium tremens. The sound of the traffic jarred my already jagged nerve system. Trying not to shake too much, I was ushered into the presence of the great Sandrich. He took one look at me and commented, "Screwball." After finishing the last close up of the test he was making, he turned to me and asked to see my credits. I had brought a list, along with the lyric writers involved. It was a list of hits, and current ones at that. He asked if I would like to work with Frank Loesser. I replied that I was sure of myself with Johnny Mercer, Johnny Burke, Mack Gordon and Eddie DeLange. He told me he would be in touch, and with a sigh of relief, I left the sound stage. A couple of belts in an adjacent saloon stopped the shakes, and soon I was back in Manhattan, being driven in style in a Paramount Cadillac limousine back to Rose Stewart's dwelling.

Flush with success and the impending hope that a major motion picture studio might be desirous of his services, Van Heusen put aside (temporarily) the lush life to concentrate on his next major project. It seems that he would at last be repaying Jack Robbins for the luxuries bestowed upon him in Havana, as Robbins asked Van Heusen to provide the music for the 1940 version of Billy Rose's *Aquacade*. It was a massive production involving singing, dancing, and swimming routines. The original *Aquacade* opened in Cleveland, Ohio, at the Great Lakes Exposition of 1937. It then moved to the New York World's Fair in 1939, where it was considered the most successful exhibit at the Fair. The New York production featured Olympians Eleanor Holm, Johnny Weissmuller and newcomer Esther Williams. An enormous Art Deco 11,000 seat amphitheatre was designed by architects Sloan & Robertson. The pool and the 300-by-200-foot (61 m) stage could be hidden behind a lighted 40-foot (12 m) high curtain of water. It was, in short, a spectacle.

The music for the 1939 edition was written by Dana Suesse. Dubbed the "girl Gershwin" by the press, she composed such hits as "You Ought to Be in Pictures" and "The

Night Is Young and You're So Beautiful." Apparently wanting to capitalize on the popular success of Van Heusen, Rose had Robbins lure him with the money only Rose could supply and by offering him his choice of lyricists — Joe McCarthy or Oscar Hammerstein II. Van Heusen selected McCarthy because of his kindness to Van Heusen when both worked for Jimmy Monaco.

Billy Rose was a powerful producer, and working with him was an outstanding opportunity. The experience for Van Heusen turned out to be less than memorable, but it was revealing:

> We worked in his living room surrounded by about a million dollars' worth of Old Masters (paintings). The little creep would sit there while we worked, once in a while offering some pearl of criticism. I knew about the stories of Rose cutting in on a lot of hit songs and I was determined his name wouldn't get on any song of mine. But, sure enough, when we'd finished a couple, the phone call came from Jack Robbins:

> Mr. Rose insists his name be on the songs as a collaborator. The fact that this miserable man, one

of the richest men in the theater, wanted to chisel in on our work infuriated me. I sent Rose the thousand bucks he had advanced me (which I borrowed from a local bookie) and got out of there. Then Joe McCarthy, who needed the work, agreed Rose could share his credit and that's the way it was – Lyrics by Billy Rose and Joseph McCarthy. So I finished the score but twenty eight years later, when it was time to renew the copyright, I had a lawyer get Rose's name off those songs. McCarthy was dead then but I got Rose's name off even though Joe wasn't around to see me squelch the egomaniacal midget – Billy Rose, a Double A ASCAP writer with his name on countless lyrics he never wrote. A miserable man.

Perhaps this affront affected the normally unflappable Van Heusen more than he knew. Perhaps he was distracted by the lure of Hollywood. Whatever the reason, the music Van Heusen wrote for *Aquacade* was not among his finest work. A May 27, 1940, *Time* Magazine review noted, "No tune this year has the lilt of last season's "Yours for a Song" (reminiscent of Johann Strauss' 'Tales from the Vienna Woods')." The four songs written for the production were: "Eleanor, I Adore You" (written for Eleanor Holm), "There's A New Gang on the

Way," "When the Spirit Moves Me," and "You Think of Everything." They would mark the only time that Van Heusen would work with McCarthy, and the last time Van Heusen would work with a lyricist other than Johnny Burke or Sammy Cahn for an extended project.

The forgettable *Aquacade* did not deter the Paramount executives. Van Heusen still had songs on the Hit Parade and was clearly a protean talent. Richard Murray, a Paramount executive, called Van Heusen and informed him that Sandrich wanted him to write songs for a motion picture to star Jack Benny, Fred Allen and Mary Martin. The movie was *Love Thy Neighbor*. His fee would be $5,000.00, plus transportation and royalties. He could also choose his own lyricist. Van Heusen chose Johnny Burke: "I called Johnny and begged him to take a reduction in pay [he was commanding $20,000 per film] and work with me in *Love Thy Neighbor*. He agreed and I was set for my first motion picture. That was the beginning of a collaboration that lasted for seventeen, eighteen years."

The die was cast for Van Heusen to enter that phase of his career where he would achieve his greatest success. Indeed, the success he would enjoy in Hollywood would dwarf that of New York. However, Van Heusen did not seem to charge into this new battle with his usual enthusiasm. He could not wait to leave Syracuse to get to New York City. But, he did not have the same restless sensation to leave New York City for Hollywood: "I was used to the action in New York. There's no city like New York when you're 26 years old and you own the world. You've got hit songs and, God Almighty, you're making dough and you are really somebody. Being in New York like that was the best thing in the world to be and that's what I was."

Van Heusen's attitude, though, seems to contradict his actions in response to Paramount's interest in his work. He scrambled for a delay in his date with Kornheiser. He begged Burke to make sacrifices to join him. For being one of Sinatra's role models of cool, he was acting decidedly "uncool."

For all of his posturing to the contrary, Van Heusen must have known that what was in store for him was a chance at immortality. But, being "true to his code," it would have been untoward to let anyone know how important this might have been to him. His instincts were right. It was his collaboration with Johnny Burke that would propel Van Heusen to heretofore unheard-of heights. Ken Bloom, in his work, *The American Popular Songbook,* described a "recipe" for

Johnny Burke as "the down home values of Johnny Mercer, the romanticism of E.Y. Harburg, and the gentle humor of Frank Loesser – plus a dash of impish whimsy and a dollop of self-deprecation."

John Francis Burke was born on October 3, 1908, in Antioch, California. His father, William Earl Burke, was a structural engineer, and his mother, Mary Agnes Mungovan Burke, was a schoolteacher. While John was still very young, his family moved to Chicago where he studied piano and drama while attending Lindblom High School, from which he graduated in 1924. Following graduation, Burke attended Crane College in Chicago for one year, then attended the University of Wisconsin, where he played piano in the college orchestra. In 1926, Burke returned to Chicago to work as a staff pianist and song plugger for the Irving Berlin Music Corporation. Burke eventually was transferred to the New York offices of Irving Berlin where he continued as a pianist and also worked as a vocal coach.

Burke was hired by the Fox movie studio in 1930, and the same year he composed the music for a tune called "Boop-Boop-a-Doopa-Doo Fox Trot" (lyrics by George A. Little). The song was featured in the February, 1930, release *Let's Go Places* by actress Dixie Lee, who seven months later married Bing Crosby. Burke was a victim of Hollywood's fading attraction to musicals, and unable to find a market for his songs, he returned to Tin Pan Alley in 1933. Burke viewed this period of his career with characteristic self-deprecation: "Getting that Fox contract was really a freak. I went to the coast, and, of course, wrote a couple of things. But I'll admit they were very mediocre. The Fox people let me out after six months."

Following his return to New York City, Burke focused his attention exclusively to writing lyrics. In this, he found unwitting common ground with Van Heusen, who also scored his first hits writing lyrics rather than music. Burke wrote, "I returned to New York and had to start all over again. The publishers didn't take to my lyrics at all. I wanted to write like Gilbert of Gilbert and Sullivan fame. Wanted to write with my tongue in my cheek – not too sentimentally."

In spite of the publisher's reluctance, Burke scored a number of hits with composer Harold Spina. In 1933, he wrote "Annie Doesn't Live Here Anymore," popularized by Fred Waring's Pennsylvanians. Fats Waller had hit recordings with two other Spina/Burke collaborations, "You're Not the Only Oyster in the Stew" (1934) and "My Very Good Friend, the

Milkman" (1935). Other hits included "The Beat o' My Heart," recorded by Ben Pollack and His Orchestra (March, 1934), "I've Got a Warm Spot in My Heart for You," also recorded by Pollack in July, 1934, "Irresistible," by Hal Kemp and His Orchestra (October, 1934), "It's Dark on Observatory Hill," by the Dorsey Brothers Orchestra (January, 1935), and "You're So Darn Charming," also recorded by Hal Kemp in August of 1935. Recalls Burke of his work with Spina, "The publishers kept turning us down. They accused us of writing over everyone's head. They complained that the songs were too tricky."

Hollywood seemed undaunted by the supposed complexity of these tunes, focusing rather on their successes, and Burke was offered a contract from Paramount Pictures in 1936. Paramount paired Burke with composer Arthur Johnston. Johnston was Irving Berlin's personal arranger, pianist and musical assistant. (Recall that Berlin, like Jimmy Monaco, wrote all of his music using the "black keys" and therefore required someone with musical training to transpose these songs in more accessible key signatures.) Johnston was noted for writing Bing Crosby's first hit in 1931, "Just One More Chance" with lyricist Sam Coslow.

In 1936, Burke and Johnston were asked to provide a song for a yet-to-be named Bing Crosby movie. For some time, Burke was unaware of whether the song had been accepted by Crosby. His concerns were allayed when Crosby not only decided to include the song, but also use its title as that of the film – *Pennies from Heaven*. However, in true Crosby fashion, Burke only learned of this good fortune when he attended a screening of the film. The song was a massive hit for Crosby, and it was nominated for an Academy Award, eventually losing to Jerome Kern and Dorothy Fields' "The Way You Look Tonight." Proving he was no "one hit wonder," Burke followed that success with the beautiful "The Moon Got in My Eyes" from the 1937 film, *Double or Nothing*.

Crosby took to Burke very quickly. He found his wit contagious and was a welcome visitor to the Crosby compound. Burke provided the voice for Crosby's most famous film songs, and it is difficult to know whether this simpatico relationship was a product of nature or the close friendship the men enjoyed. Crosby referred to Burke as "The Poet" and "one of the best things that has happened to me." It was Crosby who introduced Burke to his wife, Bessie, when she won a contest to appear in one of Crosby's motion pictures.

Crosby was working on a film called *College Humor*, and Paramount sponsored a contest to find "Miss College Humor." The winner was Bessie Patterson from Tucuncari, New Mexico. Her prize was a bit part in the next Crosby opus, *Rhythm on the Range*. Because she was underage, her part in the publicity tour for the film was limited – almost as limited as the brief appearance she made in the film itself. Nevertheless, Burke was instantly attracted to the beautiful and intelligent girl. Bessie attended the University of Southern California, and completed a three-and-half-year course in one year.

Bessie and Johnny were fixtures at the Crosby social group known as the "Westwood Marching and Chowder Club" – a mummers society. A sort of proto-Rat Pack, this group of extraordinarily talented individuals put on musical programs in the vaudeville vein for a group of fortunate invitees. Participants included – Bing and Dixie Crosby, Johnny and Bessie Burke, Johnny Mercer, Joe Venuti, Fred MacMurray, Jimmy Monaco, Andy Devine – at one performance, Tommy Dorsey and Spike Jones were part of a five piece band. It was truly a remarkable time.

There were two aspects of Burke's craftsmanship that inured him to Crosby – his economy of words and his wit.

With regard to the first, Crosby was notorious for not wanting to sing the words "I love you" and he was clear in his edicts to his lyricists that such a phrase was forbidden. In the hands of a lesser lyricist, the challenge of writing a love song without using the word "love" would result in a wordy, rambling mess of a lyric. Burke thrived under this prohibition, creating some of his most memorable and creative lyrics – "It's Always You," "Sunday, Monday or Always," "Moonlight Becomes You," "But Beautiful," "The Moon Got in My Eyes," "It Could Happen to You" – all love songs, without the word "love."

Burke's wit was multifaceted – he could be deadpan, subtle or overtly aggressive. Crosby referred to him as "the most enthusiastic rib artist I've ever known." It did not matter to Burke the location nor the victim – loved ones were especially vulnerable. Crosby tells the story of a party he gave for airmen who served in the Second World War. Everyone was having a wonderful time, and Burke decided this would be the time to strike. Crosby described the scene: "He (Burke) found two or three of my guests leaning against a bar, and asked, 'Having a good time?' 'Wonderful,' they said. 'You know of course that Bing just does this for publicity. Actually, he's quite a louse.' His rib began to pick up pace, and he ran me down in every conceivable way. For a while they tried to laugh it off; then they began to see red. Finally they swung on him and he yelled for help."

His pranks could be elaborate, taking sometimes several months to play out to their conclusion. Crosby recalls another complex gag, this time victimizing Bessie. Following Bessie's arrival in California, Crosby had employed a young lady named Pat Friday to sing on his radio show. Bessie then remarked that she, too, knew a girl by the name of Pat Friday. Johnny interrupted her and claimed that she won a contest sponsored by NBC that would pay $18.75 to anyone who knew another girl named Pat Friday – it was called the NBC Pat Friday Contest. Bessie was thrilled and went on to write NBC a letter informing them of her acquaintance. Well, weeks went by and Bessie heard nothing from NBC. When she inquired of Johnny about the contest, he asked if she had sent any Campbell's soup labels, as according to Johnny, that was one of the requirements of the contest. She had not, but immediately thereafter sent one to NBC. When another week passed with no contact from NBC, Bessie was losing her patience. She told Johnny in no uncertain terms that NBC was an unprofessional organization, and she was shocked to learn that they could have risen to such national prominence if this contest was any example of their business dealings. Calmly and without the hint of expression, Johnny asked her if she sent in a chicken gumbo label, as that was a critical part of the contest. Again, she did not, but dutifully complied with this latest "requirement." This went on for nearly a month, with Bessie getting angrier and Johnny calmly informing her of additional contest "rules." The issue came to a head at a bowling date with Bing and Dixie and Johnny and Bessie. As Crosby recalls, "One night the four or five of us, including Bessie, were bowling. She's (Bessie) a powerful girl. Beautiful but strong. We were talking as we bowled. For some reason we hit upon the subject of ribbing people. Bessie looked at us scornfully and said, "Nobody would go for those ribs you (Johnny) pull. Anybody with sense would know when you're ribbing. I could tell by your faces. I could tell in one minute if any of you were ribbing me." She had a bowling ball poised, ready to hurl it down the alley and just as she drew her arm back, Johnny asked quietly, 'Did you ever hear of Pat Friday?' Pausing at the top of her swing, she went white. Then she threw the ball down the alley so hard the pin boy was almost decapitated by the whirling pins. Then she got her coat and stalked out of the place. It took Johnny quite a while to edge his way out of his quarters in the doghouse and back into his own home."

Burke's love of a good joke should not be mistaken for an unserious nature or an unwillingness to stand up for his beliefs. Bessie Burke recalled that despite Burke's slight, 145-pound appearance, he would not back down from a fight, despite the odds. "I'd put him up against any man twice his size. He would really tear into anyone when he thought he was right and other guy was wrong."

The final ingredient in this doomed potable was Burke's streak of perfectionism. Van Heusen recalled, "Nobody else wrote words like that. Nobody had imagery like Johnny did. And getting those great words out led him to punish himself until he died. Johnny tortured himself because he couldn't live up to his own expectations of himself. He was such a perfectionist that he felt a guilt about what he thought were his shortcomings and he blamed his body – his physical side – for letting him down. He'd get himself put into traction, get shots for muscle spasms, take every pill there was and in the end he proved himself right: he finally was not well enough to work at anywhere near his best."

"Burke was meticulous about grammar and rhyme and form. He was a real poet, a very talented man and he worked his ass off. There never was a false rhyme with Johnny. He would never write near rhymes like 'down' and 'around.' 'I don't believe in poetic license,' he said. He wrote a song once with Jimmy Monaco, called "Only Forever", which ended with a grammatical error – 'only forever, that's putting it mild.' He worked for weeks on that lyric but there was no way around that 'mild.' It haunted him. It embarrassed him. Every time he heard someone sing, 'that's putting it mild' he'd go up the wall. That's the kind of guy he was. He would stay up all night fighting for just one word."

Following his successes with Arthur Johnston, Burke teamed with former Van Heusen associate Jimmy Monaco. Having apparently escaped from the fleabag motel of his New York days, Monaco travelled west to Hollywood and found renewed success in the movies. Burke and Monaco contributed the music and lyrics to the following Crosby movies: *Doctor Rhythm, Sing You Sinners, East Side of Heaven, The Star Maker, If I Had My Way,* and *Rhythm on the River* (1940). Monaco and Burke received an Academy Award nomination for "Only Forever" from *Rhythm on the River*. It lost to "When

You Wish Upon A Star" from *Pinocchio*. Monaco and Burke also provided the music for the first of the iconic "Road" pictures – Bob Hope and Bing Crosby's first journey was on the *Road to Singapore* in 1940.

The music that Burke and Monaco created for Crosby were essential elements in creating the Crosby image, and they cultivated a musical style that shaped and defined American popular music, including "I've Got a Pocketful of Dreams," "That Sly Old Gentleman from Featherbed Lane," "An Apple for the Teacher," "A Man and His Dreams," "April Played the Fiddle," "I Haven't Time to Be a Millionaire," and "Too Romantic."

Despite this success, Burke was drawn back to New York City where, according to Van Heusen, he simply happened into Remick out of the blue and asked him if he had any songs. Following the composition of "Imagination," "Oh, You Crazy Moon," and "Polka Dots and Moonbeams," in 1940, the Monaco-Burke collaboration was on borrowed time. Burke and Monaco were to contribute songs to only three more Crosby films – *If I Had My Way, Rhythm on the River* and *The Road to Singapore*. The details of the end of the collaboration are not known, but it can certainly be assumed that the move

197

from Monaco to Van Heusen would not have been made without Crosby's imprimatur. Monaco continued to work in Hollywood until his death in 1945. It certainly could not have been pleasant to lose the Crosby franchise, and Monaco would not work with as talented a lyricist as Burke. The only indication of Monaco's reaction was that Monaco felt that Van Heusen "stole" his lyricist (Burke). This reflection came courtesy of Earl Wentz, the New York-based musician/producer responsible for creating musical revues of American popular composers that have been wrongly forgotten. In 2005, Wentz' American Composers Series paid tribute to Jimmy Monaco with "Ragtime Jimmie."

In a sense, Monaco's conclusion is not entirely without substance. Van Heusen was given his choice of lyricists for *Love Thy Neighbor*, and he made a concerted effort to woo Burke. Nevertheless, given Van Heusen's fond regard for Monaco, it is unlikely that this maneuver was intended to harm Monaco for no other reason than Van Heusen never thought his move west was going to be permanent. For him, New York was the center of music, and Hollywood was full of "phonies."

SIXTEEN

Jimmy Van Heusen preparing for flight
Courtesy of Van Heusen photo archives

Swinging On a Star

The financial success Van Heusen enjoyed from his hit songs enabled him to live "the good life" – the best food, booze, and women were all within his reach. This financial freedom also permitted him to indulge his most identifying and reckless habit – flying. For Van Heusen, "Come Fly With Me" was not merely the title track of a Sinatra concept album, it was a literal invitation to his life.

How did this come about? How did a boy from Syracuse choose to embroil himself in the dangerous and relatively inaccessible world of aviation? Van Heusen certainly craved adventure – movement. He also valued freedom. An ability and willingness to fly meant he was subject to no one's schedule but his own. It was the assurance that no place could hold him and no location could trap him. So, the first capital purchase Van Heusen made was not a fancy car or showy apartment, but a two-place Luscombe Silveraire. He took lessons with his friend Larry Taylor at Floyd Bennett Field. Taylor never doubted Van Heusen's nerve, but he thought a more pedestrian physical limitation would have compromised Van Heusen's ability to pilot – his sinuses. Since childhood, he suffered from terrible, sometimes crippling sinus headaches. The remedies at the time were limited to common analgesics and heat compresses. The only possible permanent remedy was a radical new treatment. Van Heusen said, "In that operation, they'd make a hole about the size of a dime in your forehead and wash out the frontals. Then they'd put on a silver or plastic plate to cover the hole. I'd escaped that operation by a hair's-breadth several times in the past. It was a messy bit of surgery. I was afraid of it and I wasn't sure it would work anyway."

It was a bit of good fortune that Van Heusen's flying led to the possibility of relief for his ailment. Van Heusen insisted on flying his plane from New York City to Hollywood, much to the chagrin of the studio executives: "I didn't fly at night so the trip took me longer than I expected. The studio executives were mad as hell about it when they found out. They said I was endangering my life – which they didn't much give a damn about – and thereby endangering an expensive motion picture production – which they cared very much about." This "tweak" of the studio was ostensibly a display of bravado and insouciance – a reminder to Paramount that this gig was no different to him than any other. More likely, it was a way of Van Heusen to retain control of at least one aspect of his journey into the unknown.

It was, however, a refueling stop prior to his final descent into Los Angeles that impressed Van Heusen. It was a deserted strip of land noted as "Palm Springs."

"It was hot – it felt like about 180 degrees. But suddenly I felt a clearness in my nose and a lightness in my head and I realized that, for the first time since I was 8 years old, my sinuses had cleared up. It was an exhilarating feeling.

"I asked the guy at the gas pump what caused by sudden burst of health and he explained that we were just at the edge of the California desert. He pointed to San Gorgonio peak and the other mountains which stopped off the damp ocean air of the coast.

"This must be a great place to live," I said.

'Well, yeah,' he said, 'but there ain't much doing and it gits hot like it is now in the summer. Winter's nice, though.' The heat didn't seem to be anything but a boon to me as I breathed deeply, conscious of each breath. As I rolled down the runway and headed for Los Angeles, I made a note: Palm Springs might be a very nice place to live someday."

The Hollywood of 1940 was riding a creative apex. The year 1939 is considered by many film historians to be the finest year of filmmaking in Hollywood's history. Among the brightest stars of that year: *Gone with the Wind, The Wizard of Oz, Stagecoach, Beau Geste, Goodbye, Mr. Chips, Gunga Din, The Women, Wuthering Heights, The Roaring Twenties*. In case one is in need of further evidence, consider: *Ninotchka, Only Angels Have Wings, Drums Along the Mohawk, Mr. Smith Goes to Washington, The Hunchback of Notre Dame, Allegheny Uprising, The Adventures of Sherlock Holmes, The Hound of the Baskervilles, Stanley and Livingston, The Man in the Iron Mask, Dark Victory, Of Mice and Men, Young Mr. Lincoln, The Rains Came, Midnight, The Private Lives of Elizabeth and Essex, Union Pacific, Babes in Arms, The Little Princess, Another Thin Man, The Story of Vernon and Irene Castle, The Hardys Ride High, Golden Boy, Dodge City, Gulliver's Travels, The Light That Failed, The Adventures of Huckleberry Finn, The Old Maid, Son of Frankenstein,* and *Destry Rides Again.*

Hollywood was not merely succeeding artistically. It was succeeding financially, as well. The website *filmshow.com* estimates that in 1940 there were approximately 17,500 movie theaters in operation – one for every 8,000 people. Out of a total population of nearly 130,000,000, nearly 55-60 million Americans attended the movies each week. Moreover, the demographic was shifting. While the urban movie palace still dominated the landscape, more people were moving from cities to the "suburbs." Movie studios would need to adapt both creatively and financially to this new market.

It was the stars, more than anything that drew the people to the theaters, and they were compensated handsomely – not unlike today. The biggest stars in 1939-1940 Hollywood were Claudette Colbert, Mickey Rooney, Shirley Temple, Clark Gable, Gene Autry, and, of course, Bing Crosby. Crosby and Colbert commanded roughly $400,000 per picture. Van Heusen was used to high profile musicians and composers, but this amount of compensation was beyond anything he would have confronted. The stakes were decidedly higher.

Beyond the pressure of working for highly compensated people, Van Heusen was also entering a Hollywood in transition. For years, Hollywood studios would distribute its films through a practice known as "block booking." A studio would sell its films in a "block," packaging the marquis titles with those of lesser quality. The theaters had to accept the block packaging or they would not have access to the quality films. All of the studios employed this tactic, thereby creating unfair market manipulation. This attracted the notice of the federal government, and antitrust litigation ensued. Ultimately, in 1940, the studios entered a consent decree with the government, which limited the block booking to no more than five films. Bereaved of a built-in marketing tool, the studios had to sell their films the old-fashioned way – by creating a quality product that appealed to the people. This burden fell disproportionately on the stars.

Van Heusen arrived in Hollywood in July, 1940. Already released that year were *Pinocchio*, *The Grapes of Wrath*, *The Shop Around the Corner*, *His Girl Friday*, and *Rebecca*. There was work to be done, and after his welcoming dinner with Johnny and Bessie Burke at the Knickerbocker Hotel (where he would take up residence), they went immediately to work. It was their first extended collaboration. Of this collaboration, Van Heusen stated, "Collaboration is a delicate thing – a mixing and melding of two crafts and it is necessary for collaborators to work closely together. It's curious – almost mysterious – but sometimes you can read lyrics and they don't make much sense until you put them together with the music. It's like working out a very difficult puzzle."

Van Heusen was a sympathetic collaborator to different composers for the simple reason that at one time he was a lyricist, but also self-aware enough not to intrude on his partner's province:

Lyrics are the toughest part of song writing. It's like writing a sonnet – the sonnet is difficult because it has a tough rhyme scheme and it still has to make sense. Lyric writers work to a definite form which is very brief, very constricted – yet the lyrics have to be poetic and original, too. Because I wrote both words and music for such a long time, I understand the problem. [Recall that Burke started out composing music.] That's why I always do everything I can to help the lyric writers I work with. I throw in lines, look up words, do anything I can to help and occasionally come up with something. I've always been of use to the writers I've worked with. I'm a decent editor and I can help that way too. I'll write maybe six or eight tunes to the same bunch of

lyrics and then we'll juggle the words around,
trying eight or a dozen approaches until we come
up with what we think is the best.

The movie project for which Van Heusen and Burke were retained was the latest Jack Benny film, *Love Thy Neighbor*. The film had hoped to capitalize on the "feud" between Jack Benny and fellow radio personality Fred Allen. In addition to Benny and Allen, the film starred Mary Martin, Rochester and Virginia Astor. It was a typical Mark Sandrich-directed madcap caper, with mixed identities and the like. It was not a musical, per se, but, like the upcoming Road comedies, it was a comedy film with a couple of song and dance numbers thrown in to break up the often thread-bare plots. For *Love Thy Neighbor*, Burke and Van Heusen wrote three numbers: "Do You Know Why?", "Dearest, Darest I?" (where Burke was given the opportunity to play like Gilbert mixing Old English thou's and 'ests with modern colloquial idioms), and "Just Like Love."

Love Thy Neighbor was a modest success. It was another reminder that the successes of radio did not always translate to the big screen. Jack Benny was a genius, to be sure, but his wit was infinitely more suited for a more intimate medium like radio or television. Van Heusen and Burke's tunes were well-crafted but not necessarily the most auspicious start for the team. By way of comparison, Crosby's competing film, *Rhythm on the River*, was blessed with the masterful Monaco-Burke composition, "Only Forever" (which was nominated for an Academy Award).

Despite this less-than-stellar effort, the tunes written for *Love Thy Neighbor* were widely recorded. Unfortunately, they were not widely heard. *Love Thy Neighbor* was released on December 17, 1940. On January 1, 1941 there would be a seven month ban on the broadcast of any songs composed by ASCAP writers.

The battle, per custom, was over money. ASCAP members were determined not to permit the radio medium to take advantage of them, as many felt the music publishers did in the early part of the century, and ASCAP felt it needed to take a proactive stand to protect their interests. The first battleground related to live performances. Musicians and composers were paid their licensing fee for the live broadcast, but had that broadcast been a ticketed performance, the composer would have received a portion of the proceeds from the door. As a radio broadcast presumably reached millions of listeners, such receipts, had the broadcast been a concert, would have been vast. The broadcasters countered by claiming there would be no way to estimate accurately the number of listeners, and, more important, the broadcast to such vast numbers of people provided the composers with publicity they would have never had have without the technology of radio. A compromise was reached whereby the composers received a portion of the advertising purchased for the broadcast. Like most compromises, no one was happy.

As Earl Rickard recounts in *Musical Chairs Part I*:

In 1932, the broadcasters came to an agreement with ASCAP for 3 percent of advertising income, rising in 1935 to 5 percent. Five years later, with the Big Band Era in full swing and ASCAP looking to raise the fee, broadcasters decided to start their own licensing agency: Broadcast Music Incorporated (BMI). The new agency began business on April 1, 1940. Later in the year after the broadcasters refused to agree to ASCAP's new demand of 7.5 percent, ASCAP refused them the right to play ASCAP music.

On the first day of 1941, all recordings of ASCAP tunes were banned from network radio stations. Of course, musicians and singers could perform any ASCAP tune at a live performance, unless the performance was broadcast on a network. At the same time, any uncopyrighted musical composition, such as "Auld Lang Syne" (Guy Lombardo's theme song) or one with an expired copyright could be played on the air. The ban led to swing arrangements of everything from the "The Anvil Chorus" to the "Song of the Volga Boatman." Freddy Martin's band scored a huge number one hit with "Tchaikovsky's Piano Concerto in B Flat."

Nineteenth Century tunesmith Stephen Foster shot back into national prominence thanks to his music "being in the public domain" – copyright expired. With the updating of old music and BMI licensing new music everyday, ASCAP's unplayed tunes failed to hurt the networks. Instead, the ban stopped the flow of income to ASCAP members. By July 1941, the music war had taken its toll; ASCAP lowered their demands to 2.75 per cent, much less than the 5 percent pre-strike fee. Mutual Network accepted the offer and began playing ASCAP songs again. NBC and CBS continued the war until October when they both settled on the ASCAP offer of 2.75 per cent. The radio war ended. ASCAP had gambled and lost.

The entire episode could not have been timed more poorly for Van Heusen, who was just at the cusp of achieving superstardom. The following is his take on the ASCAP/BMI war:

> The broadcasters had come up with a deal, a marvelous deal, for ASCAP, and if that had been accepted ASCAP members would be a whole lot richer today. But Gene Buck, representing ASCAP said, 'You have to accept our deal. We're the ones who have the music, If you don't use our music, you'll be off the air.' You tell that to some tough businessmen, a guy like General Sarnoff, and it's a wonder you don't get killed for an answer, I don't mean to call Buck a bum, but that's what he did.

> "So the broadcasters formed BMI. BMI couldn't get the music they were accustomed to – the music of Berlin, Porter, Gershwin and the rest – so they had to go to other sources. They went down to Nashville, Tennessee, and got country and western music written by guys who weren't even considered by ASCAP. Country and western music was yokel stuff. I remember Cole Porter wrote a western called "Don't Fence Me In" which was a big hit and he was ashamed of it. But BMI took country and western and they took what was called 'race music' – Negro songs, which incidentally, included most of the blues. That's

why the music we hear today is rock 'n' roll –
that's what race music was. That's nothing new.

BMI had a brilliant administrator named Robert
Burton. Under Burton, BMI assessed every
member of the broadcasters' association and took
the money to get a well of music together. They
got race music and they got country and western
and a large catalogue of Latin American music.
Burton absolutely clobbered ASCAP. How? BMI
spread around millions of dollars. You probably
couldn't prove it, but everybody thinks BMI paid
to have its music recorded. BMI got to the A&R
guys, the men who decide what's going to be
recorded. If you give an A&R guy $10,000.00 to
record a song, that's what's going to be recorded.
Nobody wanted to record those songs and nobody
wanted to play them on the air. They wanted to
play Cole Porter, not some songs written by Joe
Schmoe. That's when payola started and that's
why we're hearing all this country and western
and rock 'n' roll stuff now. It was started by
money – the bank.

Johnny and I were both worried about the ASCAP
fight – there was nothing else to talk about in the
music business all that year. But I don't think any
of us thought our ASCAP songs would actually be
barred from the air. We were sure that the

broadcasters would run into a wall unless they broadcast ASCAP music. We thought the public would scream and holler when they couldn't get Arlen and Porter or even Burke and Van Heusen. When the time came, the public didn't have anything to say about what it got.

Van Heusen and Burke's shared love of night life and, in particular, hard drinking made their collaboration simpler, to be sure. However, one taste separated them for the time being – Hollywood. Van Heusen was not overly enamored with Hollywood. Throughout his time on the West Coast, he was anxious to return to New York, or, at least, escape from Los Angeles:

"When there was time off from the composing labors, I would hop into the Luscombe and explore the Golden State. It soon became apparent that the city of Los Angeles was the very least part of that magic place called California, and within very little time I was aware of the wonderful city of the West, San Francisco, the beauty that is the southern coast line near La Jolla and the northern coast line called the Big Sur and the wonderful cities of Carmel and Monterey, and other resort communities and mountain resorts like

Arrowhead, and then always remembering the desert that opened up my nostrils and lungs, the then sleepy town of Palm Springs."

This constant desire to return to New York irritated Burke to no end, as he had plans to draft Van Heusen into the Crosby empire, writing songs for the Crosby musical vehicles. It would be an interesting exercise in counterfactual history to speculate how Van Heusen would have fared in the New York landscape. Most of the giants had moved west – Arlen, Berlin, Porter, Kern. His collaborators were all in Hollywood. New York would soon be dominated by the musicals of Rodgers and Hammerstein. It is not unfair to assume that Van Heusen might have found Manhattan to be a less than satisfying venue.

Burke knew Van Heusen represented an upgrade from Jimmy Monaco, and also that his unique gifts would complement Crosby perfectly. Burke also knew that the one thing that might keep the stubborn Van Heusen in Hollywood would be the opportunity to work for Bing Crosby, who at the time was the biggest star in the world. For Crosby's part, he had only recorded one Van Heusen song, "It's the Dreamer in Me" – and that was not even the music of Van Heusen but

Jimmy Dorsey. However, Crosby could not have been unaware of the incredible streak of hits written by Van Heusen, and the thought of getting this hit-maker on his team was tempting. Crosby relied on Burke and valued his opinion, but certainly would not commit without a meeting. Van Heusen would not commit unless he felt the meeting would result in a deal. Crosby, of course, preferably felt he was beyond having to audition for songwriters.

Enter Johnny Burke and his Irish malarkey.

Burke arranged a meeting between the two men at Del Mar racing track, some 20 miles north of San Diego. Crosby was seated in a plush box, which stood to reason, as he owned the establishment, along with Pat O'Brien, Jimmy Durante, Oliver Hardy and Charles S. Howard. Upon meeting Van Heusen, Crosby looked at him and said, "Howdy . . . so it's Shake Down the Stars, kill all the babies, and stamp on all the flowers . . . is it?" Van Heusen recalled:

> He was referring to the lyrics of a then current hit
> of mine that he hated, and because it was
> published by his friend Rocco Vocco and probably
> been requested to sing it on his radio program.
> His opening line about the lyric assured me that

the song would never get sung, at least by him. And so it never was. That was Bing's way of telling me he wanted no part of a lyric like that. But I got along with him in an instant. We had instant rapport and we had a rapport for a lot of years.

Still, Van Heusen was savvy enough to know that rapport was not the same thing as a signed contract. Despite Burke's entreaties that he and Van Heusen were a lock to write for Crosby's new film, Van Heusen dismissed Burke's statements as self-serving: "Johnny kept trying to cement me in. He wanted me to stay in Hollywood because he felt he was lucky with me and he wanted to make it a permanent collaboration. I couldn't see it. Hollywood just seemed the world capital of phonies to me. I hated the place."

Bessie Burke recalled, "Jimmy was very quiet and retiring in those first days. He seemed on the edge of things. I don't mean he was pushed there – he put himself there. He was the quiet observer – that's how I remember him as against what he was later."

Van Heusen was no fan of the society to which he was introduced:

"I didn't get into the social life at all, and I couldn't take the Hollywood phoniness. One of the first parties I went to . . . I'll never forget. I was horror struck – not that I'm a Puritan, because I sure wasn't, but it just about floored me. It was a party for Edmund Lowe, a sit-down dinner. It was his birthday. I forget who had the party but Dixie and Bing were there and Johnny and Bessie. I sat across the table from Edmund Lowe and his wife and she would up the party by taking the birthday cake and dumping it on his head. And he called her a fucking cunt right out loud. I was shocked. It distressed me that this was the kind of fun that indulged out there. I had never heard anyone use that kind of language to a woman. Eventually I was the biggest hokey bum in Hollywood. It took me a couple of years to get acclimated – but I never talked that way to a woman.

Jimmy repeated his "threat" to leave that the moment *Love Thy Neighbor* was completed that he would be returning to New York City. Burke again told him that the Crosby picture was theirs for the taking. So confident was Burke that he advised Van Heusen to sign with Larry Crosby (brother of Bing) as his agent. When Van Heusen agreed to this business arrangement, Burke knew he was tantalizingly close. One last meeting at Crosby's house on 603 North Oakhurst in Beverly Hills:

"Johnny tells me you're heading back East."

"In a couple of weeks, I hope."

"Well, don't get too far away, Jim. I want you and Johnny to do the songs for my next picture. It's in the works now – *Road to Zanzibar.*

"Sounds good."

"We'll get you more money than you got for the thing you're on now."

And with that, a legendary collaboration was born. Burke and Van Heusen celebrated the success by frequenting one of Burke's haunts – the It Café in the Hollywood Plaza Hotel. The It Café was managed by Burke's old high school friend, Jack Clark. Of Van Heusen, Clark recalled, "Jimmy was around the saloon a lot after that. He fit right in with the guys who used to make it their headquarters – it was about the swingingest hotel you could imagine."

Clark was another colorful character in Van Heusen's world – a world that seems to be populated exclusively by such creatures. Clark wrote about the bar scene that Burke and Van Heusen inhabited:

We had the aviation guys – the pilots from Lockheed and the aviation missions who came from all around the world to buy war planes from Douglas and Lockheed and Vultee. We also had American Air Lines pilots and stewardesses, too. I gave a special reduced rate to the stewardesses because they were all pretty and it was nice to have them around to make a run at. Fred Corcoran of the Professional Golfers' Association used to fill the house with golfers when the Los Angeles Open was on. [Corcoran was a public relations dynamo for the PGA. His principal claim to fame was organizing celebrity golf matches to elevate the public perception of the game. In 1940, he scheduled a match among Gene Tunney, Babe Ruth, Gene Sarazen and Jimmy Demaret. In 1941, he somehow convinced Babe Ruth and Ty Cobb to play a three course "tournament" to resolve their baseball rivalry. (Cobb won).]

Then, because of Johnny Burke, I met all the music guys. When Tommy and Jimmy Dorsey had their bands in town, they'd finish up at the

Palladium and come in to unwind. Many's the night Tommy Dorsey'd order up a few bottles of pinch-bottle scotch and we'd close the place to outsiders and get down to some steady drinking – Joey Bushkin and Ziggy Elman and all the guys. About that time, Jackie Gleason and Cully Richards, another comic, used to appear at Slapsie Maxie's and they always stayed with me. They spent a lot of afternoons drinking and flying kites from the roof. Jimmy, being a pilot, a good drinker and a great musician, fit right in with everyone.

After finishing the deal, Van Heusen boarded his Luscombe and flew back "home" to New York City. While in New York, Van Heusen took in the current Broadway shows – Rodgers and Hart's *Pal Joey*, Cole Porter's *Panama Hattie*, Vernon Duke's *Cabin in the Sky*. Van Heusen recalls:

Sometime during every night, I managed to get to The Famous Door or The Three Deuces. All the best musicians were on 52nd Street or had just left or were about to retire. All the good ones were on the street – then Earl Fatha Hines, Benny Goodman swinging away in his great way, Bunny Berigan, Art Tatum, Horace Heidt, Gene Krupa whamming away at the drums, Pee Wee Russell

220

and Louie Prima – they were all of them there at one time or another. Bobby Hackett was at Nick's in the Village, along with Mugsy Spannier and Eddie Condon and the rest. I can't remember whether Jimmy and Tommy Dorsey were in town – Frank was singing with Tommy's band by then – but if they weren't everybody else was. The street was a marvelous place until the war came along and ruined things.

SEVENTEEN

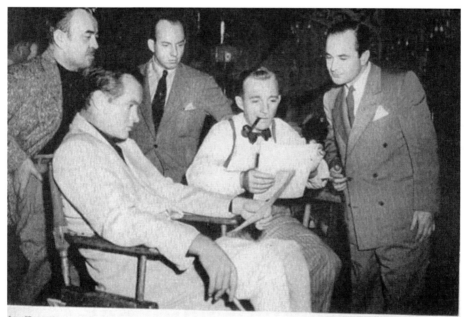

...he *Zanzibar* road, Bing and Bob Hope pause for singing details from composer Jimmy Heusen (center) and lyric writer Johnny Burke, right. The late Victor Schertzinger watches

Press Clipping of Road To Zanzibar.
Courtesy of Bing Crosby Enterprises

You're Dangerous

The war was still several years from directly touching American lives. However, with Poland, Czechoslovakia, and France in the hands of Nazi Germany, and more of the Far East succumbing to the Empire of Japan, it was unlikely that America would remain at peace. On September 16, 1940, Congress enacted the Selective Service and Training Act, which required enlistment of all males from the ages of 21 and 36 for possible selection into the Armed Forces. Van Heusen dutifully complied, along with nearly 20,000,000 other men, but in the back of his mind, was contemplating a strategy that would keep him safely from deploying to foreign lands.

Van Heusen's politics were something of a mystery. With the exception of the John F. Kennedy presidential campaign, there is hardly any public record of his political leanings. And, while Van Heusen perhaps admired the Kennedy image, it can be fairly assumed that his participation was at least, in part, consequence of his friendship with Sinatra, whose influence was brought to bear on a great many show business luminaries to support JFK.

More than likely, Van Heusen knew that exposing his political beliefs in Hollywood was at least off-putting to the 50% of the people with whom one disagreed, or, at worst, dangerous, something to which those blacklisted actors can attest. That was certainly a more credible explanation than to think Van Heusen had no political leanings. His generation was not possessed of the nihilistic belief that the political process was futile, and Van Heusen himself was far too opinionated not to express that opinion at the polls. More than likely, Van Heusen became a member of Nixon's Silent Majority, watching from his Palm Springs compound, with quiet disdain and resignation, the transformation of the nation of his youth from Norman Rockwell to Timothy Leary.

However, in 1940, the only political negotiation that concerned Van Heusen was the internal wrangling with Paramount for his just wages for his contribution in the new Crosby film. At the meeting with Jacob Karp, the head of Paramount's legal department, Van Heusen surprised and shocked both Karp and Burke by insisting upon an increase in pay from $7,500 to $15,000. The original offer of $7,500 was a substantial increase from his pay for *Love Thy Neighbor*. Karp's thrust that the film was an opportunity to work with Bob Hope and Bing Crosby was successfully parried by Van Heusen, who knew that since he was who the stars wanted, Paramount had little choice but to capitulate to his demands. Before the meeting ended, Van Heusen and Burke were being paid $15,000, but Karp told Van Heusen he would never again work for Paramount. A sullen Burke followed Van Heusen out of the office and to his waiting car:

> Johnny wasn't very happy about the whole thing, but I was in sort of a mood and didn't give a shit whether I got the job or not. I was still enchanted with New York and I figured I could go back there and do another show or just write a few more hits. I was having a ball in New York and I wasn't too thrilled with California. I knew Crosby had asked for us. That meant Paramount had to hire us so I just held them up. Johnny didn't say so but I knew he didn't want me to make an issue about the money because he wanted us to get in solid with Bing so we would be his constant writers. Karp was mad as hell and so was everybody else – but he never did live up to his promise of never

letting me work at Paramount again, not even when he became head of the studio. Eventually, our price per picture went up to $75,000 or $80,000 for both of us.

Van Heusen sought to make his latest trip to California more comfortable by bringing some of the comforts of home – in particular, old friend Jack Gale, a New York madam named Dolores, and one of her "employees." They joined Van Heusen at his new digs at 505 North Camden Drive in Beverly Hills, and as Van Heusen so eloquently stated, "I was no longer lonesome and writing well."

While Van Heusen was sleeping (or not sleeping) soundly, Burke was on edge. Burke knew Van Heusen was playing a dangerous game with Crosby, and he had no intention of ruining a chance at superstardom because Van Heusen had carnal urges:

> Johnny Burke was beside himself, however, fearing that holier than thou Hollywood and above all Bing Crosby would learn of my not so chic companions. Beyond his hearing, we used to joke about the BBC Club . . . the Brushed Off by Crosby Club. Johnny Burke also knew that any

infraction of what Bing considered proper conduct by anyone near him, he would immediately join the BBC Club. Many a former friend of the Groaner's never knew what happened, the Crosby coldness was legendary, and some discovered years later of some slight action on their part that displeased the Despot. He was probably the single most important music business star, apart from the movies. His Kraft Radio programs presentations of a song could start substantial sales the following morning. Burke was fearful of my flamboyant living. Larry Crosby acted as my agent, as well as Johnny's, and there was just so much that Larry could explain away regarding my conduct, Johnny said. I understood, but surreptitiously arranged for Larry to meet the little lady that had arrived with Dolores, and it was instant romance. Naturally he never knew that she had never accepted the filthy lucre. But, he did know something that scared me: A New York vice cop, who regularly used to visit the bordellos and either shake down the madams, or simply instill the fear of God into the poor creatures that worked there, had found a letter in Dolores' place with the imprint of Bing Crosby on the envelope. He had opened it up, unbeknownst to the madam, and had seen on a Bing Crosby personal letterhead a letter from me, to the

Madam. He pocketed the epistle, and on a trip to the West Coast, the cop presented it to Everett Crosby. Everett blustered about that pimp Van Heusen bringing disgrace to the Crosby escutcheon, and presumably Larry retrieved the damning document and prevented my banishment to Siberia. In later years Bing's reaction to such an incident would have been just a giggle, but in those days, Burke and I felt the cold draft of fear that we would lose the best dispenser of songs in the world.

There was to be no banishment. Instead, Van Heusen entered the exciting world of Bing Crosby and the "Road" pictures. The "Road" pictures could fairly be considered the first "buddy" pictures. Two guys, usually ne'er-do-well con men, stumbling into misadventures, ending up with the girl and treasure to boot. The facsimiles have been produced countless times and we can look back to Hope and Crosby for providing the template. The films were formulaic, light affairs that seemed like the perfect tonic for a society consumed with a world at war. Each film targeted a specific genre for satire. The first film in the series, *Road to Singapore,* was a send-off of Far Eastern themed movies. The next film, and the first Van

Heusen-scored affair, *Road to Zanzibar*, put Hope and Crosby in Africa being alternately conned and romanced by Dorothy Lamour and Una Merkel, encountering cannibals, slave traders, and fighting gorillas.

> It was a straight-forward job. The script indicated the song spots and Johnny and I went home and went to work. In the Road pictures, we always wrote a double song for Bob and Bing to sing together, a ballad, a love song and a rhythm song. . . . Everything was designed for laughs. Bing would sing his ballad but it was always one chorus over lightly – the quickest possible rendition and then back to the laughs. Dorothy Lamour would sing a perfectly beautiful ballad in each picture but when she sang it, Bob Hope would respond by making faces and contorting his body as though he were consumed with passion and the thing became a long belly laugh. On the concerns of writing for Lamour's limited vocal range Van Heusen was typically gallant, "Lamour was so beautiful you couldn't expect her to be a great singer, too."

> In *Zanzibar*, there was something a little different. The script called for a long sequence of jungle music. What it was a long line of natives carrying

stuff for a safari through the jungle – and it took a lot of doing. "African Etude" [the eventual title for the song] was about 200 bars long – the music was like a big long tape work which could have stretched out about sixteen feet – about six times as long as an ordinary song. It had to have a lot of native stuff - ATTOO BOMBA, ATTOO BOMBA in it. We had to get a drummer to demonstrate it. In the picture, Bing sang it backed by the Hall Johnson choir.

We also wrote an opening song for Bing, "You Lucky People," but that wasn't too hard. We did "Birds of a Feather" for Bing and Hope, and "You're Dangerous" for Dorothy Lamour. Then I wrote a pretty little ballad tune and that turned out to be a terrific job mostly because we couldn't think of a title. One finally came to me and I threw it at Johnny and he liked it, "It's Always You."

We worked mostly at Johnny's living room then. He had a big grand piano with a bar off one end – like a professional bar. Bing'd drop around a lot of times while we were working but mostly we worked all night long. Johnny drank coffee – gallons of it – but I can't drink much of the stuff and I'd just fight off sleep, or maybe I took a Benzedrine once in a while.

When we finished the songs, we took them to Bing. The musical end of the picture was Bing's province – Bing was the music man. After that, we demonstrated the songs and taught them to Hope and Bing and Dorothy and then we were set until the recording date."

It was at the recording date with Crosby for "You Lucky People" that Van Heusen learned two very important lessons about Hollywood:

I didn't say anything but I guess Bing saw it in my face. He said, 'What's the matter?' I said, 'I don't like this arrangement. It's ticky-tacky. It creaks like a barn door.' And Bing said, 'Who can you get to play it right?' I said, 'Tommy Dorsey's at the Palladium,' and, bang! That was it. Bing cancelled the whole recording session and walked out. 'Get Tommy Dorsey' he said and a couple of days later we recorded with Dorsey. The studio had a fit. They lost a whole recording date and that costs money.

I learned from that and I never criticized a studio band harshly again. They're the men you have to work with and, after that, I was a little more vocal beforehand to make sure the arrangement was the way it should be before we started. I had no idea Bing would cancel when I said I didn't like the thing. I was astounded when he said, 'Forget it' and walked out.

Road to Zanzibar was a box office success, with the team of Hope and Crosby scoring another hit. Burke and Van Heusen's songs, while a significant improvement over those from *Love Thy Neighbor*, did not yield any blockbusters. This was due in no small part to the ongoing ASCAP dispute, which would not end until July, 1941 – some three months after *Road to Zanzibar* opened in April, 1941. This was most unfortunate, as unlike their score for *Love Thy Neighbor*, *Road to Zanzibar* contained a true gem – the lovely ballad, "It's Always You." Van Heusen always had a soft spot in his heart for this number, and he indeed regretted its lack of airplay during the ASCAP strike. In a 1981 interview for the "Swing Thing" radio program, Van Heusen stated that so convinced was he of the quality of "It's Always You" that following his return to New York after completing the score, Van Heusen would follow

Benny Goodman from venue to venue with the chart for "It's Always You" cornering Goodman to read and play the chart. It worked, and Goodman's 1942 recording with Helen Forrest was quite well received, if not widely heard.

Adhering to the strict Crosby protocol that no love song could contain the phrase "I love you," Burke fashioned an appropriately sentimental lyric to fit Van Heusen's graceful, yet challenging, melody. The song's title phrase contains a daring interval between "it's" and "always" that in the hands of a lesser singer will sound forced, strained and result in a butchering of the most critical phrase of the entire song. When performed by a Crosby or Sinatra, the interval places an aural explanation point on the wit and charm of Burke's non "I Love You" iteration.

It was the type of risk that Van Heusen was able to take, knowing that the first exponent of his song would be of the caliber of Bing Crosby. However, it was not Crosby who would have the hit recording of this song, but rather Frank Sinatra with the Tommy Dorsey Orchestra. His 1941 recording, re-released in 1943 due to the musician's strike, spent seven weeks on the Billboard charts, achieving a top spot of number six. Sinatra would also record it with a swinging Sy Oliver arrangement in his 1962 album "I Remember Tommy."

EIGHTEEN

Jimmy Van Heusen's Luscombe Silvaire plane crash outside Nashville, Tennessee.
Photo courtesy Van Heusen Photo Archives

The Man With The Golden Arm

As was his habit, following the completion of work on a film, Van Heusen fueled his plane and headed back to New York City. Despite admonitions from Burke that such escapades were foolhardy, Van Heusen and arranger Graham Prince took to the skies for the trip east. The trip was rather mundane until he became aware of a sharp decline in his fuel supply somewhere between Nashville and Knoxville, Tennessee. Van Heusen located an emergency air strip at the town of Smithville and began his descent:

> There was nothing but hills and little mountains in
> sight. I picked a wheat field for a landing – the
> best choice I had although the wheat was about
> three feet high and the field angled upward at
> almost 45 degrees. Since the Luscombe didn't
> have retractable landing gear, I knew I had to
> have speed enough to wipe out the wheels to
> avoid an ass-over-applecart landing, which is not

advisable at any time. I dived at the bottom of the hill between a couple of trees, lifted the nose and pancaked into the field.

Because I was so intent on making a proper landing, I forgot to lean back in my seat on impact and my body was thrown forward against my hand on the stick. A lot of bones in my right hand were broken. Graham, who was a flyer, had enough sense to sit back in his seat and wasn't even scratched.

I was out for a few seconds. The first thing I heard was a reedy voice, 'Be ye hurt, boy?' An old woman, with a pipe in her mouth peered in at me. I was covered with blood because I had knocked out the instrument panel with my head but we followed the little backwoods lady to her cabin and got me cleaned up a bit. A short walk down a creek bed was a farmer with a truck. He took me to a doctor. Graham stayed behind to get the plane trucked out to a field where it could be put together again and I went onto New York to get myself put together . . . That's the only crash I've ever had although I've had small accidents on the ground. It should have been a non-injury landing – if I'd had sense enough to sit back in my seat. I was lucky at that.

Van Heusen's luck was limited, to a certain extent, as the hand that was broken in the crash was his right hand – a particularly debilitating blow for a pianist. But, Van Heusen was being paid not to play the piano but to write songs – a task for which both hands were not necessary.

Nevertheless, studio executives at RKO were decidedly upset. RKO borrowed Van Heusen and Burke from Paramount and had paid a hefty fee for their services. They were tapped to write the songs for two upcoming Kay Kyser films – the 1941 film *Playmates* and the 1942 film *My Favorite Spy*. While the producers were convinced of Van Heusen's ability to continue, Kyser did not share their confidence. It was Kyser's co-star in *Playmates*, the legendary John Barrymore, who ultimately set Kyser to the right concerning Van Heusen's future employment. Barrymore is said to have chastised the producers thusly, "Attendez, you sweet-scented bastards. Yon minstrel doth not need his hands to compose music. Van Heusen can fart better melodies than any tunesmith now alive can write. Any lard head knows that."

Recalling this incident, Van Heusen stated, "An exaggeration. But one of the nicest compliments I've ever had."

Van Heusen's score for *Playmates* was not one of his better efforts. "How Long Did I Dream?" was a bland ballad. "Romeo Smith and Juliet Jones" and "Que Chica" were similarly disappointing. "Thank Your Lucky Stars and Stripes" was the first foray Van Heusen made into patriotic song. The tune was catchy, and Burke's lyrics were appropriately patriotic without being jingoistic. The gem from the movie was "Humpty Dumpty Heart." This gentle ballad was a hit for Bing Crosby and Glenn Miller, and the high point of the film, musically. It was a bit of a step down from "It's Always You" – a fine song, but just a few degrees from a bona fide classic. Miller's recording reached number 23 on the Billboard charts. The film was noteworthy, though, more for preserving Barrymore's only on-screen "To Be Or Not to Be" soliloquy than Burke and Van Heusen's songs.

My Favorite Spy was another forgettable Kay Kyser vehicle, which only earns attention today from those searching for the Bob Hope/Hedy Lamarr classic of the same name. Burke and Van Heusen's contributions were, again, less than stellar. "Just Plain Lonesome" and "Got the Moon in My Pocket" were mediocre tunes, and they seem to reflect a general feeling of disenchantment or at least a lack of inspiration from the RKO/Kyser films. This might have been lingering ill will toward the lack of confidence shown in Van Heusen's ability to compose while nursing his broken hand. It might have been a consequence of Van Heusen's attempts to balance his work at Lockheed Martin with his composing career. Nevertheless, the tunes were moderate hits. Kyser's recording of "Got the Moon in My Pocket" was ranked number 17 on the Billboard charts for two weeks in 1942, and it was recorded by several artists including Bing Crosby, Woody Herman, Freddy Martin and Teddy Powell. Freddy Martin's recording of "Just Plain Lonesome" was ranked number 24 on the Billboard charts for one week in 1942.

Whether or not the scare in Tennessee was the impetus for Van Heusen's eventual permanent move to the West Coast is unclear. Nevertheless, following the commutes involving *The Road to Zanzibar*, Van Heusen became convinced it was time to move. The move seemed as much psychological as geographical for Van Heusen:

> It wasn't until my second trip to Hollywood for
> my second picture that I began to seriously think
> of remaining permanently on the West Coast, and
> maybe obtaining a house in the desert. My first

few encounters with the Hollywood and movie making life and work had sent me flying back to civilization, and the only town in the world, New York. I was like all New Yorkers in those days, in that I considered everything outside of New York completely provincial, or as somebody put it, "everything outside of New York is Bridgeport." But now I was beginning to encounter blizzards and zero temperatures on some of my return trips to the Big Apple, and the ever recurring sinus trouble and the haunting of the doctors' offices and once in a while, the hospitals. The West, and particularly Palm Springs, was walking around with me in memory. The remembered comfortable climate and the thought of the relief from the running nose were the convincers of this dyed in the wool New Yorker as he shivered and shook with the cold. I returned to each successive movie chore with less and less reluctance, and then when the World War II news grew worse and worse, and it was plain to see that California with it sunshine and then smogless days was the perfect place to practice my flying technique, I bought my first home in Palm Springs.

NINETEEN

Jimmy Van Heusen as test pilot for Lockheed in Burbank, Ca.
Photo courtesy of Van Heusen Photo Archives

Thank Your Lucky Stars and Stripes

After the passage of the Selective Service Act in 1940, Van Heusen did all he could to avoid being called up to the armed forces. This is not to say that Van Heusen did not desire to serve his country during the inevitable war. Like most other endeavors, he wanted to do it on his terms. His terms were flying. To this end, Van Heusen had been accumulating hours of flight time from flying to and from New York and Hollywood in preparation to join the Army Air Corps as a Flying Cadet. By this time, he had accumulated something of an impressive airplane collection. Van Heusen recalls owning "the Luscombe (his first plane), a Stinson Voyager, a Ranger-Fairchild, a Stinson 5M8A with a Jacobs engine, we called the bucket of bolts. I rented other planes too." Moreover, Van Heusen took additional courses in aviation, including one in aerobatics until he was, in his words, "as comfortable on my back as I was right side up." So committed to flying was Van

Heusen that during the war years when flying was forbidden within 500 miles of the coast, Van Heusen rented an apartment in Phoenix, Arizona, moving his fleet of planes to points east.

More important, though, was that his flight time threatened his relationship with Johnny Burke: "Burke took a very dim view of my flying, so I told Johnny he should forget about me as his collaborator and latch onto some other composer. I think he did talk it over with a couple of guys but he finally decided to stick with me." Burke was quite justifiably concerned both with Van Heusen's personal safety but also the practical difficulties in collaborating with a composer living some 500 miles away, albeit part-time.

But, the best laid plans . . . for all of Van Heusen's machinations, schemes and air time, he could not overcome that most imperious of foes – bureaucracy.

> They [the Army] said I was too old. The age limit was 26 1/2 and even though I was practically a professional pilot, they turned me down. They said they wanted the younger guys – the hot rodders who made the best fighter pilots. In view of my advanced age, the guy said, my best chance was with the Ferry Command which was just being formed in Long Beach, California. I beat it

down there and got a warm welcome. They
needed pilots to deliver aircraft to the Allies and
the officer in charge said that with my ratings, I'd
be a cinch to make captain in sixty days.

However, Van Heusen did not immediately commit to
Ferry Command. It was, of course, a military institution, and
Van Heusen's own memories of military organizations was not
fond. And, his own experience with authority was less than a
satisfactory fit for the armed forces. Nevertheless, Van Heusen
felt it his patriotic duty to contribute more to the war effort
than patriotic songs, and he reluctantly prepared himself to
accept the Ferry Command position. An alternative
opportunity, though, would present itself during one of Van
Heusen's many late nights at Jack Clark's It Cafe. As was often
the case, the night was one of booze, music and largesse
maximus – put all on Van Heusen's tab.

Van Heusen's behavior was not lost on two gentlemen
at the It Cafe that evening. Elmer McLeod, chief production
pilot of Lockheed Aircraft Corporation, and Steve Parker,
assistant chief production pilot, were intrigued by Van
Heusen's piano playing and soon engaged him in conversation.
When the topic turned from music to flying, Van Heusen

informed the men that he was to join the Ferry Command. McLeod and Parker immediately attempted to dissuade Van Heusen from his chosen course of action. Why fly around the world, when you could work fifteen minutes from home at Lockheed's Burbank facility? That was a powerful argument to the notoriously travel-adverse Van Heusen.

Before Van Heusen agreed to McLeod's terms, he needed to inform Johnny Burke, who reluctantly gave his assent. Van Heusen's plan had to be top secret, as no studio would ever permit an asset to subject itself willingly to the risks of test piloting. In an ironic twist, Van Heusen insisted that his flying be conducted under the name "Edward Chester Babcock" and not "Jimmy Van Heusen." In such a way, the studios would not know of his work and his "Hollywood" identity would not be broadcast to the other pilots.

The Burbank facility of Lockheed Martin was a sprawling complex, and the immense requirements of the American war effort would strain every resource the massive corporation could muster. Its success was a critical component to American victory, as Lockheed and its sister aviation companies provided the production superiority that would ultimately tilt the balance of power permanently in favor of the

Allies.[7] Lockheed would exceed expectations, its factories churning out countless aircraft, many multiples beyond its peacetime production. As Lockheed president Robert Gross stated in *Of Men and Stars:* "One word, production, characterized the war period. The air industry was called upon to build thousands of something it had only built dozens of before. It was like a youth who is suddenly expected to go to college before he has graduated primary school."

With these increased demands, it was vital to find pilots – and plenty of them – to test fly the mass produced aircraft. Lockheed employed countless production pilots, those individuals who were charged with flying the finished aircraft and insuring they could operate properly. Van Heusen was among their ranks. However, he had some distinct advantages over his colleagues – namely, his familiarity with more modern aircraft (as opposed to the myriad of local crop dusters pressed into service) and his instrument rating, i.e. an ability to fly using only instruments rather than relying solely on sight.

---

[7]   So important was Lockheed's Burbank facility that Walt Disney constructed an immense lifelike city on top of the complex so that, should Japanese aircraft fly overhead, they would mistake it for a small town rather than an aviation facility. After the war the city was removed for the hefty sum of $200,000.00.

Van Heusen's first responsibilities were limited. He rode in the bomb bay of a B-17 or Hudson Bomber as they flew over the Mojave Desert and would jettison from the craft parachutes weighted to simulate a man pulling the ripcord as he tossed them from the plane. Much to Van Heusen's horror, more than a comfortable amount of the parachutes failed to open. This led to a change in Van Heusen's flying philosophy: "Right then and there, I decided I'd stick with any plane I was in even if some very large flames were licking at my ass. I wouldn't jump out with a chute for all the money in the world. I never have. I'm scared to death of it."

Van Heusen was next assigned to the "test and delivery" department. During this rotation, pilots were to conduct a production test on aircraft to determine if any mistakes were made on the assembly line. These errors would be remedied and the planes would be forwarded on to delivery. On his first day in the department, he was playing checkers with Willie McConnell, a slightly deaf but seasoned pilot who was planning to test fly a P-38. Van Heusen was to be co-piloting a C-60, commonly known as a Lodestar. Van Heusen was ordered to take off in the C-60 as McConnell awaited his turn to take off. Van Heusen's plane had several problems and was ordered to land. As he was landing, he witnessed a horrible spectacle:

> Just as he [Willie McConnell] broke ground, I heard the unmistakable sound of an engine missing fire. Maybe because of Willie's deafness, he didn't compensate for the loss of his engine in time and the torque of the second engine flipped a wing tip onto the concrete runway. You could hear the scream of the metal and a stream of sparks shot out from the plane -- then the P-38 was just a ball of fire two hundred feet high hurtling down the runway until it crashed into [other planes]. All of them exploded into flame right before my eyes. In that instant, I knew I was not cut out for this line of work. I got out of the C-60 and, when the excitement was over, went to Elmer McLeod. 'I want out,' I said. 'Get me out of this. I'm too much of a coward for this kind of flying.'

Easier said than done. Lockheed personnel informed Van Heusen that should he leave his job, he will be subjected immediately to the draft -- at Lockheed's request.

The P-38 was the aircraft most often flown by Van Heusen. In all, Lockheed produced over 11,000 of these planes, with over 9,000 of them built at Burbank. The P-38 was the only aircraft produced throughout the war, from Pearl Harbor to V-J Day. The single seat fighter was primarily used in the Pacific Theater of operations, and it was the principal aircraft there until the arrival of the P-51D Mustang.

Van Heusen's request for transfer notwithstanding, he appeared to be held in high regard by his fellow pilots. Herman "Fish" Salmon was a legendary production and test pilot who worked with Van Heusen. He recalled, "Nobody knew Jimmy was James Van Heusen, of course. Later on, we got quite a few Hollywood pilots and the word leaked out about who he was. He was quite famous as a songwriter. He was a good pilot – one of the first really qualified pilots we had at Lockheed. He may have been scared but I never felt it. He did a very good job and he flew every airplane any of the rest of us did. I'm sure that if he wanted to get out of anything by taking advantage of who he was, he could have done so very easily but he never did."

TWENTY

Edward Chester Babcock test pilot, Jimmy Van Heusen songwriter.
Courtesy of Van Heusen Photo Archives

Good Time Charlie

Van Heusen's identity was ultimately revealed after the bombing of Pearl Harbor and entry of the United States into the Second World War. The revealer was none other than "master schemer" Johnny Burke, who thought that having a genuine war hero as a composer might increase the stock of Paramount Studios, and by extension, the songwriting team. "Little did the studios know what a sissy and coward I was and how much I wanted to get into the Army where I thought I would be safe," Van Heusen recalls with trademark sarcasm and deadpan. But, Van Heusen's fears were not without merit, as the mortality figures for test pilots bear witness. And while aviation is a risky profession on its own, Van Heusen discovered another factor at play in his risk assessment:

> I was at Lockheed for more than two and a half years and I was scared shitless all of the time. The

planes were made by women – Rosie the Riveters, you remember those guys – and the final inspection was made by women, too. I'll never forget one time I was checking a plane on the ground and when I shook the empennage, there was an awful racket. They took the tail section off and found some broad had riveted her lunch pail right into empennage. We'd find condoms and douche bags and all sorts of things. It was pretty clear what had been going on. I figured there wasn't a riveter alive who can aim a rivet gun properly while being fucked. I figured if the broads were kissing and hugging and all that instead of paying attention to their work it was only a matter of time until I'd get a sick airplane and bust my ass. We had a lot of close calls. As it was about ten percent of the pilots got killed.

Van Heusen advanced in the test pilot program. He was promoted to the rank of first pilot and given the responsibility to train all new pilots to become instrument rated. As the realities of war progressed and military technology advanced, nighttime air raids and operations took on increasing importance and the aviation firms had to create weaponry to meet these needs. This naturally required instrument ratings for their test pilots. To enable Van Heusen to train these men,

Lockheed converted the single seat P-38 into a dual seat plane. Van Heusen was cramped into the makeshift rear seat, which presented a great problem should an emergency exit be required. Standard procedure was for the pilot to turn the plane upside down and bail out. Van Heusen would then be required to stand up, buckle in his parachute (which he kept in his lap) and then climb out, a process to which Van Heusen remarked, "I always had the feeling it wouldn't work." Fortunately, he would never be put to the test.

Not that there was not a concern. Teaching instrument rating was difficult and dangerous. The pilots were being trained while literally flying blind wearing Polaroid goggles. When things began to go awry, Van Heusen would need to move quickly, and awkwardly. "I learned to land a P-38 by using only the throttles and the wheel – no rudders or brakes – while reaching over the guy's shoulders. The crop-duster types didn't believe their instruments and, after I nearly choked them to death, grabbing the wheel and throttles away from them, [they] were always surprised to find themselves upside down or in a dive when they got their goggles off."

The production pilot experience might be described using that old adage, "hours of boredom interrupted by minutes of terror." As he recalled,

The pilot house at Lockheed was a large former private residence of some ancient and it had been used for years as such, even though large factory assembly line type buildings were erected during the years and now that war was upon us, there were around 125,000 employees laboring at the location at Burbank airport. With about 120 production pilots, about half of whom were inhabiting the pilot house on each shift, the waiting for the loudspeaker of the dispatch office bellowing your name was about all that interrupted the intense boredom. The long lounging periods were usually punctuated with mud fights, water fights, hot seats, hot feet, and general harassment of anyone who fell asleep. Since I was trying to live two or three different lives simultaneously, and was working at two distinct jobs every day, my moonlighting at Lockheed (if songwriting was my main occupation), really robbed my pale psyche of its proper rest. Usually I had been up most of the night previously catching up on the composing chores, and if I happened to be on my early shift at the pilot plant, perhaps I had slept from two or three in the AM until four AM when I had to rise to make it a five AM to Burbank. Many is the hot foot I suffered, or an entire fire would be lit under your wooden chair, resulting in a very hot ass. Cardboard containers of water were slung in mock battles and in every really energetic engagement handfuls of mud would sail across the room.

The stress of his working conditions, lack of sleep and dangerous occupation certainly took its toll on Van Heusen and he sublimated it with his ether of choice – alcohol. As Van Heusen himself said, "When I was at Lockheed, I thought I was going to be killed every day and when I got home from that job, I'd drink with both hands." Ralph Harris, his old Syracuse chum who joined him on the West Coast, recalls, "Chester was working very hard at Lockheed and I worked odd shifts – a lot of time at night -- at a defense plant. We were heavy drinkers. When Chester wasn't on a picture, if he didn't have an assignment, we had a regular routine. In the late afternoon, we'd take a bottle of Gordon's gin which makes, as you know, fourteen martinis. (As an aside, this author did not know that, but on the late Mr. Harris' advice, I undertook to confirm this fact. He was correct). We each had seven. Then, every night but Monday, we'd go to Chasen's. We'd have two martinis at the bar and then have dinner. Chester usually had a bottle or two of beer. After dinner we'd have some cognac and then go back to the house and get out a bottle of cognac and drink it. Then, if he felt like it, Chester would call a girl - otherwise he'd go to bed. We did that every night."

Once Burke conveniently revealed Van Heusen's whereabouts to the studios and Lockheed generally leaked the true identity of Edward Chester Babcock, there was no reason not to let his fellow pilots enjoy the fruits of his Hollywood labor. And so the Van Heusen hospitality was revealed. Jack Clark, who joined Lockheed with Jimmy, recalls, "You'd just go over and make yourself at home. Jimmy might still be asleep but three or four of us would open up the liquor and start drinking or take a swim or have something to eat. Anyone who was a friend knew he was welcome. It would go on night and day – anything you wanted to eat or drink. He was running a free hotel – the best one I've ever seen. God knows what it must've cost him."

No one will ever know how much it cost Van Heusen, because he himself might not have known. More significant, he would never have let anyone know if he had. It was his pleasure to host people and to make them at home. Such was his way with people. In addition to his generosity shown to his friends, Van Heusen's reputation as a party host grew exponentially during his years at Lockheed.

An individual only identified as a "music man" by Van Heusen biographer Robert de Roos stated, "I've known a few great hosts in my time, but nothing ever like Van Heusen. He used to have all those people around – during the war there were a lot of flyers – and right under the phone was what Jim called "the hooker booker," a directory of all the best pros in town, and all his friends were at liberty to call for their services at any time. There were always girls around, any kind the guys wanted, Negro girls and Chinese and lesbians, all kinds. Jimmy's the only man I've ever known who paid for his guests to get laid. One time I took a girl home so Jim wouldn't pay and he bawled the hell out of the girl for taking my money."

Van Heusen's parties were certainly wild, but never out of control. He and his friends knew how to drink. As Don Rickles observed about parties with Sinatra, "this wasn't amateur hour." Even the one violent incident Van Heusen could recall was cast with the veneer of the alcohol-laced humor of a 1950s film:

One night an officer of the Ferry Command pulled a knife on a kid P-38 pilot and tried to remodel his face. It was a mistake. The kid pulled the officer into a bedroom, locked the door and proceeded to turn him into mincemeat. We finally broke down the door and the place looked like a slaughterhouse. All the furniture was broken and the entire room was painted with blood. We got the victim back to his post in Long Beach where he was listed as the casualty of an automobile accident. Nothing ever came of the incident because the commandant of the Ferry Command was asleep in another of my bedrooms with one of the girls.

It was not only Van Heusen's house that served as the site of good times. His membership in the exclusive Lakeside Country Club also inured to the benefit of pilots and Hollywood chums alike. Membership in the club was purely social for the non-golfer Van Heusen: "Johnny Burke made me join because that's where Bing and Bob Hope belonged and a lot of the producers and directors we did business with, and actors. That was the thing to do. I did all the things that were the things to do in those days. I never got out to the first tee but we played the bar pretty good. Then, when I was at Lockheed, Lakeside was only a few minutes away from the field and it was the only decent place around to eat. I used to take some of the pilots over to lunch to drown our cares in a flock of double martinis."

It is not surprising that the country club set did not suit Van Heusen, but for reasons other than what might one expect. It was not the stuffy atmosphere or rules and regulations, per se, that drove Van Heusen from Lakeside, but something far more sinister. "I found out Lakeside barred Jews. Over on the other side of town, near Fox, Hillcrest Country Club barred gentiles, and that's the way it went. Anyway, I didn't like the bigoted atmosphere I found and after the war I resigned quietly. I simply got tired of hearing 'anti' remarks with my booze. Dean Martin, a few years later, also got tired of the anti-Semitism, and he resigned by throwing his golf bag through a plate glass window, which I thought was a nice gesture."

Van Heusen's service was not limited to his work with Lockheed Martin. Despite his long hours at the airstrip and in the studio, he still made time to accompany Bob Hope, Bing Crosby, and comics Phil Silvers and Rags Ragland when they entertained troops at local bases. "These tours were always a lot of fun because we'd be entertaining the GI's or raising money for some cause." Van Heusen recalls. "Sometimes it would be a golf exhibition. I didn't play golf – that's always seemed to me like an unnatural way for a man to bore himself – but they'd roll a piano out onto the tee and I'd play a few tunes and Bing would sing."

While Hope, Crosby, and Silver need no introduction, Ragland was one of those many burlesque entertainers lost to history. It is fortunate we have Van Heusen's own biographical sketch: "Rags Ragland was a good comic out of burlesque. He traveled with just a small bag which held his toothbrush and a few bottles of whiskey - no clothes. When he needed a shirt or some underwear, he'd buy some and throw the old stuff away. Poor guy drank too much and finally drank himself to death." Filtered through the impersonal prism of the written word, it might appear Van Heusen was apathetic about Ragland's death. This is not the case. In fact, Ragland's untimely death in 1946 at the age of 40 of liver and kidney failure due to alcohol abuse was a blow to Van Heusen's social circle. Ragland was a favorite of Sinatra (who paid for Ragland's final medical care) and was Silvers' friend, vaudeville partner, and favorite comedian. Only days after

Ragland's death, Silvers, true to a contractual commitment, opened his nightclub act in New York City, which he was to have shared with Ragland. Leaving the set of his current film, Sinatra flew to New York City to support Silvers and, in fact, performed many of their old USO routines with Silvers. After a triumphant opening show, Silvers, tears in his eyes, ended the performance by asking of the audience, "May I take a bow for Rags?" Those were different times, to be sure.

Van Heusen continued his service at Lockheed Martin until the Allies' victory over Nazi Germany. With different priorities and standards, changes were made, and it is best to listen to Van Heusen's own voice telling about the end of his test flying career:

> After VE Day, the [Lockheed Martin] brass at Burbank, decided there was not the need for so many production test pilots since fighter and bomber pilots with the least seniority were discharged, and as luck would have it I was included in the unfortunate group. Unfortunate, that is, if you were under 45 years of age, because you were automatically 1A in the draft board records. With the pretty pep talk that was given each guy came a document that he had been

discharged honorably and without prejudice. Nothing was mentioned of the hair-raising heroics performed by each and every one of them in flying those female-fashioned flying machines. Just that he had been a test pilot and had done his job well, and the draft board would be notified. Naturally, I received an immediate reclassification from my draft board and could see myself trudging through the slop and sludge of Southeast Asia in the U.S. infantry. I figured I had been a hero, and although no bullets had been chasing me, the fatality figures demonstrated the dangerous endeavor of test flying. This fact meant nothing to the fellows at Selective Service, and off I went trying to find another flying job that would defer my induction into the arms.

The first places I picked were the airlines, and although I was now a pro pilot with considerable qualifications, every personnel director turned me down. I was too set in my ways of flying. The airlines liked to train you in their own way and I was too experienced to be remolded. Not even a co-pilot job on a dinky line was available, and after checking with my original love, the Ferry Command in Long Beach (which, I discovered, was not taking any more pilots after V-E Day), I reluctantly sought out the other airplane factories.

Boeing, in Seattle, took on one or two of my buddies but there was no place for Chester. Having a couple of friends that were working as test pilots at Consolidated Aircraft in San Diego (they made the PBY and B-24 bomber), I scurried south.

Brad Woolman, one of my San Diego pilot friends, was a mortician, and his family owned the then large Bradley Woolman Mortuary, now being managed by his wife. After filling out forms, another out of work pilot, Jack Clark, and I left the employment office at Consolidated Aircraft and accepted the invitation to visit the undertaking establishment. Stops at saloons en route were frequent enough to cause the arrival at the somber stairway that lead to forbidding double doors, of four men who were obviously drunk in midafternoon. To make some character with his wife, Woolman questioned her about the services then going on in the chapel. Sure enough, it was Jim Something-or-other, a friend of the family, a plumber. Yes, she had personally given him a facial and a manicure and a hair-do. After the people filed out, there I stood, as man and wife morticians talked shop in front of the open casket. What a great job she had done said the husband. In between compliments on the corpse, the organ loft was pointed out to me. Up I went, followed by my friend who was the son of a Methodist bishop, and proceeded to play "Mairsy Doats and Dozy Doats" on the elegant organ as the bishop's son recited two burial services. No attention was paid to our send off for Jim the plumber, so engrossed were the man and wife mortician team in their handiwork.

The organ loft was as close to flying as I got in San Diego, and no other factory was hiring. Eventually, I got a flying job that was considered essential at Central Airport in Los Angeles. My duties were to drop "sky hooks" as they were called then, which were small sized parachutes with a weight attached. The purpose was to arrive at the exact kind of chute for the exact type of supply that would be dropped by plane to isolated areas, for troops or behind the lines supply. The chore seemed silly, but sure enough I was reclassified, as the experiments were deemed essential.

His stint at Central Airport ended the wartime service of Chester Babcock. From thereon, he could, in his words, "fly for fun and fun alone." The work Van Heusen did for Lockheed Martin was extremely dangerous. While Van Heusen's writings and words refer to a desire to avoid the draft, it would seem that if true cowardice were his motivation, he chose a uniquely foolhardy means of doing so. There were means available to Van Heusen to remain in the United States and serve in an entertainment capacity. And, while he certainly contributed in such a manner, his own choice was much more dangerous and risky. Military aeronautics in the early days of the Second World War was still in its infancy. The Air Force as a separate branch of the military did not exist. The last air combat the world had seen involved biplanes and triplanes with mounted machine guns and bombs being tossed from the cockpit by the pilot. By the end of the Second World War, the jet age was upon us. Van Heusen and the rest of the test pilots at Lockheed Martin ushered in that age and endured the birth pains of the modern military aviation era. While there were no medals on his chest, Van Heusen made an important contribution to the American war effort.

The Lockheed schedule permitted Van Heusen to continue to write for the movies. "Four days a week, I went to work at Lockheed at 5:00 am and was sprung at 1:00 in the afternoon. Those days, I could make it to the studio in the afternoon or even a late lunch. Three days a week, I went to work at 1:00 in the afternoon and worked until dark."

This was a fortunate occurrence, for in 1942, Burke and Van Heusen were about to compose the music for what would be the first iconic moment of their partnership. The "Road" series of pictures generated significant revenue with the first two entries. They were lighthearted comedies and exposed the country to the fact that Bing Crosby, in addition to being a brilliant vocalist, also possessed keen comic timing and wit. The next entry in the series, *Road to Morocco*, would be a landmark - the pinnacle of the Hope/Crosby wit, a wonderful cast, a decent story, and a remarkable score by Van Heusen and Burke.

Road to Morocco represents the most complete film score Van Heusen had composed to date.   After some interesting moments, the music portion of the film gets off to a rollicking, swinging beginning with "The Road to Morocco." This jaunty, catchy Van Heusen melody is the perfect frame for some of the wittiest lyrics Burke had ever crafted. The scene with Crosby and Hope singing together, riding a camel, has become for many the iconic image from the entirety of the Road picture series. With the Paramount desert as a backdrop, the two stars trade lines, tearing down the fourth wall, letting the audience in on inside jokes, and otherwise tossing off witticisms: "Where we're goin', why we're goin', how can we be sure?/ I'll lay you eight to five that we'll meet Dorothy Lamour" and "We certainly do get around/Like Webster's Dictionary, we're Morocco bound."

Crosby's standard "devil may care" number is the overlooked "Ain't Got a Dime to My Name." It is an interesting song – there is a rapid fire succession of notes and words, akin to nervous chatter – then the song stops, and Crosby tells us not to worry, as the tune's refrain of "Ho hum" is elongated over two whole notes. He considers the problem, and then decides, it is just not worth worrying about. Van Heusen and Burke wrote a beautiful song for Lamour called "Constantly." In any other context, it might have been a hit song, but the song served more as a backdrop for Hope and Crosby clowning than anything else. Hope is entranced by Lamour's serenade to him, while Crosby is infuriated to discover that Hope is not in danger (as Crosby was led to believe) but rather in the lap of luxury, about to be married to Lamour's Princess Shalimar. Crosby's slow burn during this song demonstrates remarkable timing and sense, as in the hands of a lesser actor, the scene could easily have degenerated into overdone farce.

However, the crown jewel of the movie, "Moonlight Becomes You," almost failed to make it from Burke's workroom. Van Heusen recalls having difficulty composing the requisite ballad for Crosby to sing. He composed several melodies, but none really were thought to be adequate to Burke. Van Heusen then stumbled across a fragment of a lyric by Burke in a notebook: "Moonlight becomes you/It goes with your hair." Immediately, Burke shot back that Crosby would never sing such an effeminate song. Van Heusen persisted and Burke, perhaps for lack of any better alternative, completed the lyric. Van Heusen's masterful melody followed soon after.

As Burke had predicted, the difficult part would be pitching it to Crosby. As Van Heusen stated, "The Groaner abhorred mushy love lyrics. He refused to come right out and sing, 'I love you, my dearest one' or anything like that. But the judicious use of the word 'if' sometimes saved a lyric from his taboo. In 'Moonlight Becomes You', for instance, the lyric says, 'If I say, I love you/I want you to know/It's not just because there's moonlight, although/Moonlight becomes you so'...that 'if' saved the bacon."

And what bacon it was! "Moonlight Becomes You" is an inspired, beautiful melody without a hint of pretense or cliché. With its leaping intervals and diminished cadences, it decidedly has the characteristics of a Van Heusen melody. However, this song has a remarkably strong bridge – in fact, it can be argued that the bridge provides the moments of highest drama in the song. In his superb arrangement of the song for the 1965 Frank Sinatra album *Moonlight Sinatra*, Nelson Riddle has Sinatra open the song with bridge before launching into the opening lines of the chorus.

Much to the relief of the team, "Moonlight Becomes You" was an unadulterated hit. While Van Heusen and Burke were away cavorting with Kay Kyser, Mr. Crosby was away shooting a film, *Holiday Inn*, from which came the immortal "White Christmas." It would, of course, become Crosby's greatest hit and the most popular record in the world by many standards. It was not lost on Van Heusen that he had not had a success to rival his New York hits while in Hollywood, and Crosby was enjoying a monumental success with a composer Van Heusen felt to be one of the great masters – Irving Berlin. "Moonlight Becomes You" crept into Billboard's Top 10 on December 19, 1942, courtesy of Glenn Miller's recording with

Skip Nelson. Crosby's recording would enter the Billboard Top 10 the week of January 16, 1943, and would remain in the Top 10 until April 3, 1943, achieving its highest rank of 4 on February 27, 1943. For many of those weeks, the Miller and Crosby recordings of "Moonlight Becomes You" both occupied spots in the Billboard Top 10 during the same week.

For its own part, the movie was a tremendous box office success. Along with "White Christmas," it catapulted Crosby into the stratosphere of fame. Van Heusen and Burke were more than happy to hitch their wagon to such a star.

The next film featuring the music of Van Heusen and Burke was the first Technicolor vehicle for Bing Crosby - the 1943 biopic of composer David Decatur Emmett, *Dixie*. This hopelessly dated, politically incorrect, but good natured movie also starred "Road" alumna Dorothy Lamour. There were six original songs for this film - Van Heusen and Burke's most ambitious effort to date: "She's from Missouri," "Miss Jemima Walks By," "If You Please," "Kinda Peculiar Brown," "A Horse That Knows Its Way Back Home," and the classic "Sunday, Monday or Always."

If Van Heusen and Burke did not believe that the unions had it in for them when their first films fell victim to the

ASCAP/BMI feud, they had to think it was the case when their finest composition for Bing Crosby to date might face a grim future because of the Musicians Union strike of 1942-1943. This strike crippled the recording industry, as no orchestras or session players could be found. Record companies with established stars like Bing Crosby and Decca could simply re-release their older platters. However, in the case of a young Frank Sinatra, who had just broken with Tommy Dorsey to chart his own path, it was particularly devastating. Necessity being the mother of invention, arrangers came up with a unique solution – the use of a chorus to mimic the instruments of the orchestra. When crafted properly, the arrangements were surprisingly effective – the listener soon forgetting he is hearing a choral (rather than orchestral) arrangement. Sinatra's first 10 sides with Columbia employed this approach, and "Sunday, Monday or Always" was so popular Crosby was persuaded to record it with the Ken Darby Singers. The record was Van Heusen and Burke's first number one hit for Crosby. His recording lasted 18 weeks on the Billboard chart in 1943, where it remained at number one from September 11 to October 23. Sinatra's recording was also quite successful, entering the Billboard charts on September 9 where it lasted four weeks, peaking at the number nine position. Once again, a Van Heusen and Burke song had two separate versions in the Billboard top 10 during the same week – the Groaner's impeccable musical instincts were paying off.

The influence of "Sunday, Monday or Always" existed far beyond the major hit for Crosby. It remains a favorite of jazz singers and instrumentalists, having been recorded countless times. Paul Desmond was said to be obsessed with the melody, such that the bridge to his landmark "Take Five" is a clear homage to Van Heusen's tune. It was clear, though, that Van Heusen was crafting music of a different and more sophisticated quality than the standard in Hollywood.

Nevertheless, those talents would go largely unnoticed if not more the power of Bing Crosby. With the successes of "White Christmas." "Moonlight Becomes You," and "Sunday, Monday or Always," Crosby was at the top of the music and film world. While his closest rival was perhaps Frank Sinatra (the positioning of the various male crooners was not yet finalized), even he conceded the superiority of Der Bingle when he sang these lyrics from a parody of "Sunday, Monday or Always":

Everytime I sing,

I'm compared with Bing
by Dick Haymes, Dick Todd, and Como
Bing's four boys are sublime
But they won't give me time
Dick Haymes, Dick Todd, and Perry
I'll never sing like Bing
I know I don't compare
I'll grant them he's got voice
If they'll grant me, that I've got hair
But then why all this fuss
There's room for all of us
Dick Haymes, Dick Todd, and Como
There's just one Crosby
There's room for all of us

This tune titled "Dick Haymes, Dick Todd and Como" had lyrics specially written for Sinatra, detailing his current attempts to remain, at least the second best vocalist in the country. In his liner notes to the Frank Sinatra collection "The V Discs," Will Friedwald opines that the lyrics were written by Sammy Cahn. There is no reason to doubt this contention. Sammy Cahn was, even at that time, a part of the Sinatra circle, soon to be writing many hit songs for his films with Jule Styne. And, as many can attest, Cahn was well known for his ability to write witty parodies of popular songs. This tune certainly fits that bill.

TWENTY-ONE

Jimmy Van Heusen and Bing Crosby
Photo courtesy Van Heusen Photo Archives

Something in Common

Van Heusen knew that so long as he produced music of a high caliber he would always be a welcome member of the Crosby court. Burke, however, wanted a bit more insurance: "Johnny always said 'Blood is thicker than water,' and was convinced that having Larry Crosby [Bing's brother] as our agent helped us with Bing. I don't think Larry did that much for us. We pretty much got our jobs on our own and certainly Larry couldn't have persuaded Bing to work with anyone he didn't want." This view is confirmed by Bessie Burke who claimed that "Crosby never gave his friends the star treatment. They were always good friends. I don't think Bing would have liked anybody who was sycophantic. He would never have people around who were trying to get something from him."

The relationship between Van Heusen and Crosby was decidedly different than his relationship with Sinatra. With the latter, there was more a relationship of equals, with Sinatra often referring to Van Heusen as his "brother." Van Heusen's relationship with Crosby was decidedly different. While Van Heusen was never overly deferential to anyone when it came to his music, it was fair to say that he was in awe of Crosby's star power. And, it would stand to reason. As a Hollywood neophyte, he was awarded the hottest songwriting assignment imaginable. Fresh from New York City, he was writing songs for filmdom's brightest star.

Moreover, Van Heusen knew Crosby and he were different people. In his view, Crosby was "a very autocratic man and the casual, carefree attitude he presented was a façade which covered a highly-motivated and well-ordered creature." This was in direct contrast to the lifestyle and personality of Van Heusen. Those activities he enjoyed with Crosby were clearly more of a bow to the inequality of the relationship than a reflection of friendship. For instance, he joined a prestigious golf club (but hated golf), invested in the Del Mar racetrack (but rarely gambled), spent summers at the Crosby ranch in Rancho Santa Fe. The awkwardness of the last activity was not lost on Van Heusen who recalled of his time at the ranch, "I was more used to bordellos and saloons than to a strict household. There were jokes about my silence but I decided that if I didn't say anything I couldn't say the wrong thing."

While Van Heusen certainly had immense respect for Crosby, he had genuine affection for his wife, Dixie. Wilma Winifred Wyatt was an aspiring actress and singer when she met and married Bing Crosby in 1930. Her career would take a back seat to that of her role as Hollywood hostess and mother, but by all accounts, her life was not happy. She battled alcoholism throughout most of her short life, which ended tragically in 1952 from ovarian cancer, only days short of her 41st birthday. Van Heusen had occasion to see Crosby's relationship with his children and Dixie, and saw Dixie as being something of a safe harbor for Bing's children from his authoritarian ways:

> Dixie was a fabulous, marvelous woman. She was beautiful and charming and a good mother, a real and regular dame. She always put me at my ease and she used to sit down on the piano bench and sing when I played a song she liked. She could sing. The boys of Bing's first family were always catching hell from Bing. He believed in the old woodshed. I don't know whether he swung a belt or a board but he used to punish them regularly and I can remember the boys coming out yelling

that it hurt like hell. They used to spend summer vacations working with the ranch hands on Bing's ranch up near Elko, Nevada - backbreaking work that was supposed to be just the things for growing boys. They hated it and some of the boys grew up to hate Bing, too, and had to be head-shrunk out of it later. Bing loved them but he just couldn't show it. They adored Dixie and when she died, they lost their only touch of tenderness.

It is unlikely that Van Heusen was quite as frank with Crosby as he was in this interview in the late 60s. There is only one recorded recollection of Van Heusen expressing dismay to Crosby about his treatment of his children. Following an incident where some poor publicity came to the Crosby's courtesy of his son's shenanigans, Van Heusen reminded Crosby that his children were only doing what he did at their age, and Crosby should show some degree of leniency. Crosby ended the conversation by telling Van Heusen that that was exactly what he did not want his children doing – that is, taking after their father. There were certain lines that were not to be crossed, and it may have been that Van Heusen found himself too close to a particular line for comfort.

It was a testament to Van Heusen's personality that he was able to juggle the egos and personalities of Hollywood, and remain on friendly terms with nearly everyone. That was in no small part due to his generosity and openness as a host. It seemed that wherever Van Heusen was, his home was the base of operations. And so it was in Hollywood. Whether entertaining pilots from Lockheed or stars, musicians and the like, Van Heusen relished his role as host. In the early 40s, it was commonplace for Van Heusen's home to be a stopover for Sinatra, Sammy Cahn, Polly Adler, Phil Silvers, and others. Of that group, Van Heusen had a particular fondness for Phil Silvers. At that time, Silvers was under contract with Metro-Goldwyn-Mayer, but he was being used only in bit parts, and so had yet to achieve any real fame. Sgt. Bilko was still over a decade in his future. Nonetheless, his talent was evident to Van Heusen: "Phil would always perform. He was funny as hell – he did all the things then that he does now. We called him the best living-room performer in the world."

On one of his journeys to the Van Heusen house, Silvers came upon a melody Van Heusen had composed several nights before, which was still on the piano. Silvers asked Van Heusen to play the melody, as he had crafted some words to it:

If I don't see her, each day I miss her.

Who wouldn't miss that Irish kisser?

Believe me, I've got a case, on

Bessie with the laughing face.

Van Heusen tells the story:

> "Ho Ho Ho," I cajoled, "But why Bessie . . . do you mean Johnny Burke's wife Bessie?" "Of course," he reminded me, "It's her birthday Saturday and we are both invited to a party at the [Crosby] house. Wouldn't it be great if I got up and sang this song after the cake?" "Yeah, if we can come up with a funny, but I mean funny, lyric." "No, it should be beautiful, like she is," he objected. So, there he sat, occasionally asking me to play the tune for him, sweating out what he thought was a lyric.
> "We can help," I said after seeing his amateurish efforts. "And maybe Sammy Cahn, who arrives every day, can throw in a line or two, and tonight while I'm working with Burke, maybe he can take time out and polish this pretty putrid ode to his wife."
> "OK, but the title remains," said the fledgling funster turned lyricist.
>
> After Phil Silvers departed, sure enough Cahn arrived, and I showed him his friend Phil's feeble efforts. He threw in a couple of better lyric lines

and though he knew the whole project was slightly stupid and in some areas absolutely awful, he couldn't think of anything better for a title or improve any of the inanities inherent in the wordage. It would have to wait for the master's touch that night, and as suspected, Burke supplied the release lyric, which is the only decent language in the whole thing, and tidied up the rest of the lines:

Did you ever hear mission bells ringing?
Well, she'll give you the very same glow.
When she speaks, you would think it was singing.
Just hear her say, "Hello."

Saturday arrived and there at 603 North Oakhurst Drive in Beverly Hills, which was the Burke household, stood Phil Silvers, very seriously singing "Bessie with the Laughing Face." Bing Crosby's presence seemed to mean everything to Phil. He directed his performance not to the guest of honor, Bessie, but to Crosby. Although there was not an intentional humorous line in the lyric, lots of belly laughs were forthcoming. Phil bowed, but I could see he was not trying to be funny. He was disappointed, and was grumbling to himself as I immediately went into a medley of Cole Porter songs. Phil was crushed, I could see, and felt guilty for allowing him to carry the gag so far. The evening ended with the pleasant little prank completely forgotten. The only one who didn't forget was Phil.

It never occurred to me when I couldn't find the manuscript on which the melody was written, either on the piano or anyplace in the house after the party and it was time to go home, that Phil had pocketed his precious piece. This was made known to me with a thundering thud of a shock a couple of weeks later when I received a phone call from a music published by the name of Ben Barton. He published Sinatra songs, and had been present at a party at the Sinatra home on Valley Spring Lake in the Toluca Lake district of San Fernando Valley. It was the birthday of their daughter Nancy Sinatra, Jr., and the adults celebrated after the little one had been bedded. Phil Silvers was a guest, and very quietly had taken Axel Stordahl (Sinatra's arranger-conductor then) into a corner and showed him the piano copy of the melody I had written. No title was inscribed at the top, because I had no intention of the 'Bessie with the Laughing Face' wordage being permanent. Phil asked Axel to play it for him while he vocalized a song written especially for the occasion called, "Nancy with the Laughing

Face." Axel played, all too well I guess, and Phil sang the same song with only one word changed, Nancy replacing Bessie, and the assemblage cheered. No one had the slightest knowledge of the songs previous performance under slightly different conditions and reactions. Later I realized that the whole gimmick assumed a charm and innocence when sung to a cute little girl, a kind of garb that disappeared completely when delivered to an adult. That made the whole difference, and Phil bowed and bowed, and consented to the host's recording the song. The call from the publisher was to tell me how beautiful the record had turned out and where could he send the contracts for me to sign, and also send the proofs for the published song copies.

"Hold it", I said, "I can't sign anything. I'm contracted to another publisher. Put some other name on that song and I'll assign the royalties to little Nancy for her future education or whatever she wants to do with them." "OK, send the assignment, but sign the contract with your own name and we'll just put Phil's name on the song." Naturally, he did not live up to his promise. My name appeared on the music copy big as life, but Sinatra's stature stopped any punitive action on the part of my music publisher. I said I was sorry and all was forgiven. Furthermore, Sinatra was singing and recording almost everything I was writing for Crosby, and there were hits galore. Sinatra was too important a plug to alienate, just because one little item slipped into his company. Sinatra was delighted with the gesture of giving the loot to Nancy, Jr., and it also enriched an already budding friendship between the two of us.

"Nancy" was a hit for Sinatra, ranking as high as 10 on the Billboard charts in November, 1945. However, it had a rather circuitous route to the charts. The song was introduced in April, 1944, on a broadcast of Sinatra's Vimms radio show. He recorded it in July, 1944, for the V-Disc program. Sinatra then attempted a recording for Columbia in late 1944, which was never released until 1994 as part of the "Columbia Complete Recordings" package. It was only when Silvers and Sinatra toured Europe in June, 1945, when the first request from servicemen was for "Nancy," did Sinatra re-record "Nancy" in August, 1945. Sinatra would record "Nancy" twice for his Reprise label – in 1963 as part of the *Sinatra's Sinatra* sessions and once in 1977 for an aborted album featuring songs titled with ladies' names. It remained, throughout the majority of his career, an important song for him, referring to it as a good luck charm. It was a concert mainstay, with Sinatra even including it as one of the eleven selections for his 1971 "retirement" concert.

Nineteen-forty-four would be a most busy and profitable year for Burke, Van Heusen, and Crosby. The year began with their being assigned to provide a song for the screen treatment of the Ira Gershwin/Kurt Weill musical *Lady in the Dark*. It was unfortunate that most of that masterful score was excised from the film, with only "The Saga of Jenny" and "Girl of the Moment" remaining. (The exclusion of "My Ship" is borderline criminal.) Still, Van Heusen and Burke were more than up to the task with the contribution of "Suddenly It's Spring." Whether Van Heusen was subconsciously channeling Weill is debatable, but the opening measures contain a tricky interval that could easily have come from the German's pen. The remainder of the song contains those intricate phrases and beautiful resolutions of seemingly impossible melodic mazes that were to become (if they were not already) the Van Heusen trademark. Burke's lyric is conversational and measured.

Lady in the Dark only required one song from the team. Their next project of that year, *And the Angels Sing*, had no fewer than eight tunes. While not a true musical, the film starring Dorothy Lamour, Betty Hutton, and Fred MacMurray served as little more than a vehicle for Lamour, Hutton and Diana Lynn (The Angel sisters) to sing. Fred MacMurray's role as scheming manager offers a bit of weight, but largely the movie is good-hearted fun. Van Heusen and Burke seem to be particularly inspired writing for Betty Hutton as she is the recipient of two of the cleverest songs in the movie – "Bluebirds in My Belfry" and "His Rocking Horse Ran Away." The latter, a peon to the woes (and joys) of motherhood was a rollicking, swinging, catchy tune that was one of the finest unions of lyrics and melody that the team produced. The lyric truly showcased the ingenuity of Burke. Each verse tells of the destruction that a rather precocious little one is wreaking on the household. At the beginning of each phrase of the chorus, the first word of each measure is an action word (wham, crash, etc.). Van Heusen's first note in each is a fortissimo blast (ably communicated by Hutton's powerful alto). Remarkably, Burke never repeats an exclamation, despite have some fourteen instances to do so:

Bang went the bridge lamp, **down** went the table, **crash** went the china tray . . .

Rip rip went the curtain, **wham** went the window, **crunch** went the new buffet . . .

Slam went the screen door, **smash** went the mirror, looks like I'll soon be gray . . .

Wham went the dish pan, then came a holler, up went the neighbor's shade . . .

Clang, clang, clang went a cowbell, **whee** went a whistle, I nearly had a stroke . . .

Bam went the book case, **boot** went the fruit bowl, **boom** went the glass bouquet . . .

The song is truly fun, and it is difficult not to smile, if not laugh out loud, at Hutton's performance in the film. Anyone with a rambunctious child can sympathize with Hutton's plight and loving acceptance. The song proved to be a big hit for Hutton, staying in the Billboard Top 10 of 1944 from July 29 to September 23, peaking at number 7.

The jewel of the film, though, was the ballad the team wrote for old friend Dorothy Lamour. Composed to suit her limited vocal range, "It Could Happen to You" was a song Lamour could finally sing without the competing egos of Hope and Crosby. It was a beautiful melody with equally beautiful lyrics. In his work, *American Popular Song*, Alec Wilder chose it as singularly demonstrative of Van Heusen's characteristic of "chromatic bass lines." Wilder explains:

> (Van Heusen) loves diminished chords not for themselves but in order to make chromatic bass lines. In all of his songs you will find him, thank heaven, very respectful of bass lines.
>
> Some writers settle for scale lines, but Van Heusen is more fond of chromatic lines. And, in order to have them, he must have diminished chords. So, when he reaches one he must find a way for his melody to move, with them as the foundation. In "Darn That Dream" he moves one way, and with "It Could Happen to You" he moves another. In the key of G he moves to an F natural in the second measure, F being one of the notes of a G-sharp diminished chord. He drops to E, but

moves up to B, another note of the chord. Then, in the third measure, where he uses an A-sharp diminished chord, he lands on G and arrives at C-sharp, another note of the chord. It makes not only for a logical bass line but for a more experimental melody. More power to him!

In addition to the complex melody, Burke's lyrics are also noteworthy once again for their ability to convey a love song without using the word "love." In fact, any hint of romance is referred to by the impersonal pronoun "it." The bridge lyrics are Burke in his purest form – measured sentimentality: "Don't count stars or you might stumble/ Someone drops a sigh and down you tumble."

The song proved to be yet another hit for the team, with Jo Stafford's recording reaching the tenth spot on the Billboard charts on September 21, 1944. The song has remained a standard, with exceptional recordings by Crosby, Sinatra (with string quartet from his classic album *Close to You*), The Four Freshmen, and June Christy (among many others). In a sign that the baby boomers may finally be growing up, Barry Manilow included it in his album of love songs, *The Greatest Love Songs of All Time*.

TWENTY-TWO

Jimmy Van Heusen at work
Courtesy of Van Heusen Photo Archives

Going My Way

By 1944, among his many costumes, Crosby had worn a fez, a yachting cap, a straw hat, and blackface. The public was used to seeing Bing in lighthearted, comedic, and musical roles. While his turn in *Road to Morocco* demonstrated his comic acting chops, there was little to suggest that Crosby was prepared for a dramatic role. This did not deter director Leo McCarey from making good on his "threat" to use Crosby in one of his motion pictures. In his autobiography, *Call Me Lucky*, Crosby recounts the story of how he became a part of *Going My Way*:

> When he (McCarey) came over, he told me, "After you hear the idea I have for you, maybe you'll think it isn't 'now.' I want you to play a priest." "Now what kind of a priest could I play?" I asked. "I'd be unbelievable, and besides, the Church won't like that kind of casting." "I think it would," he said. "I've talked to some pretty wise priests in

this diocese and they think you can handle the character I described." I said, "Let's hear it."

Leo told me a terrific story. It wasn't the story he eventually used, but when he was through, there wasn't a dry eye in the house – his or mine. In his preliminary take-out of his idea, I played a priest all right, but from there on it wasn't much like *Going My Way*. Looking back, I don't think he had a story at all. He just made one up as he went along. Nevertheless, he had me transfixed. When he finished, I was sold. I said, "I'll be ready in the morning."

Crosby was certainly the linchpin to the production, but in Leo McCarey, Van Heusen and Burke found a director who had a genuine interest in music. While this might have been comfort to some, Van Heusen saw it as less than ideal. "Right from the beginning, I knew he was one of the millions of people who think they are songwriters or want to be songwriters. Burke figured McCarey wanted a hand in writing the score and that we'd have to put his name on our songs. We set to work and wrote a complete score and McCarey turned it down. Then we knew we were in trouble." Van Heusen recalls the intercession of noted Hollywood tunesmith Buddy DeSylva to finally free them from McCarey's oversight. (For his own part, McCarey would continue to dabble in music, earning an Oscar nomination for his lyrics to Harry Warren's "Our Love Affair" from *An Affair to Remember*.)

The working title of *Going My Way* was "The Padre," and Van Heusen claims that he and Burke came up with the title to the film, and, by extension, the title song. "After all, that's what the guy is trying to do, trying to get several sorts of sinners to 'go his way,' said Van Heusen. Of all the songs written for the film, "Going My Way" is perhaps the most complex musically. As with most Van Heusen melodies, it is eminently hummable but not easily hummable. The absent minded singer could easily find himself lost in Van Heusen's melodic maze. It is a testament to the genius of Crosby that his performance seems so effortless (if not a bit thin in the high register of the penultimate measures). At first blush, Burke's lyrics tend to stray into the saccharine, until you realize he is not writing a love song, but an invitation to the path of salvation. In that context, "Rainbowville" and "Dreamer's Highway" are not only excused but demanded.

The only true "love song" of the movie, "The Day After Forever," is a similarly intricate song. Van Heusen starts the song on the third (rather than the tonic or even dominant), so the tune has the feel of having begun in the middle of things. This trick permits him to maintain some degree of suspense as the listener is not yet able to determine exactly where the melody is going. His move from the sixth to the seventh in the measure reading – "I'll be loving you AND THEN," is unexpected and adds a dramatic sweep to the opening phrases. Of course, this song is introduced by a wayward young girl, singing the tune to Bing's Father O'Malley. As he gives the girl a much needed vocal lesson, he appears to be singing the song to her as well. That being said, Burke had to write a suitable love song, but not one that would scandalize his (and Crosby's) strict Roman Catholic faith. With its understated but persistent longing, "The Day After Forever" is an appropriate paean to the eternal nature of love. Both Crosby's and Burke's knuckles go unrapped.

In the movie subplot concerning Crosby's effort to get one of his songs published so that he might earn enough money to relieve his indebted church, it is "Going My Way" that Crosby plugs to the publisher. It is given a full symphonic arrangement, with a vocal performance by opera star Rise Stevens. "Going My Way," however, is deemed too high brow for the publisher and is rejected, even after the amazing performance. Wry smiles between composers and lyricists throughout Hollywood followed that exchange, it is certain.

However, the good guys do win in the end. Still a bit downhearted after the rejection, Bing and the kids are encouraged to sing another song. One of the children suggests "The Mule Song." That was the children's moniker for what would be known was "Swinging on a Star." Crosby launches into its opening measures, and the rest is musical and movie history. They get the money, save the church and arrange for Father Fitzgibbon's elderly mother to visit for the Christmas holiday. It is a wondrous movie, and even in this jaded time, can manage to warm hearts and coax tears. If you can hold it together with the strains of Too-Ra-Loo-Ra-Loo-Ral in the background and Father Fitzgibbon, head down, incredulously making his way to his 90-year-old mother, whom he has not seen in 45 years, tearfully embracing the other, then you had better hope the soul transplant list is short.

"Swinging on a Star" was so lighthearted, cheery and uplifting, never would one expect the heartburn it induced in its creators. Charged with writing a musical version of the Ten Commandments, Van Heusen and Burke seemed resigned to the fact that a literal incarnation of McCarey's wish was not going to come true. Burke ruefully acknowledged that the original version of the Ten Commandments was written by a fairly successful lyricist. Their labors yielded nothing, and the pressure was mounting.

One evening, while dining at the Crosby house, Van Heusen and Burke overheard a heated "discussion" between Bing and his son, Gary. The younger boy was not at all happy with having to go to school, and Bing, after seeing the day was not going to be won with rhetoric, finally told his son, "So you want to be a mule, be a mule." That was all the inspiration Burke needed. As Van Heusen recalls:

> Burke suddenly looked at me as though he
> wanted to kiss everyone. Naturally, he felt that
> way because Bing had given him the handle for
> the song we were finding increasingly more
> difficult to write. 'Don't you see,' he exclaimed.
> 'Do you want to do something decent and good or
> do you want to be a mule, or pig, or whatever.'
> 'Yeah,' I said, 'but what's the title?' 'Doing
> Something Decent or Rolling with the Righteous,
> or Associating with the Stars, maybe Would You
> Like to Swing on a Star.'

And that was that. The original title was "Would You Like to Swing on a Star," and the first copies bore that inscription. Under my urging, however, a little later, Johnny changed it to "Swinging on a Star." His complaint was that this line was only mentioned once at the end of the song and the other title was mentioned three times. It didn't make any difference, the song was more than a hit, it was an epidemic.

An epidemic. A phrase Van Heusen would use to describe a runaway hit. And "Swinging on a Star" certainly was such a hit. Crosby's recording of it entered the Billboard Top 10 the week of June 24, 1944, at number three. It remained in the Top 10 for 19 weeks, reaching number one on August 5, 1944, and keeping the top spot for nine weeks. The film was, of course, a financial and critical success. McCarey made so much from his share of the film that he was able to produce the sequel, *The Bells of St. Mary's*. *Going My Way* was nominated for 10 Academy Awards, including Best Actor for Bing Crosby and Best Original Song for "Swinging on a Star." It was Burke's third nomination. He had previously been nominated in 1938 for "Pennies from Heaven" and in 1940 for "Only Forever."

It was a triumphant Oscar night for *Going My Way*, winning seven Academy Awards, including Best Picture, Best Director (Leo McCarey), Best Actor (Bing Crosby), Best Supporting Actor (Barry Fitzgerald), Best Screenplay (Frank Butler and Frank Cavett), Best Original Story (Leo McCarey), and Best Song ("Swinging on a Star").[8] It was something of a coming out party for both Crosby and the team. Crosby's acting bona fides were validated, in spades. Indeed, he remains the only man whose chief profession was not acting ever to win the Academy Award for Best Actor. On the heels of their commercial successes for Crosby in 1943 and 1944, the Academy Award for Burke and Van Heusen marked the final validation of Mark Sandrich's excursion to New York City to poach the composer of "Imagination" from the New York music scene.

Ever the nonconformists, Burke and Van Heusen did not spend Oscar night with the other nominees at the site of the awards ceremony, Grauman's Chinese Theater. The thought of spending all evening cooped up backstage was too much for either to bear:

---

[8]   Frank Sinatra was honored at that same ceremony for his short subject "The House I Live In."

In those days, instead of the nominees sitting in the audience as they do now, they were all herded around backstage. With ten songs nominated, that meant twenty songwriters would be milling around waiting to find out who won.[9]

Johnny and I said to hell with that kind of crap. Johnny suddenly invented a death in the family and left town and I went to St. Vincent's Hospital for a checkup. I listened to the radio broadcast of the awards with a group of nurses and when we heard that I'd won with "Swinging on a Star," I was the toast of Bed Pan Alley. I was a hero among the nurses and I got my first taste of how important the Academy Award is to most people. I liked the feeling.

There was a poignant moment in the life of Theodore Roosevelt following the American victory at San Juan Hill observing the United States battle flag raised over newly conquered Cuba. Knowing that the era of the isolationist United States was over, he commented to himself that nothing

---

[9] The songs nominated in 1944 were impressive. They included, among others, "I Couldn't Sleep a Wink Last Night" (Jimmy McHugh/Harold Adamson); "I'll Walk Alone" (Jule Styne/Sammy Cahn); "I'm Making Believe" (James V. Monaco/Mack Gordon); "Long Ago and Far Away" (Jerome Kern/Ira Gershwin); "Now I Know"(Harold Arlen/Ted Koehler); and "The Trolley Song" (Ralph Blane/Hugh Martin).

will be the same. And, indeed, for the United States 1898 was a watershed year in its history – it marked its entry into the world of empire and the nasty business of geopolitics. It had, for lack of a better phrase, "grown up."

While certainly infinitely less significant in the scheme of things, 1945 was such a year for Van Heusen and Burke. They were now Academy Award winners, and "players" in the Hollywood game. Legendary radio host Jonathan Schwartz liked to joke that Van Heusen remained 19 years old for his entire life, and to a certain extent he is exactly right. However, in 1945 he certainly made a gallant charge at 20. The first step toward adulthood was the formation of his music publishing company with Johnny Burke.

Van Heusen, ever the generous and charitable one, seemed to have real difficulty in spending his own money on business. It was nothing to drop several thousand for a party, aircraft or home. However, an investment? That was something entirely different. His reluctance to spend, it could be said, prevented him from moving into the stratosphere of wealthy musicians, a la Irving Berlin, Johnny Mercer, or, more recently, Sir Paul McCartney or David Bowie. Van Heusen's former business manager, Edward Traubner, recalls a vain attempt to get Van Heusen to invest in lucrative land in California:

> I once tried to invest some money for him in a piece of land in Tarzana, right next to the boulevard. There were thirty acres of bean fields and every inch of it could have been built on. In a few years, it was worth $600,000. But Jim went to [Mouse] Warren, a former boss, and asked him about it. 'Remember Florida', Mousie said. 'Everybody went broke on land down there.' Mousie was a music man and he didn't know anything about investments but Jim listened to him.

This was the mindset facing Burke when he approached Van Heusen about his publishing idea. Van Heusen was reluctant at first, but the prospect of investors such as Bing Crosby and famed music publisher Buddy Morris made the idea much more palatable. Van Heusen also insisted upon placing their previously written works into the newly formed company. And, in his boldest suggestion, Van Heusen felt they should make a play to get the rights to the songs from *Going My Way* from Paramount.

This would prove to be a difficult task, but fortunately, the team had a strong ally in Crosby. Crosby was no fool, and he realized that the possible profits from those smash hits would enrich his coffers for years to come. He also had the utmost confidence that Van Heusen and Burke would assuredly produce more such hits in the future. So, Bing had a plan. He would suddenly become unavailable for recording dates. Studio musicians would be assembled, sit for several hours awaiting Crosby, but there would be no Bing. Not wanting to run afoul of his contractual obligations, Crosby would attend the recording sessions, it was just that he needed a bit more time or would warm up and then remember meetings and depart. The message was more than subtle, and Paramount's attorneys met with those from Burke and Van Heusen Music Company, and soon after they acquired the publishing rights to the songs from *Going My Way*. Then, Bing sang.

Burke and Van Heusen Music opened with a roar. They placed Hoagy Carmichael, Bob Wells, and Mel Torme under contract. Paramount's Sidney Kornheiser was its general manager. There were offices in New York, Chicago, Cleveland, and Hollywood. The one time song plugger and copyist was now in charge, and despite his initial reluctance, it seemed Van Heusen enjoyed the role of businessman:

> I spent money with both hands, but I couldn't get rid of it fast enough. At the end of eight months when we declared a fiscal year, there was $800,000 in profits in the till - all from three little songs from Going My Way. Of course, we got to keep very little of that because the taxes were like 92 or 94 percent. But the company was a good one and we made a lot of money for a long time - a lot more money than I would have made as a simple songwriter. It was all gravy and I adored it and I loved being president of the company.

Despite the financial success, Van Heusen and Burke were not content to rest on their laurels. All the talent in the world was useless if no one was publishing or performing your songs. Burke seemed to be more conscious of that than Van Heusen, as evidenced by his more sophisticated political moves in Hollywood, e.g. forming the publishing company and hiring Bing's brother as his agent. And, true to form, Burke managed to wrangle an invitation for Van Heusen and him to attend a party at the home of Henry Ginsberg, the executive head of Paramount Studios, and one of the five moguls of Hollywood, along with L.B. Mayer, Jack Warner,

Harry Cohn and Darryl Zanuck. Ginsberg, it was said, wanted to hear the new songs the team had penned for Crosby. Van Heusen refused to attend with Burke. He gave no reason, other than he simply did not want to attend. And, as the party progressed and Ginsberg requested the tunes be performed, Van Heusen was nowhere to be found, and Burke was compelled to reveal the true reason for his partner's absence. Not surprisingly, Burke felt that Jimmy had blown it for them (again).

"The next day Ginsberg made a point of finding me. I tried a weak joke like 'You don't sing as good as Crosby,' or something equally inane, and he laughed," Burke recalled. "Eventually, we got to be good friends. But, he never lifted a hand to help any deal I was trying to make." It did not appear, though, that this stemmed from any personal animus. "He (Ginsberg) said he disliked the stooges and sycophants that followed the other heads of studios, and also didn't approve of hiring relatives. I worked on the lot by the grace of Crosby or got hired because I had hit songs." It reinforced Van Heusen's belief that parties and invitations were all fine and good, but no one is going to perform or publish a garbage song as a favor.

But, it certainly did not hurt to be friends with the boss. And, like his affairs with Crosby and Sinatra, Van Heusen became friends with one of the most powerful men in Hollywood, simply by being an affable, available person with whom they could party:

> Because I was single-o, and had no one to report to at any time, I was "available Jimmy" to the Groaner and finally to Ginsberg. I would accompany him to many Hollywood parties that his wife Mildred refused to attend. Consuming the joy juice at every soiree usually resulted in my slightly drunkenly playing someone's piano. I never played my own songs, but would claim authorship of "God Bless America"[10] or "Stardust" and then launch into a medley of Cole Porter or Harold Arlen songs. Ginsberg, in his cups, liked to "get on." He was a ham, and only liked to "perform" with two songs, "Embraceable You" and my song, "But Beautiful." As I would play them, accenting the melody because occasionally he attempted a musical tone, he would recite the lyrics partially, and other lines and nonsensical phrases of language would come out, the utter foolishness of which was sometimes laughable.

---

[10]   In a 1978 interview with Jonathan Schwartz, Van Heusen claimed "God Bless America" was the finest song ever written.

Following their success with *Going My Way*, the team gave two songs to the RKO Randolph Scott/Dinah Shore Alaskan oater *Belle of the Yukon*. The movie was not a commercial success, but the Van Heusen/Burke contributions "Like Someone in Love" and "Sleighride in July" survived the chilly fate of their introductory vehicle. Both were introduced in the film by the lovely Ms. Shore, and she herself had a hit record with "Sleighride in July." It was also honored with an Academy Award nomination. And while it is clearly a lovely tune, and Burke's ironic allusion to a sleigh ride in July is a wonderful lyrical device (despite its propriety in context), the true gem from this file is "Like Someone in Love."

This tune, like "Darn That Dream," has enjoyed broad pop/jazz crossover popularity, with recordings by Bing Crosby, Frank Sinatra, Ella Fitzgerald, John Coltrane, Stan Kenton, Coleman Hawkins, and Stan Getz (among many others). The appeal to jazz artists is explained in part by the linear structure of Van Heusen's melody, permitting the artist to utilize all variety of harmonies in a chromatic bass line. It offers a suitable vehicle for the artist to express his creativity in fashioning harmonies while providing an interesting enough melody in its own right. Wilder notes the influence of Kern in the melody, calling it "simply lovely."

As Van Heusen and Burke entered into the business end of music with their publishing company, Crosby ventured into the world of motion picture production. The year 1945 saw the first entry from Bing Crosby Productions, the biopic of John L. Sullivan, *The Great John L.* For their part, Van Heusen and Burke contributed a fine song, "A Friend of Yours," introduced by the lovely Linda Darnell (dubbed by Trudy Erwin). Relatively speaking, the song was not a hit, but it did demonstrate the team's ability to produce consistently high quality material, even when being pulled in many different directions.

It is comforting to say that the notorious "sequel," with all of the pejorative connotations, is a creature borne of modern Hollywood mediocrity. That, however, is not the case. Case in point: no sooner did the closing credits conclude to *Going My Way*, than Leo McCarey was ready to shoot its sequel, *The Bells of St. Mary's*. It would again star Crosby, this time matched with one of the hottest talents in Hollywood – Ingrid

Bergman.[11] Indeed, when Bergman won the Best Actress award for her role in *Gaslight* (1944), she told the audience at the awards ceremony, "I'm glad I won, because tomorrow morning, I start shooting the sequel to '*Going My Way*' with Bing Crosby and Leo McCarey, and I was afraid that if I didn't have an Oscar, they wouldn't speak to me."

Among the other Oscar winners to contribute to *The Bells of St. Mary's* were, of course, Van Heusen and Burke. Asked to recreate the magic of "Swinging on a Star," they very nearly did it with "Aren't You Glad You're You." The song was another hit for Crosby, and it garnered the pair their second nomination of the 1945 Academy Awards season. Burke's lyric is slightly reminiscent of the internal rhymes of Lorenz Hart, as he extols the virtues of having a nose, ears, and other things that "make you, you." Van Heusen's melody is as easy going as the upbeat Father O'Malley. It seems to be taking the listener on the very same walking journey described by Burke's lyric. It is at once appropriately childlike, but yet sophisticated enough for appreciation by adults – note Van Heusen's key

---

11   The Bells of St. Mary's was actually written before Going My Way.

change in the second iteration of the main theme – that ain't kids' stuff (pardon the grammar).

The filming of *The Bells of St. Mary's* proved to be a real delight for Van Heusen, who seemed to be justifiably enchanted by Ms. Bergman (but, in all honesty, how could you not have been?) He recalls, "Ingrid was the darling of everyone who worked. Furthermore, every Saturday, her cooks and servants set up a smorgasbord lunch for everyone. It was delicious, and she couldn't have been more delightful and friendly."

Indeed, Van Heusen and Burke's contract called for them to write two songs for the film – one for Crosby and one for Bergman. The song for Bergman, "Bluebirds on a Blackboard," was dropped from the film. Van Heusen believed that the great disparity in the singing voices between Bergman and Crosby was the reason for the song's deletion. That hardly seems plausible, though, as the studios certainly were aware of the vocal limitations of the actors before assigning the team their songwriting duties. In any event, the old standard "The Bells of St. Mary's" was used in its stead. This is rather unfortunate, as it is a beautiful, wistful melody by Van Heusen and contains a touching, bittersweet Burke lyric. If it is true the song were to have been performed by Bergman, its exclusion is mystifying, as the tone of the song would have revealed a different side to the strict nun, which might have made for a more complex interaction between the carefree Father O'Malley and Sister Mary Benedict:

Verse:

I had a kind old teacher.

She loved to watch kids play.

Each afternoon when lessons were done,

She always used to say:

Refrain:

Bluebirds on a blackboard,

They never sing.

You must get out to hear the real thing.

Any schoolboy knows the reason

Why the schoolhouse keeps him in.

But is it wrong if his dreams go fishing

With Huckleberry Finn?

And sailboats in an inkwell,

Where can they go?

That's why the rain makes puddles, you know.

So, if your mem'ries get so grown up,

They forget how to climb a tree,

That's bluebirds on a blackboard, to me.

The song, was eventually published in a folio of children's songs (*Bing Crosby's Songs for Young Hearts*) written for each of Johnny Burke's children and Van Heusen's nephew. Van Heusen and Burke would return to this theme of lost childhood in their later song, "The Magic Window," from *Little Boy Lost*.

As was typical of most of the women in Van Heusen's life, both professional and personal, he was somewhat protective toward Bergman, as evidenced by his opinion about the "scandal" involving her relationship with Roberto Rosselini. "I've always thought that the impression Ingrid created in that picture, the image of a straight-forward, dedicated, beautiful nun, contributed to the public outrage when she later ran away with Roberto Rossellini," Van Heusen recalled. "Nobody wanted to believe Ingrid was a normal woman with normal juices after that role. Or maybe straight-forward, beautiful women aren't supposed to have any juices."

However, lest we think our hero has gone soft, he does recount one episode from filming that could only have come from Van Heusen:

Not only did her (Bergman's) shoes come off but also most of her makeup and she appeared as the epitome of pale innocence and beauty in her nun's outfit. Barney Dean, who was always hired as a gag writer on every Hope or Crosby picture, and I were on the set watching a scene between the angelic Bergman and the priest, Crosby. As the cameras rolled, I whispered to Barney. 'Would you still want to fuck her if she were really a nun, Barney?' Without hesitation, he whispered back, 'I'd want to fuck her if she was a rabbi." We got to laughing so hard, they had to break the scene and we got some very dirty looks from Leo McCarey, the assistant director, and everyone else on the set. We finally had to leave until we could get over our giggles.[12]

Despite the paucity of their output in 1945 (six songs), two were nominated for Academy Awards – "Sleighride in July" from *Belle of the Yukon* and "Aren't You Glad You're You" from *The Bells of St. Mary's*. There was much gold for *The Bells*

---

[12]   This was not the only instance of tomfoolery on the set. As the production was overseen by a Roman Catholic priest, the temptation for joking was too great for prankster Crosby. Crosby and Bergman both requested McCarey allow them one more take for the touching farewell scene between Father O'Malley and Sister Mary Benedict. Straying a bit from script, Bergman and Crosby ended the scene with a passionate kiss, much to the dismay of the present clergy!

of St. Mary's, both through Oscar nominations and box office. In current dollars, *The Bells of St. Mary's* grossed $279 million, making it the 51st successful film in history. It was nominated for eight Academy Awards, including Best Picture, Best Actor (Crosby), and Best Actress (Bergman). However, there was to be no treasure trove of statuettes for this picture, only a single win for Best Sound. It was the year of Billy Wilder's masterful *Lost Weekend*. Van Heusen and Burke were bested by Rodgers and Hammerstein's "It Might As Well Be Spring." There was certainly no dishonor in that. The sting of defeat was dulled a bit by the fact that two other songs published by Van Heusen and Burke ("Doctor Lawyer Indian Chief" and "I'll Buy That Dream") were also nominated. Van Heusen still reflected rather ruefully on the loss, saying, "Four strikeouts, and I wasn't to get another Oscar until the Sinatra years."

TWENTY-THREE

Jimmy Van Heusen and Johnny Burke working on another standard
Courtesy of Van Heusen Photo Archives

Moonlight Becomes You

The Sinatra years would not formally start until 1955 when Sinatra would pair Van Heusen with Sammy Cahn for "The Tender Trap" and the television production, *Our Town*. The germ of the relationship formed when Van Heusen would sneak copies of sheet music to Young Blue Eyes in New York City in the 1930's. During the 1940's, when Sinatra was making movies at RKO Studios, he (along with his tunesmiths Sammy Cahn and Jule Styne) were frequent guests at Van Heusen's Palm Springs home.

Thus, Van Heusen takes credit for introducing Sinatra to the Palm Springs area. He recalls, "Sinatra discovered Palm Springs by way of my first home there on Cabrillo Drive. He had come down as a guest, and since I had to be away for some time, he asked for and was given the house for a whole month. He stayed there by himself, with only the occasional company of four waitresses that occupied the house to the east of mine on the other side of two vacant lots. He became enchanted with the sunshine, and when I returned, he was completely suntanned and determined to build his own home in the same community."

It is likely that Van Heusen's month-long departure from his Palm Springs home was due to his commitment to write the songs for a British movie, *London Town*. It was to be one of four major projects the team would release in 1946 – the others being Hope and Crosby's *Road to Utopia*, Betty Hutton's *Cross My Heart* and an ill-fated Broadway endeavor, *Nellie Bly*. There would be much activity in 1945 and1946, most of which required extended travel either to London or New York. There would be the added stress of London and New York audiences. All of these hurdles, it would seem, the team would be well-equipped to climb. However, Johnny Burke was laboring under a burden that threatened to destroy all the team had worked so hard to achieve.

Only a tormented soul could create the lyrics of the variety and scope of Burke: the soul plumbing depths of "Here's That Rainy Day," the hopeful sweep of "Swinging on a Star," the bittersweet nostalgia of "The Magic Window," the romantic pastels of "Moonlight Becomes You," the manic humor of "His Rocking Horse Ran Away," or the wit of "Road to Morocco." Burke either shone very brightly or was tucked away in shadows. His demons and angels constantly waged a war, and as fearful as it was, the demons seemed to have much more ammunition.

In September, 1940, not long after Van Heusen began work on his first picture, Burke's father committed suicide by hanging himself from a tree in the yard of the home that Burke had purchased for him in California. Van Heusen recounts Burke having to remove the body from the tree by himself and waiting for the fire department and other authorities to arrive. It was, naturally, a singularly traumatic and sorrowful occurrence that would haunt Burke with feelings of guilt for the remainder of his days. To Burke, had he not moved his father from Chicago to the West Coast, this might never have happened.

Guilt led to depression which led to sleep disorders for Burke. Van Heusen said that, in turn, led to drug dependency. "Our song writing modus operandi was a nocturnal one, and gallons of coffee would be consumed by that great Irishman through the wee hours. Now, whether he was wide awake from the caffeine in the coffee or not, he was drowning his consciousness with Seconal, and soon his body was adjusting to quite a quantity of them that must be consumed before the arms of Morpheus enfolded him."

In addition to the medication, Burke also was a frequent imbiber. That alone would have been troublesome given what Burke endured, but in conjunction with the medication, it was utterly disastrous:

> It got to be a psychological problem and put together with the amounts of booze he gulped of an evening, the scares endured by his wife began to increase in number. One time the house was nearly burned down. Another time, and because he genuinely enjoyed shocking people, he took two handfuls of sleeping pills and swallowed them in front of his wife, Bessie. His wife, alarmed at the amount, and his eventual passing out, called all his doctors. He had a string of doctors, well acquainted with Johnny not on just a professional basis, but as friends. In the wee hours, I was summoned to the house, and arrived to see a psychiatrist, who had been treating him, a surgeon, then head of St. John's Hospital, a proctologist and a couple of internists. The head shrinker said Johnny would be all right because

his body was so accustomed to the barbiturate that he could have taken a hundred without dire consequences. However, all his doctor friends agreed that Johnny wouldn't last the year. He would kill himself.

Work was still the most important thing to Burke, and despite his physical and emotional troubles, he continued to be capable of producing lyrics of superior quality. "Johnny was a very strong man, and he was able to pull himself together after one of these spells and you'd think everything was all right. For many years, we functioned as top writers with Johnny working at about one-tenth capacity," Van Heusen recalled.

Laboring under these conditions, Burke undertook the team's burdensome 1946 workload. The first 1946 release featuring Van Heusen and Burke tunes was the latest installment in the "Road" series – *Road to Utopia*. To call it a 1946 release, though, is misleading. The movie was actually filmed in 1943. However, it was not released until 1946 because of Paramount's desire not to "waste" the immense power of its three stars – Crosby, Hope and Lamour – by having them all appear in one feature. However, the public loved the Road films so much, that the clamoring from fans and theater owners compelled the release of this film in 1946. According to Lamour, *Going My Way* was a significant reason behind Paramount's failure to release *Road to Utopia*. It was her belief that Paramount wanted nothing to interfere with the Academy's impression of Crosby's portrayal of a priest. His con-man, lothario "Duke" was truly a far cry from the kindly, heroic Father O'Malley.[13]

Lamour's song, a racy number titled "Personality," was the big hit from the film. It was not without controversy, though, as Van Heusen remembered, "The Hays Office or the Green Office that monitored the morals of each script and read and approved the pages before they were shot was a constant problem in the comedies of Hope and Crosby. What would now be considered perfectly proper in a script, in those days, could be blue penciled as off-color and completely out of line." The lyrics of songs were not exempt, either, and "Personality"

---

[13]   The observant viewer, though, would notice several references that suggest the 1946 release was not timely. For instance, Crosby makes his entrance singing (off-screen) his 1943 hit "Sunday, Monday or Always." Had this been truly made in 1946, it would have made infinitely more sense to have him sing "Swinging on a Star." Furthermore, in the Crosby-Hope duet, "Put It There, Pal," Hope's character (named "Chester") congratulates Crosby on his film Dixie. Again, it would have been infinitely more appropriate for Hope to have mentioned Bing's Oscar-winning role in Going My Way – derisively or otherwise!

was okayed. On the screen, however, due to a musical phrase and some snake hips staging it became a salacious sight, according to the censors, and a fight followed to keep the sequence in the picture. The lyric read: "When Madame Pompadour/Was on the ballroom floor/Said all the gentlemen, obviously/The Madame has the cutest (then followed a slightly strip tease musical phrase)/Personality." On the musical phrase that preceded the title "Personality," Lamour wiggled her posterior and delivered a grind and a bump, saying choreographically what precisely Madame's "personality" really was. Naughty for its time, but retained in the picture because of the argument that it couldn't be bad or it would have been censored while still in script form." "Personality" was a vindicating experience for Lamour, as it showed her ability to carry a song unfettered by the clowning of Hope and Crosby.

"Personality" would be the only hit from the film, but it would not come from Crosby, Lamour or even Sinatra. Instead, it came from the chops of an old Van Heusen friend, one more accustomed now to writing hits rather than singing them – Johnny Mercer. Mercer's recording for his fledgling Capitol label was a number one hit. (To be fair, Dinah Shore and Bing Crosby also had top ten recordings of the tune in 1946, but the Mercer platter was the definitive popular recording).[14]

The remainder of the score from *Road to Utopia* was very strong. "Put It There, Pal" – the requisite Hope-Crosby "buddy song," is as witty as "Road to Morocco," and, in fact, would serve as the team's unofficial anthem for years to come. The faux-vaudeville "Goodtime Charlie" is light and fun. "It's Anybody's Spring" is vintage Burke – measured sentimentality, returning to the Crosbyian "Ain't Got A Dime to My Name" bonhomie bohemia.[15] "Would You" is another serviceable Lamour vehicle. However, the Crosby ballad "Welcome to My Dream" deserved a far better fate than that which it earned. Opening in a minor key, the melody mimics that of an art song. It is a haunting, beautiful tune, rich with Van Heusen harmonics, melodies and daring intervals.

---

[14]   Van Heusen claims to have played the piano on several sessions for Capitol Records, including the first big hit for Capitol, Johnny Mercer's "Strip Polka."

[15]   This song is sung by Crosby and Hope during a talent show on the ship on which they both stowed away. Crosby is confident of his victory, only to see top prize go to another contestant. Disgusted, Hope tells Crosby the next time he's bringing Sinatra.

Road to Utopia was a smash for Paramount, but would mark the team's only real success in 1946. Van Heusen and Burke were drafted to write the score for the British film *London Town*. It was considered to be the first British film musical, and it was produced by the massive J. Arthur Rank Company. To refer to it as a dismal failure might be too kind. So upset with the quality of the production, choreographer Agnes de Mille paid the producers $5,000 to remove her name from the film credits. It was considered to be the greatest "flop" in the history of the Rank Company. Fortunately, the team was spared a bit of the embarrassment, as the film was not released in the United States until 1953 – and even then under a different title – *My Heart Goes Crazy*. It was not so much that the movie was objectively poor, but so much money was invested into it that it would had to have been a blockbuster to muster a profit. Burke and Van Heusen wrote a grand total of seven songs for the film, which represented one of their most ambitious endeavors to date (*And the Angels Sing* merited eight contributions from the team). The songs, "You Can't Keep a Good Dreamer Down," "The 'Ampstead Way," "Any Way the Wind Blows," "So Would I," "My Heart Goes Crazy," "If Spring Were Only Here To Stay," and "You Ought

To See Me On Saturday Night," were certainly decent, and Crosby managed to wrangle something of a successful recording of "So Would I."

The team's last cinematic endeavor for 1946 was a Betty Hutton vehicle entitled *Cross My Heart*. It was another failure. Indeed, Ms. Hutton found the movie so distasteful that she ranked it as her worst, and in certain recollections she failed (perhaps deliberately) to recall her participation in it. Once again, however, Van Heusen and Burke's participation in the film, confined as it was to songwriting, escaped the critics' wrath. To be fair, though, when Hutton offered this unofficial ranking in 1948, she was in the middle of a row with Paramount. The songs for Hutton – "It Hasn't Been Chilly in Chile," "That Little Dream Got Nowhere," "How Do You Do It?" and "Love is the Darndest Thing" were carefully tailored to her trademark manic style. "Love is the Darndest Thing" is an echo of "His Rocking Horse Ran Away" except this extols the joys of married life, instead of motherhood.

If there could be a third recipient of Van Heusen's writing, beyond Crosby and Sinatra, it would have been Betty Hutton. She was certainly a bankable star, and Van Heusen and she certainly enjoyed a warm friendship. In reviewing correspondence in Van Heusen's archives, a 1950 thank you note from Hutton to Van Heusen was found referring to a Christmas gift, best wishes to him for a speedy recovery from back ailments and signed "Betty the Witch." Following the success of "His Rocking Horse Ran Away," Burke and Van Heusen had Tiffany's design a broach specifically for Hutton commemorating the hit recording. It was a rocking horse. From it, a chain led to a little boy who appeared to be flying off of the horse. You pinned both rocking horse and boy separately from each other so it appeared as if the boy was in flight after having been thrown from the horse.

Beyond the friendship, the Van Heusen-Hutton collaboration yielded another important fruit. The frantic songs that Van Heusen wrote for Hutton served as prototypes for the swinging numbers that he would be called on to write for Sinatra. "Come Fly With Me" and "Come Dance With Me" have more in common with the songs he wrote for Hutton than most anything written for Crosby. The Groaner, while a ballad singer par excellence, was not known for hard-swinging arrangements, unlike Sinatra. It was fortunate that Van Heusen had the opportunity to write for someone with such a divergent style.

It is something of interest that great songs have survived mediocre or sometimes downright forgettable movies or shows. Van Heusen seemed to have his share of those with "Darn That Dream" and the soon-to-come "Here's That Rainy Day." It was sometimes through sheer force of the greatness of the song that it was able to throw off the rock to which it was shackled. However, with regard to those Van Heusen songs of 1946 that earned radio play and even sales, it was more through business acumen than anything else. Van Heusen recalls, "Although some of these pictures were just fair and some of them were failures, we saw to it that all the song pluggers of our music company pushed at least one song from every score. Sometimes records were made by each and every one of the great bands they had in those days. I would see Tommy Dorsey or Benny Goodman and personally play the score of a whole picture to get them noticed."

Sandwiched between these cinematic millstones, was Van Heusen's second (and Burke's first) essay upon the Broadway stage. It was Burke that had the calling to travel east to conquer Broadway. He was approached by Eddie Cantor with the idea of creating a musical around the idea of Nellie Bly and her journey to beat Phileas Fogg's "record" of traveling around the world in eighty days. Cantor had promised to provide the financial support, and he had purportedly secured the commitment of stars William Gaxton, Victor Moore and Marilyn Maxwell. Gaxton and Moore were established Broadway veterans, and while Maxwell was a bombshell, a musical star she was not.

Van Heusen was reluctant from the start, especially at the prospect of working with (or perhaps, under) Cantor: "I don't care who he's (Cantor) got. I know Cantor's a big star but I can't stand his kind of humor. He'll turn his gag writers loose and they'll come up with a crock of corn because that's the only thing Cantor understands." This particular concern was slightly allayed when Van Heusen was informed that Morrie Ryskind, the Pulitzer Prize writer of the Gershwins' *Of Thee I Sing* would write the book, and Cantor's gag men would have no part in it.

Still, what seemed to be motivating Van Heusen's reluctance was the frail condition of Johnny Burke. "Johnny's health was no great shakes. I knew something about the tension and turmoil of a Broadway show and I worried that Johnny might not be able to take it. And always in the back of my mind was Cantor and his awful taste. But I agreed to go because Johnny wanted to do it so much."

Van Heusen should have trusted his instincts. Whatever could have gone wrong with the show did. And, in his recollections, Van Heusen made no attempts to hide his disdain for the entire effort. The trouble started early, in the show's opening city of Boston:

> Marilyn Maxwell sang in such a whisper she couldn't be heard beyond the first row. Since we didn't have hidden mikes, then, that meant no one in the theater would hear her. Then Bing and Frank came hustling around because she was so beautiful and William Gaxton also got the hots for her. If he had a line like, 'Hello, Nellie,' he'd take her in his arms, fondle her, kiss her and keep ad-libbing as long as he could. The show was a disaster. Morrie Ryskind got fed up with Cantor's meddling with the book and he left. We should have left, too, but Cantor persuaded us to stay. By the time we tried out in Boston, I actually got down on my knees and pleaded with Cantor to close the show. If we close, there's a chance we can fix it, but we can't save it when we're playing eight performances a week. I told him, but he wouldn't listen.

Not surprisingly, things got no better in New York. Marilyn Maxwell left the show after the Boston tryout. The show opened at the Adelphi Theater on January 21, 1946, with a decidedly inauspicious but somehow fitting performance that saw scenery collapse, and in lieu of a final scene, Cantor himself delivered a monologue. Van Heusen "damn near committed hara-kari." The show mercifully closed 16 performances later on February 2, 1946. The critics were as merciless as the public, with *Time* Magazine writing, "With its weak and whiskered gags, its dime-a-dozen tunes, and its plot that has a muddled Victor Moore competing for a rival paper, *Nellie Bly* is just musical globaloney."

Once again, Van Heusen failed on the Great White Way. However, unlike his previous effort that might have been too avant-garde for Broadway, this particular show was decidedly behind the Broadway curve. Transformed by the brilliant successes of Rodgers and Hammerstein's *Oklahoma!* and *Carousel*, the tastes of Broadway audiences matured beyond screwball antics. More important, in this case, Van Heusen and Burke were as much of a selling point for audiences and producers as Louis Armstrong and Benny Goodman were with *Swingin' the Dream*. They were the hottest songwriters in

Hollywood – writing for the biggest star in films and having just won the Academy Award. It was their game to lose.

So, what happened? If Van Heusen is to be believed, there was discord from the start. He clearly did not believe in the project, and labored under a not so subtle disgust for Cantor's influence. It appeared his heart was more in Hollywood than New York, and frankly did not want to lose his place at the Crosby table (even though Crosby was an investor in the show). More important, it did not appear that Van Heusen or Burke had any real conception of the time and dedication necessary for a successful Broadway show. While the show was being produced, the team was composing music for other films and other projects. When one analyzes the great composers of Broadway, it is clear that these composers devoted themselves single-mindedly to their shows. There was very little other activity in their professional lives that took from their show. Van Heusen and Burke tried to mix Hollywood with Broadway – and that was a drink even too potent for those men.

The phrase "dime a dozen" tunes was cutting, but particularly apt in this case. With the exception of "Just My Luck," the score was largely uninspired. Burke's lyrics were leaden, free from the wit and gaiety of his efforts for the Crosby movies. Neither his lyrics nor Van Heusen's melodies captured the Gay Nineties era or even attempted to put a more modern spin on the prevailing musical style of that era (as Van Heusen and Cahn would do successfully with their tune "Thoroughly Modern Millie"). In fact, it would not be surprising to learn that these tunes were either from the Van Heusen "trunk" or sketches of unused songs from Crosby films. There is no continuity in the score. It is 12 different songs with no real connecting thread. It is unlike most Broadway scores in that regard, and it is indicative of a rather distracted approach to the entire effort.

Furthermore, Van Heusen's fears about Burke's delicate psyche were unfortunately not unfounded. Jack Clark recalled, "When that show folded it was a crushing blow to Johnny's ego. He was under great pressure and showing signs of instability. Jimmy was worried and suggested that I move in with Johnny, which I did. Johnny couldn't sleep and we'd walk around in the park for hours, but that didn't work. Then he got hold of some phony doctor who started him on some really strong barbiturates. I remember he'd take the stuff out of the capsules and mix it with orange syrup. He said it worked faster that way."

The team, though, suffered no ill professional effects from the failure. They were slated to score the next two Crosby vehicles – *Welcome Stranger* and *Road to Rio*, both released in 1947. *Welcome Stranger* reunited Barry Fitzgerald with Crosby, but the film, while a more serious turn for Crosby, was unable to capture the magic of their earlier associations. Crosby, though, through the offbeat intercession of Van Heusen, was about to begin one of his deeper associations with co-star Joan Caulfield. This beautiful blonde was a neighbor of Van Heusen in the Sunset Plaza Apartments on Sunset Strip. Not surprisingly, he struck up a friendship with the lovely lady, and in time introduced her to Crosby:

> "When I saw Bing's gaze go ga-ga over the girl I volunteered my living room as a meeting place. This was eagerly accepted and daily tennis games and swimming took place after which cocktails and sometimes dinner would be served in my diggings. Ralph Harris, now living with me, and screenwriter Liam O'Brien would make up the foursome for the tennis. Occasionally, I would play but was usually too hung over for much

jumping around. They played and I provided the background music and the martinis or scotch.

In the late 40s, Crosby's popularity started to wane, his place slowly being taken by Frank Sinatra. Crosby was certainly still a formidable star, to be sure, but something was changing. As Wilfrid Sheed wrote in his excellent book, *The House That George Built*:

> Thus, in bits and pieces, and in a deceptive fever of activity, Death began to make its presence clear to the old Hollywood. The Marx Brothers, for instance, made a new movie. For a second, it seemed like a comeback, but it was just a chance for them to take a last bow. And "Gable's back and Garson's got him" screamed the ads, but not for long. An old man returning to an old lady was really nothing to get excited about . . .And when Fred and Ginger put on their taps once again, they seemed older than time itself. . . By keeping his continuity in our eyes right through the war, Crosby did not yet seem so moribund, but the clock was ticking on him too. The remaining songwriters all wanted to grab at least one more ride on the old Bingo Shuttle, until there was hardly room for Van Heusen himself on his own life raft.

Episodes like that with Caulfield greatly assisted Van Heusen with his own flotation, as they allowed him access to Crosby in ways that his other writers could never have. Van Heusen was a swinging bachelor. Irving Berlin, Johnny Mercer, Harold Arlen, Cole Porter and Harry Warren (Crosby's other composers during the Burke/Van Heusen years) were all married men. Van Heusen offered the comfort of a nonjudgmental, at-the-ready companion for almost any adventure. And, being the consummate promoter, Van Heusen was ready to utilize this freedom to his advantage:

> By the late forties, Bing was prone to enjoy an extended bender a couple of times a year, and since this was my favorite pastime and since Bing was one of the greatest elbow benders I have ever seen, I enjoyed following him around the town. He was a great drinker. He'd never stagger and never became belligerent and his personality did an about face when he had a bottle of whiskey in him. With the booze inside, his façade of ice-cold Irish indifference melted away and he became warm and convivial and interested in other people. We had a lot of deep, good talks on those binges.

We'd close Lucy's or the Villa Nova and start out on the town. Many's the night we'd show up at someone's house at some ungodly hour and announce that we wanted to sing. Our hosts seemed happy enough about it – with me at the piano and the Groaner singing the night away. When we absolutely had to, we'd sack out at my apartment and some nights Bing would sneak into his mansion out in Holmby Hills to grab some clean clothes. Or we'd sneak in and sleep in a downstairs bedroom. We'd get in and out without Dixie or the servants ever knowing we were in the place. I had some of my best drunks with Bing. He's one of the funniest men alive when he's relaxed like that.

That Crosby was able to let his notoriously rigid guard down with Van Heusen spoke of the level of trust he enjoyed with Crosby, and would foretell the level of trust he would have with Sinatra. To be fair, his relationship with Sinatra expanded well past the boundaries of mere friendship, but the essence remained the same: Van Heusen was able to connect with his performers in a manner that theretofore was relatively unknown. He not only knew the men, but ingratiated himself into their inner personal circles, becoming a confidant, friend, and confessor.

In an undated interview found in the unpublished biography of Van Heusen written by Robert de Roos, there is this telling quote from Tony Bennett:

> If you look at the repertoire of Crosby's most famous songs, you'll find out that Van Heusen molded and helped form Crosby's musical personality – and there isn't a singer in the business who doesn't imitate Bing Crosby. The fact that Crosby and Sinatra, the greatest entertainers in America in our time, turned to Van Heusen is no accident. He's been their secret director. He showed Bing how to play it and he taught Frank to sing an awful lot of beautiful songs. I don't know how he does it. He's a master psychologist. He makes artists find themselves. And remember this: there is not relationship on this planet closer than that of a singer and his coach – the man who teaches him to sing a song. Jimmy Van Heusen taught the best of us what to do and how to do it.

This trust from Crosby was sorely needed in the late 1940s as Johnny Burke's condition continued to deteriorate.

While the team continued to produce quality songs for the Crosby films – for example, from *Welcome Stranger* they wrote the delightful "As Long as I'm Dreaming," "My Heart is a Hobo," and "Country Style" (which was a hit), it was certainly a struggle:

> It was getting to be a problem. Sometimes Johnny wasn't able to work more than about fifteen minutes at a time. We'd work a bit and then I'd go out for a walk. Come back for another go at the songs then walk again. Sometimes Johnny would be so full of drugs that he couldn't walk well. When I couldn't keep him away, he'd show up at the studio and I'd have to explain his slurred speech as due to medication he took for a cold. I had a million excuses for his slack appearance and odd speech. But his lucid moments were as productive as ever. " But Beautiful," one of the songs he wrote during those years, is just one example of Burke's writing which few lyric masters can touch. But, he'd have to go into sanatoriums for drying-out sessions with his psychiatrist in attendance several times a year. I can still smell the paraldehyde they used to ease his withdrawal from alcohol and barbiturates.

That the team continued to work was due in some part to Van Heusen's ability to play the Hollywood game. In the wake of his success, Van Heusen negotiated a six picture deal with Paramount. This contract was due in large part to the team's songwriting prowess, but also due to the fact that people genuinely liked Jimmy Van Heusen. He was a fun person to be around, and he knew how to let others have fun. His open houses were legendary, and his ability to mingle and charm at others' open houses kept him in the Hollywood mix. Van Heusen tells of his talent for partying and socializing with his usual mix of charm and humility:

Hollywood was quite a small community in those days. I guess it's even smaller now. But then the town was swinging and everybody had plenty of dough. It was a pretty chummy little community. Visiting at homes was the main thing. Night life was non-existent even though there were a couple of night clubs. People just didn't go to night clubs. They'd go to premieres or charity affairs but mostly it was parties and open houses. A lot of people had them and I was one of them. Of course, it meant a lot to be invited to certain homes. If you got an invitation from one of the bosses of a studio that was a command performance. Each studio head has his sycophants, a little social group around him – his staff of directors and writers, producers and stars. You'd wind up mostly seeing the same faces, the same producers and the directors and stars at every affair. But that was Hollywood then. You kept around the people who mattered. It was a matter of 'out of sight, out of mind' and it wasn't a good idea to be out of sight. Everything was done on a daily basis – a producer would walk into his office and say, 'We've got to have a song for this picture and I saw Jimmy Van Heusen last night. He played me a hit song. He'd be great for this. Let's get him.' Anyone you might meet who was connected with a picture could suggest you for a job. At the parties, there was always a lot of small talk with people you didn't especially warm up to and it's easier to do that when you're drinking. I'd get drunk and then I'd love everybody.

Road to Rio, the next installment in the Hope/Crosby series, was a marked contrast from the madcap mania of *Road to Utopia*. Its script is smart (as opposed to goofy) and it is undoubtedly the last quality entry of the series. *Road to Rio*, though, was most definitely a return to form for the team, which admittedly had shown signs of being "written out."

Their songs tapped into the chemistry between Crosby and the Andrews Sisters with "You Don't Have to Know the Language" and "Apalachicola, FLA." Those songs were almost too fast for Crosby, with both their rhythms and the manic energy of the sisters seemingly pulling Crosby along, the way an excited child might tug at a tired parent. Still subject to the prohibition of mentioning the phrase "I love you," Burke inserts a graceful lyric at the end of "You Don't Have to Know the Language" when he wrote, "You don't have to know the language/To know you don't want to say goodbye." Lamour's number, "Experience," can be fairly described as the son (or daughter) of "Personality" with the loaded meaning Burke gives the seemingly innocuous term "experience." And, while the listener can plainly see where the story is going in the song, Burke's denouement does not disappoint.

In all three of these songs, Van Heusen's melodies seem to borrow from his past. "Experience" is a redux of "Personality." The numbers with the Andrews Sisters could have easily found their way into Betty Hutton films. One is left with the feeling that while the songs are pleasant enough, they have been heard before. That is until Bing Crosby begins to sing "But Beautiful." At once, you are reminded of Van

Heusen the innovator – the composer of "It's Always You," "Moonlight Becomes You," "Imagination," and "Darn That Dream." Johnny Burke elegantly articulates a concept of love that could only be borne of his current travails, his lyrics taking on a decidedly darker hue:

> Love is funny, or it's sad
>
> Or it's quiet, or it's mad.
>
> It's a good thing, or it's bad,
>
> But beautiful.
>
> Beautiful to take a chance,
>
> And if you fall, you fall.
>
> And I'm thinking,
>
> I wouldn't mind at all.
>
> Love is tearful, or it's gay.
>
> It's a problem, or it's play.
>
> It's a heartache either way,
>
> But beautiful.
>
> And I'm thinking, if you were mine
>
> I'd never let you go,
>
> And that would be
>
> But beautiful, I know.

The song is without question, a masterpiece, and can genuinely be considered their finest work written for Crosby. Indeed, only "Here's That Rainy Day" could contend with "But Beautiful" as the finest of the Burke/Van Heusen catalog. Starting the chorus on an augmented fourth, ending the first A section on a third over the ninth, the omission of a traditional bridge, and simply containing an inspired melody, "But Beautiful" has stood the test of time and remained a favorite of both jazz instrumentalists and singers. It is a complex song, but that did not hinder its popularity. Sinatra and Crosby both had top 20 recordings of it in 1948, and on the distaff side, Margaret Whiting's version that same year topped at number 21. The success of the song, of course, was in no doubt assisted by the enormous popularity of the film, which was a box office smash.

In many ways, "But Beautiful" marked the end of an era for Van Heusen and Burke, as it was the last truly great song they would write for Crosby. There would be successes in the last three years of their association with the Groaner, but to be sure, the highest points were behind them.

Following *Road to Rio* was a Billy Wilder period comedy called *The Emperor Waltz*. It again starred Crosby, this time as a salesman trying to pitch the phonograph to the Austrian emperor. Van Heusen's sole contribution was the song "Get Yourself a Phonograph," which was little more than a throwaway. Burke found himself putting lyrics to Viennese operetta tunes and to the melodies of Johann Strauss. Although the film was quite successful, most critics considered it Wilder's poorest effort. Crosby had a minor hit with the adaptation of "The Kiss in Your Eyes," from the operetta *Der Opernball*.

That Van Heusen and Burke were tasked to score their next film, *A Connecticut Yankee in King Arthur's Court*, was due to the fact that the Rodgers and Hart Broadway score for the Mark Twain novel was purchased for use in the 1948 tribute film, *Words and Music*. The Rodgers and Hart score contained some of their finest work, including "My Heart Stood Still," "Thou Swell," and "To Keep My Love Alive." Inevitable comparisons would be unfavorable, and while there were some memorable songs, the score, one of their last true movie musicals, was starting to show signs of age. The movie again had its share of hits – Tony Martin and Crosby each had a successful recording of "If You Stub Your Toe on the Moon" and Jo Stafford had a hit with "Once and For Always." "If You

Stub Your Toe" is yet another iteration of "Swinging on a Star," complete with Crosby singing to a group of children. "Once and for Always" is a pleasant, but not outstanding, love song. The finest selection from the film, though, is the ballad "When Is Sometime?" The song shows that Van Heusen did not lose his gift for harmonic surprise, as the "sometime" in the penultimate measure avoids the trite sequence of notes in favor of a tricky and refreshing melodic turn.

Van Heusen and Burke rounded out the decade by contributing two songs to the third Crosby-Fitzgerald pairing, *Top O' the Morning*. This time Crosby visits Ireland as a detective, only to butt heads with the stubborn and old-fashioned Fitzgerald and to woo Ann Blyth. The film is a schizophrenic experience alternating between Crosby wooing Blyth with light-hearted Van Heusen/Burke original tunes and traditional Irish melodies and his attempts to solve a particularly brutal murder. The film suffers from attempting to blend these two seemingly irreconcilable genres. Still, in their context, the Van Heusen songs work remarkably well. The requisite Crosby ballad, "You're in Love with Someone," has an old pro's grace about it. Burke again performs the "I-love-you-prohibition" dance, but inserts more "love" per square inch than any other prior Crosby ballad. The title song "Top O' the Morning" is a jaunty gigue that the Crosby charisma more than adequately pulls off.

TWENTY-FOUR

*Jimmy Van Heusen taking part in another one of
his hobbies - photography.*
Courtesy of Van Heusen Photo Archives

Here's That Rainy Day

In his last at-bat in his Hall of Fame career, Ted Williams hit a home run at Fenway Park. In his final fight, Rocky Marciano knocked out Archie Moore to retain his title and would ultimately retire undefeated. It is unfortunate that these instances are the exceptions rather than the rule. All too frequently, the last memory of a great athlete is of a lunging strikeout, an ill-timed interception, or a powerless knockout. It is the same with artists. Would that Richard Rodgers ended his career with *The Sound of Music*. And, while the most ardent Sinatra apologist can pan gold from *Duets I and II*, in their heart of hearts, most wish Sinatra would have ended his recording career prior thereto.

Unfortunately, Burke and Van Heusen, ran into this invisible wall in the late 1940's and early 1950's, as their association with Bing Crosby came to a rather unremarkable close. "But Beautiful" was something of an aberration, as their scores for their final Crosby films seemed more to be marking time than making music. In 1950, they scored *Mr. Music* and *Riding High*, of that former, Robert Bookbinder remarks it is one of "the least satisfying" of the Crosby films in the 1950's, and "an elaborate but weak picture that is a disappointing throwback to the days when the Bingle had to attempt to make the most of silly scripts and threadbare plots." Jimmy and Johnny, for their part, did little to raise these movies above Bookbinder's analysis.

Road to Bali, released in 1952, was the last of the true "Road" pictures (the later *The Road to Hong Kong* distinguished itself by the deliberate use of "The" in the title and by having the picture released not through Paramount but United Artists). It was, by far, the weakest entry in the series, and a rather sad way for it to end. Hope and Crosby looked tired, the jokes were worn, and the music sounded stale. Of course, this was not the same America that watched *Road to Morocco* and *Going My Way*. This was an America that had come face-to-face with the horrors of war and were living with the fact that humans now possessed the ability to destroy the world. Films were turning darker, more serious. However, this change in climate cannot wholly explain the commercial failure of these films; they were, objectively, not good.

The final Crosby film to feature the music of Johnny Burke and Jimmy Van Heusen was *Little Boy Lost*. It was a largely dramatic film, but Paramount still would not risk Crosby in a role completely devoid of song, so he turned to his old tunesmiths for one last time. For this final effort, Burke and Van Heusen contributed several songs. One was particularly impressive – "The Magic Window." This hymn to the innocence of youth and the melancholia of adulthood was a beautiful collaboration that provided Crosby with a meaningful lyric and a challenging melody. The song darts from interval to interval, daringly changing keys, seemingly meandering, but resolute in its conclusion. It is our loss that this song has disappeared from popular thought. Burke's lyric, while still optimistic, is certainly darker than most of his efforts.

Truly, the "magic window," symbolic of childhood and innocence, also was a fitting metaphor for the transition in American society and culture in the 1950's. The films of the 1950's were certainly darker than their pre-war predecessors. In the 1950's, Crosby, Father Chuck, would portray a troubled war correspondent, divorcee and a broken down alcoholic performer. Frank Sinatra would forego sailor suits for roles as a presidential assassin, Army misfit, and heroin addict. The music would also change, with dreamy melodies and wistful lyrics yielding to driving rhythms and lyrics charged with sexual innuendo. Tame by our standards, but well nigh scandalous compared to stubbing one's toe on the moon.

And, of course, the performers would experience their own changing of the guard. The popularity of Crosby would wane, and he would eventually (and bloodlessly, as one author wrote) cede his throne to Frank Sinatra. And, while the world is partially divided between "Crosby people" and "Sinatra people," no such divisions occurred between the men. Sinatra routinely referred to Crosby as his idol, and unabashedly credited Crosby for heavily influencing his career. For his part, Crosby is quoted as saying, "A talent like Sinatra comes along once in a lifetime. Why did it have to be my lifetime?" Crosby would ultimately appear in Rat Pack films, television shows and even signed with Sinatra's Reprise record label.

The curtain would fall on Johnny Burke, as well. Despite his place in popular music already secure with his contributions to the Crosby legend, he found his lilting, sentimental lyrical style somewhat unsuited for the modern, atomic era. Burke would continue to write after his partnership with Van Heusen dissolved, but would write little of note. In 1955, he scored his last success by adding the lyrics to Erroll Garner's "Misty."

The collaboration between Van Heusen and Burke ended not with a bang, but with a whimper. Still stung by the colossal failure of *Nellie Bly*, Burke wanted to take another stab at Broadway. He thought he had an excellent vehicle in the 1934 French film, *La Kermesse Heroique*, (or, as it was to be known, *Carnival in Flanders*) a script Burke reviewed following one of his frequent stays in sanitariums. The treatment was written by George Oppenheimer, and more important, the show was to be produced by Paula Stone and her husband Michael Sloane, who had two musical successes with *Top Banana* and a revival of *The Red Mill* starring Eddie Foy, Jr. Due to Burke's health conditions, Van Heusen was not eager to embark on another Broadway journey, but according to his autobiography, allowed himself "to be sucked in" when he learned that the show might be penned by another composer – Herbert Fields. That Van Heusen would take the threat of another composer writing a show seems somewhat fantastical.

He had rejected shows in the past, and certainly knew that other writers would step in, should he reject the producers. However, if the sentiment is to be believed, it certainly reflects an uncharacteristic bit of self-consciousness in Van Heusen, and perhaps a recognition that his own star had faded slightly.

Van Heusen's reluctance in undertaking such a project with Burke was sadly justified. As he recalls,

> Sometimes Johnny was able to work and other times he was not. On one afternoon when I went to the Burke house, which was now in the Toluca Lake district of San Fernando Valley, I was pretty horrified to see the great Irish poet go into convulsions. Why? Well, he had decided to "cold cock" himself, and since he was made of iron, he often succeeded. But not this time, because the convulsions were simply indications that a more gradual withdrawal should have been made. Needless to say, a doctor was called and soon he was comfortable, but work that day was out of the question for even me. It really shook me up, but the secret of the situation was kept inside the family and inside me. Later, while in rehearsal and fund raising in New York, Johnny's long disappearances were increasingly hard to explain away.

Further troubles plagued the production when it was learned that the producers, though fronting two hit shows, apparently had no profit to show for their work. Apparently, the producers failed to pay their backers on those shows, and worse, had only raised approximately $50,000 of a needed $375,000 needed to make *Carnival in Flanders*. Even worse, the raised funds were used by the producers for personal expenses, which was against the law at the time, as no funds for a show were to be utilized unless and until the show was fully capitalized. Perhaps lured by the charms of Ms. Sloan and ever the sucker for a damsel in distress, Van Heusen gallantly informed the crew that he would raise the money himself. Predictably, this turned into a disaster, as the burden of writing the songs, along with raising the money, resulted in substandard production of both. Moreover, Burke found himself in the middle of another breakdown, this time ending up in a Long Island sanitarium.

Through sheer force of will, and the backing of one Bing Crosby, the show finally began rehearsals with its stars John Raitt and Dolores Gray. Burke's appearances were still spotty, and one day, the entire façade collapsed. Van Heusen recalled, "Burke arrived with a male nurse at the rehearsal, and proceeded to lecture the cast with a tongue so thick with drugs he could hardly be understood. From then on, there were no secrets, and no bullshitting the actors, the singers, the director or the producers, or anybody. Burke looked just exactly like what he was. Very sick."

Compounding their mistakes, and demonstrating, again, Van Heusen's lack of business acumen, the men dug into their own pockets for financing, and named themselves co-producers, along with Mr. and Mrs. Sloan. The move was intentioned to bring *Carnival in Flanders* to heel, but it appeared to all that they were clearly on the road to hell.

The show was to open in Philadelphia, then travel to Los Angeles and San Francisco, then return to open on Broadway. The Philadelphia reviews were disastrous. As Van Heusen wrote, "each one either faint praised us or out damned us." Worse, though, was that the head of the Los Angeles Civic Light Opera, Edwin Lester, attended one of the performances, and knew that a real clunker was coming his way. As such, he made every effort to back out of his commitment to front the travel fare for the company, knowing that without this money, the show could not go west. The company would have to resort to the courts to get the money, and by that time, the show would have been long-forgotten. Lester's ostensible excuse to the producers was that the show was "too dirty" for his audience.

Salvation came in the person of Lester Shurr, manager of the stars of the show. Shurr entreated Van Heusen to contact Walter Winchell, who, at that time had his own television show. Shurr was convinced that Winchell would enjoy nothing more than excoriating a Los Angeles producer for claiming a show was "too dirty" for Hollywood. Van Heusen enjoyed a comfortable relationship with Winchell, and upon hearing about the situation, Winchell informed Van Heusen to tune in to his nightly television spot. As recalled by Van Heusen, Winchell said the following:

> Carnival in Flanders the Broadway bound musical comedy starring John Raitt and Dolores Gray, now playing in Philadelphia, is going to have to close because the Civic Light Opera and Edwin Lester will not live up to their commitment to play Carnival this summer. Why? Lester says it is too dirty for Hollywood. Ha Ha Ha. Too dirty for Hollywood. A million dollar law suit follows immediately.

Lester had no idea that the "million dollar law suit" was Van Heusen's hyperbolic response to Winchell's question to him about what he wanted to do to Lester. Van Heusen originally said "kill him," but Winchell eased him into saying exactly what Winchell wanted him to say, that is, sue him for a million dollars. It made for a better story. And Winchell knew that lawsuits were more effective in Hollywood than death threats.

Lester suddenly found religion and provided the money for the tickets and the production. Van Heusen and Burke employed a new director, Preston Sturges, feverishly reworked music, lyrics and script, but, in the end, it was too little far too late. The company survived the West Coast tour to open on Broadway at the New Century Theater on September 8, 1953, only to close on September 12, 1953, after just six performances. The paucity of shows did little to sour the critics on Dolores Gray's performance, as she won the Tony Award that year for Best Actress in a Musical. It remains the shortest lived Tony-Award-winning performance.

Despite that accolade, the show was, quite predictably, a disaster. But, when properly considered, it had little chance from the start. Its producers were under cloak of suspicion.

The script was reworked several times, with complete changes in writing personnel. George Oppenheimer, an original writer, withdrew during the Philadelphia tryout. Dorothy Fields and her brother Herbert Fields rewrote the script prior to the West Coast run, only to have the totality of their changes discarded by Preston Sturges. Sturges replaced the original director, Bretiagne Windust. Burke was in the throes of drug addiction. Van Heusen was spread entirely too thin, acting as fundraiser, producer, and composer.

The score to *Carnival in Flanders* was by and large a poor effort on the part of both Van Heusen and Burke. There is the feeling throughout the score that a particular song was inserted or written merely because a song had to be found to fit a particular situation. While ostensibly that might be the entire purpose of a composer in musical theater, there is the unspoken rule that this particular mechanic need not be so naked. There is no need for a song to scream out, "I am a love song" or "I am a large group dance number." This would even be somewhat forgivable if the songs were decent, but Van Heusen's songs for *Carnival in Flanders* lacked grace, melody, or daring. "That Sudden Thrill" frustrates, as it is on the cusp of being memorable, but it then retreats into cliché or otherwise meanders to an unsatisfying conclusion.

Indeed, the vast majority of the songs from *Carnival in Flanders* suffer from this problem. In the memorable Van Heusen's songs, the melody may (and often does) meander, it takes twists and turns that are often surprising and sometimes dissonant to the ear – most frequently in his bridges. However, once the melody reaches its destination, the listener cannot imagine it any other way. To put it another way, you enjoyed the ride. With *Carnival in Flanders*, you are fairly upset you got in the car in the first place, and when you arrived at your destination, the place had been ransacked.

Why do we dwell on *Carnival in Flanders*? Why concern ourselves with this second consecutive Van Heusen/Burke Broadway flop (and Van Heusen's third miss)? Because during the second act of each of the six performances, as audiences were wondering to themselves if they were actually listening to the work of two of America's finest songwriters, the opening strains of a ballad to be sung by Dolores Gray were heard. It was a melancholy lament, and while it opens in a major key, it had a decidedly minor air to it, which was somehow fitting for this travesty of a show. But, this was

different, and that was evident as Ms. Gray sang:

Maybe I should have saved

Those leftover dreams

Funny

But here's that rainy day

Here's that rainy day

They told me about

And I laughed at the thought

That it might turn out this way

Where is that worn out wish

That I threw aside

After it brought my love so near

Funny how love becomes

A cold rainy day

Funny

That rainy day is here

     According to Van Heusen, that number stopped the

show every night. And, if his memory is faulty, it can be

forgiven, because a song that ingenious should stop any

performance of which it is a part. The lyric to this song is by

far the deepest and darkest ever written by Burke. There are no swinging stars or singing bluebirds. This is the confession of a man racked with guilt, pain and addiction. Burke paints in hues as dark as Lorenz Hart, as his simple, direct use of language is used to devastating effect – the ironic usage of "funny," the depiction of dreams as "leftover" and wishes as "worn out." And, of course, the title "Here's that Rainy Day." This "rainy day" does not bring "the things you want." There are no "pennies from heaven." While that earlier song eschewed the need for shelter from the rain, "Here's that Rainy Day" depicts a storm from which one will never find respite. One must wonder if, at least subconsciously, Burke was producing the polar opposite of one of his earliest hits. If this was not the reflections of man who saw his career fall from such heights, one thing is certain – this song conjured all of Burke's creative forces to produce one last masterwork from a genius.

Van Heusen's melody is every bit the work of genius that is Burke's lyric. It is funereal but at the same time lyrical enough not be maudlin. It is persistent, moving reluctantly, but inevitably forward, as the singer must do with his life. Alec Wilder described the songs as "bold" and "almost demanding its harmony's presence for a singer not to get lost in the complex line." Of the songs reviewed by Mr. Wilder, he saves his highest praise for "Here's that Rainy Day," who said, "It's a powerful and affecting song. It has great weight and authority and must have been a song written under extremely intense circumstances. In my opinion, it is a great illustration of absolute honesty, quite irrespective of its extremely innovative character as a melody."

However, because of the lack of success of the show, the song was largely forgotten. No recordings were made, and of course, sheet music sales were nonexistent. But, as Van Heusen was quick to point out, certain songs simply could not be denied. In 1954, when Sinatra was recording his classic torch album *No One Cares*, he was in need of a number to close the first side. Van Heusen suggested "Here's That Rainy Day." Backed by Gordon Jenkins' masterful arrangement, Sinatra created the first and, by all accounts, the definitive version of this song. More important, its position on a Sinatra album exposed the song to a vast audience, helping its popularity immensely.[16]

---

[16]   The Sinatra/Jenkins arrangement makes an interesting harmonic change to the ending of the song. Instead of ending the song on the major tonic, Jenkins opts to end the song on the parallel minor tonic. Given the mood of the song, it seems appropriate that it would be in a minor key, but

The end of the relationship with Burke was troubling for Van Heusen, as he lost not only a partner but a friend. Van Heusen was asked to write the introductory comments to a folio (sadly, unpublished) of Burke's work. His words were every bit as sentimental as the lyrics of their subject:

> To me, Johnny Burke was, and remains, "But Beautiful." Apart from being one of the truly great, great lyric writers, he was one of my most meaningful collaborators, but even more important, a very close and dear friend. I hope he is standing over my shoulder now, as I often stood over his, and I hope that he is wearing a "But Beautiful" Irish blush, because it is my intention to put on paper how I felt about him and his work. Start blushing, Johnny.
>
> His taste and integrity in the composition of a lyric was matched only by his taste and integrity in human relationships. I am proud his words graced my music and that the music is part of the legend and the monument to that brilliant and "but beautiful" man, Johnny Burke. A man I always called, "My Favorite Irish Poet."

Van Heusen's original melody does remain in a major key.

TWENTY-FIVE

Jimmy Van Heusen and Frank Sinatra vacationing in Spain
Courtesy of Van Heusen Photo Archives
Photographer Unknown

How Can I Replace You?

The poorly kept secret of Burke's illness made additional jobs for Van Heusen difficult to come by. His exclusive contract with Burke prevented him from working with other lyricists or publishers, and Van Heusen was feeling the effects of artistic frustration. He wrote, "In order to keep my hand in so to speak and keep my mental processes from rusting, I took to writing for other publishers and with other lyric writers." Van Heusen solved the legal problem, as he solved a similar, earlier problem with public recognition: he used a different name. Taking his father's first name and his mother's maiden name, Van Heusen, under the name "Arthur Williams," wrote several wonderful songs in the early 1950's. These included "Funny Thing" (with Carl Sigman), "How Can I Replace You" (with Sammy Gallop), and the brilliant "I Could Have Told You" (also with Carl Sigman).

However, because of the "gossipy nature" (to use Van Heusen's phrase) of the music business, his "secret identity" was soon revealed. This compelled Van Heusen to adopt another nome de plume for his continued efforts. For this effort, Van Heusen used an anagram of an old girlfriend's name, Ada Kurtz, to become "Kurt Adams." Under this moniker, he wrote "Somewhere Along the Way" with Sammy Gallop. This song became a big hit for Nat King Cole. Van Heusen recalls the unorthodox method of collaboration he utilized for these "secret songs":

> The way these songs got written was by long distance collaboration. In the case of "Somewhere Along the Way," I simply wrote a certain type of melody that the publisher requested and he took it back to New York and under my instructions, called in the lyric writer Sammy Gallop, who had written a well-known song called "Maybe You'll Be There." I instructed the publisher to tell Gallop to come up with another lyric in the same vein, which he proceeded to do, and it was duly mailed to me on the West Coast. Liking the title, because of its similarity to the song I requested him to simulate, I embarked on a rewrite of the lyric itself, which in many places was hack work. Soon,

the lyric as it now appears on the sheet music was completed. I had retained only three lines and the title of the original, but it finally satisfied me, and also Nat Cole. I received very silent and secret satisfaction while the song sailed through the airwaves as a smash hit, but could take no actual bows with anyone or at any place.

Van Heusen would certainly never say that working with a healthy (or at least non-medicated) collaborator acted as a creative tonic, but the results speak for themselves. "I Could Have Told You" and "Somewhere Along the Way" are two of the finest songs Van Heusen ever wrote. They were fresh. Their melodies were decidedly original. They were dramatic. They represented the finest concentrated period of quality work since the days of *Going My Way*. "Somewhere Along the Way" is an uncharacteristically dramatic Van Heusen work, foreshadowing more complex efforts such as "Only the Lonely," "All the Way" and "To Love and Be Loved." "I Could Have Told You" straddles Van Heusen's Crosby and Sinatra incarnations. The melody is not quite dreamy enough for Crosby, but a little too on the "easy-listening" side for the custom material he would later write. It still is markedly better than most anything Van Heusen wrote with Burke in the 1950's.

Van Heusen eventually was granted leave to write with other lyricists, but Van Heusen still was unable to make a clean break from Burke. "I made no overt move to team up with any lyricist in particular out of deference to the great Burke who was ill so much of the time, and I didn't want to appear like a deserter at such a time. This resulted in collaborations of another long distance variety." Van Heusen would merely submit a melody to a studio, and a lyric would be provided for it. There would be no meaningful collaboration, and it was clear Van Heusen did not prefer to work in this manner. But, these particular tasks were ordered up by a friend who was difficult to refuse – Frank Sinatra. Fresh from his Academy Award winning performance in *From Here to Eternity*, Sinatra was in the early stages of resurrecting his career. However, as Sinatra well knew, Van Heusen could be called upon for a favor for a friend regardless of their current station. Sinatra tapped Van Heusen to provide the title song for his medical drama, *Not as a Stranger*. The resulting effort was a decidedly inauspicious way to begin his true professional relationship with Sinatra. Van Heusen recalled the song, not for its melodic content, but because of the lyrics he was asked to review, he found Robert Mitchum's (the film's star) the finest. The publishers did not agree and settled on words by Buddy Kaye, who gained fame for his lyrics to classical melodies ("Till the End of Time," "Full Moon and Empty Arms").

His next "collaboration," for the 1954 Sinatra-Doris Day film, *Young at Heart,* reunited him, albeit virtually, with Mack Gordon. The movie told a tale far too close to home for Van Heusen, with Sinatra playing the part of a troubled, suicidal musician (named "Burke"). It is not certain whether Van Heusen knew of the story before being asked to contribute a song (although given his relationship with Sinatra, it was fairly certain that he did), but he produced a lovely, dramatic song ultimately titled "You, My Love."

"You, My Love" was the first song Van Heusen wrote specifically for Sinatra to perform in a film. However, it was a marked departure from the songs he created for Crosby, and showed Van Heusen's remarkable ability to mature and adapt as a songwriter. It must be remembered that Van Heusen was no longer writing for two goofballs wise-cracking their way through some exotic locale. *Young at Heart,* despite its title, was a rather dark tale of a troubled soul. In fact, the original ending to the film had Sinatra's character perish. A melody such as "But Beautiful" or "Moonlight Becomes You" would have been decidedly inappropriate. Van Heusen would need to more prominently feature his modern, dissonant side to reach these more modern audiences.

"You, My Love" is not as modern-sounding as his later songs for Sinatra, such as "Only the Lonely" or "When No One Cares." However, its structure, including its dramatic conclusion, announces clearly that, unlike his earlier songs, this was a song written for Sinatra, and not a Crosby song that Sinatra decided to record. The "big note" ending of this song would have been as misplaced for Crosby as placing "bub-bub-bubs" in a song for Sinatra. There are more subtle differences, as well, that evidence Van Heusen's unique ability to know his artist. The bridge ends unresolved melodically with the forgettable lyric phrase "What peace of mind, your smile unfurled." The note on "-furled" must be extended legato to the "Yes, and because of you, my love." This type of extended phrasing was the Sinatra trademark, and Van Heusen's melody highlighted this brilliance.

TWENTY-SIX

Jimmy Van Heusen and Frank Sinatra
Photo Courtesy of Van Heusen Photo Archives
Photographer Unknown

Out with Somebody Else

Sinatra called him a brother and a best friend. Van Heusen was with him almost from the beginning, never to leave his side, despite the infamous wane of his career in the early fifties. The relationship between Van Heusen and Sinatra transcended friendship and transcended artistic interest. With Sinatra, Van Heusen found the familial bond that eluded him with Crosby. Only two years separated the men. They were both peers, meaning that both men were largely at the same station in their respective arts. This was in marked difference to Crosby, who, when Van Heusen first worked with him, was a much larger star than Sinatra. In many ways, each man's ascent tracked the others. As with Crosby, though, Van Heusen knew well his place, and contented himself with being an unseen force behind the genius.

The friendship between Sinatra and Van Heusen began to blossom in the late 1940's when Sinatra moved to Palm

Springs, and the work with Crosby and Burke began to slow. During these adventures, he would prove himself to be a valued and loyal confidant, being present at many infamous events in Sinatra's personal life. The first of these was in Houston, 1950. In the hopes of landing a lucrative deal with an oil tycoon, Van Heusen convinced Sinatra to play the sprawling new Shamrock Hotel owned by Glenn McCarthy. This was clearly a vestige of his days with Crosby and Hope, who were notorious in the diversification of their interests. Sinatra, while certainly entrepreneurial in his music holdings, particularly publishing rights, did not possess the same interest in extra-musical businesses. Sinatra's career was in a decline, his marriage existed in name only, and he was in a very public pursuit of Ava Gardner. Striking it rich in the oil business did not sound like that bad of an option.

Gardner accompanied Sinatra on this trip, and quite naturally, the press was everywhere. Van Heusen acted as the able lieutenant in keeping the press at bay, and insuring that Sinatra and Gardner were able to enjoy their trip in relative peace and quiet. Still, encounters were inevitable, and Sinatra found himself on the wrong end of the society pages because of a perceived misunderstanding. These events were anathema to

Van Heusen who, shunning the limelight of the gossip pages, was much more interested in making money and music, drinking and womanizing. He wrote of the occasion:

> There was no way to win with those shit heels in those days, and back to the hotel we went, and since the boy and girl in love needed me around like a social disease, I took off every night and visited the local saloons and whore houses. They were great and wide open and soon in one little bordello, I found a lady of the evening who appealed to me and a madam who was hospitable enough to allow me to sleep there, with my love that is.

Van Heusen repeated this ritual almost every night of Sinatra's stormy Houston engagement. Van Heusen recounts the well-known story of Sinatra staring down six foot-plus Texans who would interrupt his singing with hooting, hollering, and most horrifyingly, requests for "The Yellow Rose of Texas." It was a far cry, indeed, from the swank audiences at the Copacabana. And, while Sinatra found it all too natural for his companion to frequent bordellos on a nightly basis, Gardner was intrigued by this ritual:

Sinatra didn't mind my getting lost after the shows, particularly when I told him where I was going. But Ava became curious and said, 'where the hell do you go every night, Chester?' With a non-committal answer, time and time again, her curiosity was satisfied by the thin one and he told her the details. She thought the whole idea intriguing and said she wanted to go and meet the girls. Impossible, we said, and although she persisted, there was no problem until we had a visit from a certain Sam Maceo and his wife Ms. Sedgwick. They came to the show and visit Frank, and almost immediately Miss Gardner had enlisted the aid of Mrs. Maceo in arranging a visit to my little whore house. Sam Maceo was purple, and I tried to explain that I didn't want this to happen but he sort of blamed me, because after all, I was living there. The two girls would have nothing less than a limousine ride (the car filled with champagne and caviar) off to the bordello and I felt like an idiot telling the madam on the phone who I was bringing. The name Sam Maceo was famous throughout Texas in those days, and the establishment I was patronizing nightly was probably one of many under control of his group, there in that area as well as south to Galveston. FS was not too upset as we started out, but Sam was cursing me, even though I explained I didn't want to take anyone with me. The two ladies forced the issue and arrive we did at the house of assignation. We were greeted by the madam and invited to sit and drink our champagne and partake of our caviar, and I introduced my little love, but the other girls made themselves scarce, and only an occasional face would peek around the corner of a door way. I went along to try and explain further, that the whole escapade was not of my doing. I don't think Sam ever forgave me for that, although he knew it was not my fault.

It is at this point that the author would care to beg the reader's indulgence. Sam Maceo is a notorious figure in the Texas underworld. It is not the point of this book to in any manner examine, highlight, or analyze the overdone thesis of Frank Sinatra and the mafia. It is beyond dispute that most entertainers of note in the '40's, '50's and '60's associated with individuals who had connections to organized crime. They owned and operated the nightclubs and casinos in which those entertainers performed, and consequently were vital to a successful career. The above-quoted portion of Van Heusen's autobiography is instructive in discovering the matter-of-fact manner in which entertainers and musicians dealt with those with underworld connections. To Van Heusen and Sinatra,

Sam Maceo was another guy to entertain and schmooze in the hopes of being invited back to entertain.

While he was not enjoying widespread popularity during the Houston engagement, Sinatra at least was able to sing. Van Heusen would also be with Sinatra when that ability would briefly – but terrifyingly – leave him in New York City on April 26, 1950, some two months after his appearance at the Shamrock Hotel. Playing an engagement at the Copacabana nightclub, Sinatra attempted to sing, but no sound was produced. He coughed into a handkerchief, saw blood, croaked a "good night" and immediately departed the stage. It was diagnosed as a vocal cord hemorrhage caused by hysterical aphonia. The affliction was no doubt a product of emotional stress over the end of his marriage to Nancy and his current tempestuous relationship with Ava Gardner and the physical stress on his voice. Sinatra was performing far too often, and with little rest, and he was performing numbers that were taxing his vocal cords. He was not a "big voice" performer like Frankie Laine or Eddie Fisher, yet some of the songs selected for him to perform in his waning days with Columbia were ill-suited, and it showed.

Sinatra recuperated with Van Heusen in Miami – silently, as all use of his vocal chords was forbidden by his doctors. His recovery was interrupted by news of a tryst between Gardner and Mario Cabre, the bullfighting co-star of her newest film, *Pandora and the Flying Dutchman*. It was rumored he was writing a book of poetry for her. The film was being shot in Spain, and that meant to Spain the two would go. It was challenging in 1950 to make one's way to Spain, as it still labored under the yolk of fascism through Generalissimo Francisco Franco. Visas needed to be obtained and inoculations administered. Van Heusen had an adverse reaction to the typhus shot, and suffered through symptoms from New York City to Barcelona.

Van Heusen recovered enough to be able to guide their chauffeur to the town of Tossa de Mar on the Costa Brava where Gardner was staying. No one spoke Spanish, and Van Heusen was required to adapt his rudimentary Spanish quickly to administer to the needs of Sinatra and Gardner. The trip was largely uneventful, with the three trying their best to outwit and avoid the throngs of press hoping to capture an image or two of the scandalous lovers. There was no sign of the encroaching bullfighter. In an event that gave Van Heusen much glee, the interloping toreador was nearly gored in an attempt to show-off for Ms. Gardner: "Incidentally, the Bullfighter, trying to show off in front of his adored one while they were shooting a sequence involving him and a bull, was very nearly impaled by the horns of the animal against the barrier of the ring. He, too old for the ring anymore to begin with, stopped taking chances and the movie shows him giving the bull a wide berth in every shot. He was only brave in his putrid poetry and braggadocio bowing."

Clearly unsatisfied with their Spanish adventure, Van Heusen and Sinatra headed north to Paris for their first trip to the City of Lights. The pair found infinitely more success there. They were treated as conquering heroes at Maxim's (according to Van Heusen, it was the only location that the two knew in Paris). Then, after being filled with food and drink, they set off for the famed club, Le Monsigneur. Once again, they were the center of attention, with wine flowing freely, servers waiting at their beck and call, and women aplenty. However, despite this auspicious beginning, the boys would be playing the part of Napoleon rather than Wellington:

There came out of nowhere a little girl who proceeded to sing some French songs. In between her little performances, she would sit next to me and the best I could do was hit her with my stilted Spanish. Some of it she understood, and as the evening progressed, her rapid French seemed more and more personal. I was sure I was home free as far as a romance with this little French singer was concerned. Then it occurred to me that perhaps I should get a little background and after questioning all the musicians, I discovered that the bass player could speak English. I asked him to move his bass fiddle closer to me and my girl and listen to what she was saying to me and then translate. As the evening wore on, and the bubbly flowed freely, the little lady chattered on in French, and while the bass player plucked his fiddle, he leaned his ear in our direction. Finally, while the musicians were taking five, the bass player took me aside and broke some horrible news to me. It seemed that what the little girl singer was saying all the time to me in French was that she wanted me to fix her up with Sinatra. I took this little shock in stride and informed FS that she was now with him. Via the translator, she was telling me that she had a date in mind with me and a late night club she wanted to take us to.

It was getting close to four o'clock in the morning and the Monseigneur was closing and was only waiting for the two Americans to leave, and just before the band stopped their serenading there materialized from somewhere "my date," who turned out to be another French broad who spoke no English either, and also looked like a lady wrestler. Off we went to the late, late spot suggested by the pretty little French singer, and as walked in we both knew we had made a terrible mistake. It was obviously a joint that rolled drunks and tossed them into the alley. One look and we did an about face and left. With sign language, I suggested that "my date" remain there since she looked like she belonged there. We were lucky to get out, I thought, and back we went to our hotel. I immediately figured my friend was "in like Flynn." Up in the suite, it took very little persuasion (sign language again) to get her clothes off. Very soon she was nude and dancing around the room. I disappeared into another room. The noise and racket of the lady singing and jumping all over the room which, I guess, was dancing for her, precluded any attempts at sleep and before long, two nude figures burst into the room where I was prone. Hours had passed, and certainly there had been several sessions of sex. After all, they were both in the nude. But no...she would permit no one, particularly Mr. S. to get near her, even in the raw. What was her story? Well, with some difficulty, we were made to understand that what she wanted was to audition for the great man, and nothing more. She wanted to appraise her dancing and the fact that her Abraham Lincoln was in evidence had nothing to do with them, but no touch. Exhausted, I managed to get her dressed and out of the place and on her way home. And a couple of male egos were bent and bruised a bit.

TWENTY-SEVEN

Sammy Cahn and Jimmy Van Heusen
Photo courtesy Van Heusen Photo Archives

Pardners

This flourishing personal relationship with Sinatra was complemented by a budding professional collaboration. Pleased with Van Heusen's efforts in *Young at Heart* and *Not as a Stranger*, master strategist Sinatra had his eye on uniting his old hit making lyricist from his MGM days with the hit making composer for his rival Bing Crosby. And that is how the team of Sammy Cahn and Jimmy Van Heusen was created. Why did it happen? It happened because Sinatra wanted it to happen.

With his career enjoying a second life following his Academy Award for *From Here to Eternity*, Sinatra was certain to retain complete artistic control over his recordings. There would be no Mitch Miller at his new home, Capitol Records. To complement the new sound of modern arrangers like Nelson Riddle and Billy May, Sinatra needed a new brand of song. His old tunesmith, Jule Styne, composer of such magnificent Sinatra gems as "Time After Time," "I Fall in Love

Too Easily," and "What Makes the Sunset," was leaving Hollywood to write for the Broadway stage. That left his wordsmith, Cahn, partnerless. Van Heusen was, of course, searching for a lyricist after the incapacitation of Burke. It seemed to Sinatra to be the perfect fit.

Writing specifically for Sinatra offered Van Heusen the "resurrection" of his career he desperately needed at that time. While the music he wrote with his sporadic collaborators post-Burke was impressive, it did not bring him the same attention that his work for Crosby did. His finest songs during that period – "I Could Have Told You" and "Somewhere Along the Way" were written under pseudonyms. The lovely "You, My Love" was buried under the weight of the title song for the movie for which it was written (*Young at Heart*). As such, Van Heusen eagerly attacked his first assignment with Cahn – to compose the title song for the upcoming film, *The Tender Trap*.

An Academy Award winner with composer Jule Styne for the 1954 song "Three Coins in the Fountain," Sammy Cahn had long established himself as one of the finest lyricists in Hollywood. At the time, Cahn had been nominated nine times for songs for which he provided the lyrics: "It Seems I Heard that Song Before" (1942), "I'll Walk Alone" (1944), "Anywhere"

(1945), "I Fall in Love Too Easily" (1945), "It's Magic" (1948), "It's a A Great Feeling" (1949), "Be My Love" (1950), "Wonder Why" (1951), and "Because Your Mine" (1952). Cahn also contributed the lyrics to two Broadway shows, written with Jule Styne, – *Glad to See You* (1944) and *High Button Shoes* (1947).

It is fair to say that Styne and Cahn occupied a similar position with Sinatra that Burke and Van Heusen occupied with Crosby. The two wrote the songs for most of Sinatra's MGM films of the late 1940's, including *Step Lively, Anchors Aweigh,* and *It Happened in Brooklyn.* Unlike Burke and Van Heusen, though, Cahn and Styne were personal confidants of the singer. Sinatra eagerly welcomed them (and in some manner, expected them to be) in his inner circle. As such, Sinatra had no compunctions about throwing together his two "partnerless" friends into a professional collaboration. Styne had left Hollywood to pursue more actively writing for the Broadway stage. Cahn had written several songs with Nicholas Brodzsky for a variety of films, including the Oscar-nominated "Be My Love," "Wonder Why," and "Because Your Mine," but the prospects of a long-term collaboration were dim when Sinatra intervened.

Cahn and Van Heusen wrote "The Tender Trap" at Van Heusen's residence. According to Sammy Cahn, he wrote the majority of the lyric after associating the word "snap" with "trap." He handed what was to be the first "A" section of the song to Van Heusen, who, under some pressure from his new collaborator, came up with what Cahn called "one of the worst melodies I'd heard." Cahn then continued to write the second "A" section when Van Heusen's old partner Johnny Burke walked into the room. Burke was convalescing at Van Heusen's home, which he did from time to time. Cahn welcomed the immediate distraction from his disappointment at Van Heusen's melody but also felt a sense of embarrassment – as if caught with another man's wife.

Cahn already felt somewhat uncomfortable with Burke because he felt a tinge of anti-Semitism in remarks Burke would make at his home. "When I finally made it to Hollywood I was welcome in Burke's home, but I confess I felt uncomfortable there. Everyone tended to be "Meyer" in his jokes." In his autobiography, Van Heusen delves into the various faults of many of his associates, and certainly spared no detail when describing Burke's drug addiction. Absent, though, is any hint of anti-Semitism in his recollections about

Burke. In fact, it is likely that Van Heusen would not have voluntarily tolerated the company, especially on a long-term basis, of anyone who had an engrained racist or otherwise intolerant worldview. Cahn's opinion of Burke is somewhat difficult to reconcile with the moniker Sinatra bestowed on Cahn: "The Nervous Jew." Of course, Sinatra was a client and Burke a rival.

The creation of "The Tender Trap" offered a microcosm of the Cahn/Van Heusen working relationship. Sammy Cahn was full of energy, preferring to work very quickly. He recounts a story of a young Paul Anka requesting special material from him, offering a lead time of six months. Cahn told Anka to call him about a week before the engagement, and then he would get to work. In this case, Cahn came to Van Heusen with a nearly completed lyric, and Van Heusen, perhaps feeling a degree of pressure, came up with the offending original melody. Van Heusen was used to writing with Burke (or on his own), who wrote at a painstakingly slow pace. Cahn forced Van Heusen to work a bit more quickly, while Van Heusen slowed Cahn to a less frenetic pace. True to this formula, the next day Van Heusen returned to Cahn, admitting that his original melody was not his finest work, and proceeded to play the melody that we know today.

"The Tender Trap" was a hit for Sinatra, and was nominated for an Academy Award (ultimately losing to "Love is a Many-Splendored Thing"). It marked a return of sorts for Van Heusen, who had not been nominated for the award since 1945. It was also the first popular song for Van Heusen written after his collaboration with Burke where he could use his real name. And Van Heusen's announcement to the musical world was as startling as the opening notes of Nelson Riddle's landmark arrangement of "I've Got the World on a String" for Sinatra. "The Tender Trap" is a driving, seductive song cloaked in a deceptively difficult, yet catchy, melody. The recording, featuring Riddle's swinging, brass-heavy arrangement and Sinatra's more mature coarser baritone, was a proclamation that polka dots and moonbeams had given way to shoes and rice.[17]

---

[17]   At the same session that Sinatra recorded "The Tender Trap," he also recorded another Van Heusen song – "You'll Get Yours," with lyrics by Dok Stanford. This marked one of the few instances after the DeLange collaboration where Van Heusen (as Van Heusen) wrote with someone not named "Burke" or "Cahn."

Buoyed by the success of "The Tender Trap," Van Heusen was consulted by his old friend Crosby to provide the music for a musicalization CBS had planned for the Thornton Wilder classic, *Our Town*. Crosby was slated to play the narrator. He had his pick of composer and lyricist, and after Van Heusen was selected, Crosby hoped to pair him with either Johnny Mercer or Dorothy Fields. Van Heusen began work, going so far as to meet with the CBS producer, Ralph Levy, and layout the production. Van Heusen had yet to decide upon a lyricist.

It came as something of a surprise to Van Heusen upon visiting Sinatra to learn that Sinatra's people were negotiating with NBC also to produce a musicalization of *Our Town*. Sinatra suggested that Van Heusen and Cahn would be perfectly suited for the vehicle. When Van Heusen informed Sinatra of the pendency of the Crosby project, Sinatra assured Van Heusen that his people had the inside track. Of course, Sinatra was correct. NBC's premiere event of 1955 would be its Producers Showcase production of *Our Town*, starring Frank Sinatra.

Van Heusen and Cahn wrote the score for *Our Town* in Van Heusen's newest home in Thunderbird Heights. It was an inspired collaboration. Cahn believed it to be the finest writing the team produced. It is difficult to rebut the point. Van Heusen and Cahn wrote four extremely powerful songs that perfectly complemented the multifaceted drama. They evoke Americana, pathos, hope, joy, and regret, all the while remaining firmly accessible and respectful of the text they were serving. As presented in the live broadcast, the songs are so expertly interwoven throughout the play that one could believe that Wilder himself had contemplated their inclusion from the beginning.

Of the four songs written for *Our Town*, only one, the rollicking "Love and Marriage," is widely known to those who are not Frankophiles. That is truly tragic, as the other songs represent some of the finest writing the team has done. The production's opening number is the title song, "Our Town." Van Heusen's broad, rustic melody evokes Copland, and contains many harmonic devices that elevate this song above the stock fare of the time. Van Heusen ends the first phrase of the song on a diminished seventh, building to this point by using parallel sixths. The "B" section of the song ends with a very intricate interval, jumping from the tonic (Eb) to an augmented fifth (B natural). The intricacy of the phrase is not to be overlooked, as the singer's natural tendency would be to resolve to the perfect fifth, Bb, rather than the B natural, as written. The difficulty of this phrase is compounded by the lead into the next phrase, which could properly follow either the Bb or the B natural. In another of ongoing testaments to the genius of Sinatra, he understood both the beauty and difficulty of this interval, and although it is not marked as such in the sheet music, Sinatra sings this portion of the song with a significant regard to ensure a clean articulation. The going gets no easier for the singer as the song progresses, ultimately reaching its dramatic climax on a ninth.

"The Impatient Years" was more lyrical, but no less challenging than "Our Town." Van Heusen employs an old trick, starting the song on the supertonic, giving the impression that the listener interrupted the singer in the middle of a story. And, to a large extent, this is most appropriate for the tone of the play, where we, as the audience, are eavesdropping on the residents of Grovers Corners. The song follows a lyrical, patterned format, permitting Van Heusen to build and release suspense, until the final articulation of the lovers' conviction that "Clinging together, (they're) certain, (they'll) weather, the warm and stormy, gay and impatient years." Cahn's lyrics are a fine testament to the travails of young love, taking his cue from Wilder's title phrase. The lyric is not a maudlin, brooding, or immature statement of teenage angst (even though the lovers are ostensibly in their teenage years). Rather, it is a surprisingly mature and rational view of a decidedly irrational topic. One wonders if Cahn wrote the lyric in such a manner to provide a subtle critique of the beat generation and its newest musical exponent – rock and roll.

Cahn once again borrowed from Wilder for the title of the third song, "Love and Marriage." Van Heusen wrote one of his finest, catchiest melodies, and the song was destined to become a massive hit. The jaunty, rollicking nature of the song adds to its deceptive complexity. First, the song has a range of an octave-and-a-half. It is peppered with intervals of sixths. Cahn's lyrics, while witty and charming, do the singer no favors, as, instead of providing a nice round vowel sound at the top of the phrase, forces the singer to articulate the awkward "this," "ask," and "Dad."

It remains in the popular consciousness, due in no small part to its selection as the opening song to the long-running comedy *Married... With Children*. People may think that the selection of a song from the Eisenhower 1950's as a theme song to a 1990's show devoted to the most dysfunctional family on television was ironic. If anything, it was entirely predictable because, despite the bizarre ways they showed it, the Bundy family loved each other very much. The "love and marriage" of the Bundy's of the 1990's was just as valid and authentic as the "love and marriage" in the 1950's. But here's the rub: the song in the 1950's was not about love in the 1950's, but about love in the 1890's Grovers Corners.   And it worked. Going even deeper, the song was not really about love in 1890's Grovers Corners, because it was being sung by the bride's father to a very nervous groom. It was about love and marriage in the 1850's. And it worked. In the span of three minutes, Van Heusen, with the help of Sammy Cahn, drew a line connecting nearly 150 years of love and marriage, uniting nearly five generations. He crystallized, made concrete, and since he did once attend a Seminary, made incarnate, the idea of "love and marriage," showing it was the same in 1850 as it was in 1990.

  "Love and Marriage" was honored by receiving the first Emmy Award for an original song in 1955. Sinatra's recording was a commercial success, lasting 17 weeks on the Billboard charts, peaking at fifth place. And, with such accolades for

"Love and Marriage," it is all too easy to forget what might be considered the finest song of the group – "Look to Your Heart." Cahn perfectly encapsulates the principal theme of Wilder's work with his closing verse: "Too late we find, a word that's warm and kind, is more than just a passing token. Speak your love, to those who seek your love. Look to your heart. Your heart will know what to say. Look to your heart today." Van Heusen wrote an exceptionally heartfelt melody that deftly avoids drowning the emotion of the moment with schmaltz. Indeed, in the teleplay, when recently deceased Julia Gibbs (Eva Marie Saint) looks from the great beyond onto her 12th birthday party, and asks the Stage Manager (Sinatra) what more she could have done to let her family know how much she loved them, the resulting song flows as naturally as if Wilder himself contemplated its inclusion.

With songs written, Van Heusen and Cahn participated in the actual audition process. At this point, the only role that had been definitively cast was Sinatra as the Stage Manager. There is a persistent rumor that James Dean had been cast as George Gibbs but had to be replaced due to his untimely death. As interesting as it might have been to envision two titans of cool sharing the stage, logic makes this impossible. *Our Town* aired on September 19, 1955. James Dean was killed on September 30, 1955. The world would have to wait until 1960 for such an event, when Sinatra welcomed Elvis Presley home from the Army on his television show. Of course, Van Heusen and Cahn would have their hands in that affair, as well.

Van Heusen had composed difficult songs, and all of them, at one point in the production, would need to be essayed by people not named "Frank Sinatra." Therefore, Van Heusen thought it important for the leads to be able to sing – and sing well. The first actress Van Heusen recalls seeing was Eva Marie Saint. He found her absolutely perfect for the part, but was not quite convinced of her vocal talents. Among the actors, Van Heusen was suitably impressed, but not overwhelmed, by the audition of the then unknown Paul Newman. Van Heusen's recollection of Newman's audition was somewhat muted: "He (Newman) walked in, put his feet on the table, and attempted to warble a little piece. Not a very impressive demonstration for a composer like me who wanted to hear his songs really sung."

Cahn has a somewhat different take from his autobiography, *I Should Care*:

I'll never forget the way Paul Newman
auditioned. He came to the studio, slouched
down at the piano and sang, to his own
accompaniment, one of the raunchiest smoker-
room songs I'd ever heard. No man was ever able
to make a room as blue with language as James
Van Heusen. His talent for making a room blue
with language was right up there, in its fashion,
with his musical gifts, and when he heard young
Newman's rendition he was suitable and
profoundly appreciative. 'That's the most be-f---
ing-yewtiful thing I ever heard." No prude am
I...but I was appalled by this audition song of
Newman's, though it was a clear winner with Van
Heusen. Still, I'm pleased to say that in the actual
show Paul Newman sang "The Impatient Years,"
one of my favorites – and bearing no resemblance
to the X-rated ditty Paul used to win over my
earthy collaborator.

Van Heusen resigned himself to the fact that, given the
vocal limitations of the stars, a grueling rehearsal schedule
would be required. The great choirmaster, Norman Luboff,
was assigned as a vocal coach to Ms. Saint and Mr. Newman.
However, Mr. Luboff's task was made somewhat more difficult
given the space limitations of the theater. The orchestra was

too large to be placed on set, and therefore would have to be piped in from another studio approximately a third of a block away. The overhead speakers that provided the singers with pitch and support would have to be played at a low level to prevent feedback.

A more daunting obstacle than the vocal performances of the stars, was the actual participation of the biggest star. Sinatra notoriously hated rehearsals, and the numerous rehearsals required of this production were anathema to the temperamental singer. He failed to attend several of the rehearsals, which was starting to concern director Delbert Mann and his co-stars. Producer Fred Coe appealed to Van Heusen for help:

> That evening, I went to the apartment on Wilshire Boulevard in which Sinatra was living at the time, and before many moments went by, I knew there would be trouble. He did not plan to show up for the dress rehearsal and maybe not even for the show. What had happened? Well, it was during the days when he was not as (an) important (of) a figure as he later became, and it seems he was to receive $50,000 for appearing in *Our Town*. It also appeared that he owed this same identical amount to his lawyer, Henry Jaffee, who was also a

producer of *Our Town*, being the guiding genius behind Producers Showcase. Because it was owed to him and because he felt it should be paid to him at that particular time, Mr. Jaffee commandeered the $50,000 and in essence, Frank Sinatra was to be doing the show for zero dollars. This had really disenchanted the master, and it was driven home to me, hurting every inch of the way, that this lovely score of songs I had written might never be heard. 'We'll still publish the songs, even if I don't do this damn thing, can't we?' said Frank on the phone the next night. He had failed to show up for rehearsal that afternoon and now the staff was desperate and depending upon me to deliver him for the show. 'There won't be any songs if you don't do this thing, because I'll tear every copy up and burn it.' I replied, 'I didn't write this stuff for anyone they might get to substitute for you, like Gordon MacRae, who took over when you left *Carousel*.' Then, I knew that if I didn't stay with him night and day, he certainly would not show up for any of the necessary dress rehearsals and the actual show. I walked into his apartment and planted myself and together we lived it up, partying and drinking, and staying up most of the nights. When the day for the very last run through before the actual show, I talked him into showing up. When he and I walked through the doors of the Hollywood rehearsal hall, there was a sigh of relief from the staff and also from the other actors. They had been working out with no one but his stand in, and were edgy and nervous about just how it would go with the real article. He went through the play reading all his lines from a blackboard, and when he sang, another blackboard displayed the lyrics of the song. It gave the company a lift, but was no assurance that he would really appear for the live television shooting at Burbank. Mr. Coe, who rightfully was worried to death, begged me to stay with Sinatra and be sure he got to the actual show. I promised to do so, on one condition. That condition was a violation of every contractual obligation the studio had made with the author's agent but in desperation, it was agreed upon. I was to receive a kinescope (rudimentary video recording) of the entire program. The deal NBC had made was for live TV rights only, and sets, scripts, costumes and everything pertaining to the production had to be destroyed immediately after the show. I couldn't bear the thought that this great program would disappear forever after one single showing. I exacted my pound of flesh, and it was eventually delivered to me.

The production was quite remarkable. Although a bit uncomfortable at first, Sinatra eased into his role as the Stage Manager, tempering its detached, fatalistic tone with just enough warmth to comfort the viewer in the production's most emotional moments. His singing was spectacular. The richness and power of his voice that evening was near operatic in tone. Indeed, while Sinatra's studio recordings of these songs are among the finest, it is regrettable that this live performance was lost to history, as it surpasses the studio recordings in quality. One wishes he could have sung the more dramatic, more difficult ending to "The Impatient Years" during this performance. Paul Newman and Eva Marie Saint were predictably brilliant. And, much to Van Heusen's great relief, both acquitted themselves quite well with their vocal performances.

In 1956, Cahn and Van Heusen provided additional material for yet another film incarnation of *Anything Goes*. Crosby starred again, but was joined by Donald O'Connor, Mitzy Gaynor, and Jeanmarie Zizi. All vestiges of the original plot were jettisoned in favor of a more suitable vehicle for two male leads. Fortunately, the production kept most of the original Cole Porter score. The team's contributions suffered in comparison to the original, but this was a particularly high bar to overcome. Once again, Van Heusen was placed in the unfortunate position of having his lesser caliber songs juxtaposed and somewhat imposed on the works of those composers Van Heusen held high regard – Richard Rodgers (*A Connecticut Yankee in King Arthur's Court*) and, now, Cole Porter.

The team also provided the songs for one of the last films of the Dean Martin and Jerry Lewis team – *Pardners*. This remake of the Crosby film *Rhythm on the Range* contained four original Cahn and Van Heusen songs: "Pardners," "The Wind! The Wind!" "You and Me and the Moon," and "Buckskin Beauty." All of them would easily have found their way in to a Hope/Crosby production (even though the original source film did not feature Hope). They harken back to the more easy-going crooning of Crosby than the new Sinatra sound. For his part, Sammy Cahn did his best Johnny Burke imitation with "Pardners" and "You and Me and the Moon." The songs, though, were uninspired. It was almost as if Van Heusen was overcome with the idea of past associations, those representing a musical style he had thought he could finally put behind him.

There were exciting opportunities to explore, and he was ready to go traveling.

TWENTY-EIGHT

Jimmy Van Heusen pursuing yet another one of his hobbies
Photo courtesy Van Heusen Photo Archives

To Love and Be Loved

While Cahn and Van Heusen were laboring under the fading aegis of Crosby and Martin/Lewis, Sinatra was entering the most successful portion of his already remarkable career. Since *The Tender Trap*, Sinatra had made the following films: *Guys and Dolls, The Man with the Golden Arm* and *High Society* (which also starred Crosby). More important, from 1954-1957 he had recorded the first several of his legendary concept albums – *In the Wee Small Hours, Songs for Swingin' Lovers, Close to You, A Swingin' Affair* and *Where Are You.*

To say these albums dramatically changed popular music would be an understatement. From a technological perspective, Sinatra utilized the longer playing capability of the 33-rpm record over that over that of the 78-rpm record to create a particular mood, which he was able to carry throughout a 30-40 minute time period, formulating a variety of "mini opera" of popular music.

The arrangements of Nelson Riddle (and later, Gordon Jenkins and Billy May) essentially redefined and reshaped the sound of popular music for the next decade, producing the essential versions of most of the canon of American popular music. With these stellar successes in both major mediums, it was not hyperbole to consider Frank Sinatra as the king of the entertainment world. It was now time for Van Heusen to hitch an extraordinary second ride on another legendary star. Like with his previous pilot, the trip was made so much more memorable because of Van Heusen's participation.

Cahn and Van Heusen had written five songs for Sinatra in 1955, all of which represent some of the finest work the team had done. They had given Sinatra two of his signature songs ("Love and Marriage" and "The Tender Trap") in their first two outings. In that same glorious year of 1955, they were called upon to write the title song for Sinatra's film noir classic, *The Man With the Golden Arm*, but the team missed the mark. The resulting song was recorded by Sinatra, but not used in the film. It was heard only in extended trailers. This was not altogether unfortunate, as Van Heusen's melody never really finds itself and what there is to find is out of place as a theme song for a recovering heroin addict. Cahn's lyrics, though, while not quite as dark as might be required for such a film, do a much better job of plumbing the depths of a loner. The lyrics, recycled with a better Van Heusen melody, would have made a fine torch song for Sinatra.

The Man with the Golden Arm represents the first time that a particular subject matter was beyond Van Heusen's ability as a songwriter. Van Heusen could write music for dramatic films and provide the soundtrack for Sinatra's darkest albums, but there seems to be coming in the entertainment world a darkness or seriousness that Van Heusen could not adequately convey in his music. Van Heusen's other foray into weightier material – patriotic music – produced similarly disappointing results: "Early American" and "You Never Had It So Good" (with Johnny Burke), though written at different times, appear to be more of a cardigan-ed Bob Dobbs chastising "those kids" than an effective rejoinder to the nascent counterculture issues of the mid-1960's.

And Sinatra, ever aware of people's capabilities, may have seen this in his decision not to select Van Heusen to contribute something to his 1956 avant-garde: *Frank Sinatra Conducts Tone Poems of Color*. This piece of Sinatra esoterica saw Sinatra conducting tone poems from modern musicians depicting certain colors: Nelson Riddle, Gordon Jenkins, Billy May, Alec Wilder, Elmer Bernstein, Victor Young, Jeff Alexander, and Andre Previn. Notorious by exclusion were Sinatra associates Axel Stordahl, Jule Styne and Jimmy Van Heusen. Certainly the exclusion of Van Heusen was not personal. It was perhaps a conscious attempt on the part of Sinatra to appear as musically progressive instrumentally as vocally. Time was not a factor – most of the selections are less than five minutes. That Van Heusen could not write orchestrally might have been the deciding factor. Still, given the artistic license given to Sinatra by Capitol, it would be difficult to imagine this would have been an insurmountable obstacle.

The reason might never be known, and it probably did not matter much to Sinatra or Van Heusen. They were friends, and Van Heusen knew that Sinatra was fiercely loyal to his friends. Van Heusen, too, was most certainly not a fair-weathered friend. They found in each other kindred spirits united by love of music, women, booze, and general hell-raising. However, their friendship blossomed during Sinatra's "lean years" (roughly 1948-1953). Feeling increasingly marginalized by the sunset of the soft romantic vocalist and unable to find a niche in post-war America, Sinatra saw his career fall from staggering heights to unimaginable depths. Massive theater engagements were replaced by hotel openings or small clubs. Worse, his personal life mirrored the turmoil of his professional world. Trapped in marriage, publicly pining for Ava Gardner, and seemingly impossible to befriend, Sinatra retreated to a small group of people. Van Heusen kept vigil with Sinatra, drinking, eating, talking, or simply saying nothing until the wee small hours. These times with Sinatra held no promise of lucrative movie deals or recording contracts. To all concerned, Van Heusen was befriending a fallen star, but that did not matter to him. As he would write to Nancy Sinatra, Jr., many years later: "Those were the lean years for him...although your father knew he was only as big as his last picture (he couldn't get a picture), he gave love, much of it. He dispensed it. Among the fellows. We called it loyalty or friendship or faithfulness. But it's love – love for a friend."

And so Van Heusen became almost inseparable from Sinatra during those years. It was Van Heusen who went to Houston or to Spain to chase Ava. It was Van Heusen, among others, at La Scala restaurant in New York City with Sinatra in a quasi-send off to the Academy Awards presentation that would give Sinatra his Oscar for *From Here to Eternity*. It was to Van Heusen's Palm Springs house or Van Heusen's Manhattan apartment that Sinatra would retreat after arguments with Ava, and with whom he would find solace, or, at least, a drinking partner. And, it was Van Heusen who purportedly found his friend on the floor of the elevator in that 57th Street apartment with his wrists slashed. Van Heusen apparently called a doctor, paid off a taxicab driver to take Sinatra to the hospital and paid off a desk clerk to keep the entire event quiet.

To be sure, Van Heusen never wrote about this incident, nor did he ever mention it in any recorded interview. This, alone, does not indicate that the event is a fiction. If Van Heusen found it important enough to pay someone "hush money" then, in deference to his friend's reputation (and his family), he never saw fit to reveal it. Indeed, its inclusion here is not to sensationalize but rather to reveal the depth of the friendship between the two men. When the music industry marginalized Van Heusen in the '70's and '80's, and especially when Sinatra-bashing was in vogue, Van Heusen would have been a prime target, but true to this friend, he never took the bait.[18]

It would appear George Jacobs in his memoir, *Mr. S*, has the most logical perspective on this issue: "It [suicide] didn't seem his style, but the despair was there. If it was true, then Van Heusen's mission was to never let his friend get that low again, and, to that end, he kept the booze and broads flowing nonstop."

Van Heusen was more than qualified for the task at hand. Uniformly described by all as the consummate swinging bachelor of the 1950's, Van Heusen had a seemingly insatiable appetite for women and alcohol. Crosby, no mean drinker himself, claimed to run from Van Heusen when the sun went down. He had a legendary refrigerator that he kept filled solely with martini glasses. His ultramodern bachelor pad in the Palm Springs desert was filled with the latest technology, and more important, filled with women and booze. Peter Marshall, then trying to break into the business, was a waiter at the famous Chi Chi club in Palm Springs – a favorite hangout

---

[18]   Kitty Kelley, the author of the controversial Sinatra biography, His Way, indicated that she attempted to contact Van Heusen for an interview but could not reach him.

of Sinatra, Crosby, Hope, and Van Heusen. He recalls Van Heusen's home to be full of ladies, most of them "professionals," but not secretaries or clerks. Marshall also recalled the presence of Van Heusen's old friend Polly Adler, who had since retired after a storied career dodging law enforcement and stubbornly refusing to turn on her powerful (and illicit) protectors. Now a much larger star than when he first made Ms. Adler's acquaintance, Van Heusen, nevertheless, always had a place in his home for old friends – and their baggage. Marshall described Van Heusen's home as a bustling resort, with people coming and going at their leisure. Van Heusen never kept account of the food, drink and lodging bestowed on his guests. It was certainly due to his incredibly generous nature, but also, one wonders where he would have found the time. All-night drinking and womanizing left little place for such mundane details as discovering who ate the last piece of pie. And, from all accounts, Van Heusen's appetites were not merely the stuff of Hollywood folklore – they are accurate representations of his exploits. Sammy Cahn famously remarked that the trouble with Frank Sinatra is he thinks he's Jimmy Van Heusen. And, it is also true that Van Heusen was associated with a fair number of very attractive women – Inger Stevens, Jacquelyn McKeever, Angie Dickinson, Helen Joyce, Charlotte Fairchild, Peggy Lee, and Angela Leeds, to name a few. Sammy Cahn recalled, "Long before Xerox, Chester was an innovator. He'd take a sheet of paper eight-and-a-half by eleven inches and have his secretary write down the names and telephone numbers of a hundred girls. Then he'd have that reduced so he could carry it around handily – put it onto a little card which fit in his pocket."

And while it would be nearly two decades before he succumbed to marriage, even in those swinging days, though, there was one woman who seemed to have a special place in Van Heusen's heart – Ada Kurtz. Robert De Roos writes in his unpublished Van Heusen biography of Ms. Kurtz:

> "Ada Kurtz, a very important part of Jimmy's life, a lady whom he first knew in New York, a lady who lived with him for many years, remains an enigma – quite possibly because her role is no one's business. By all accounts, Ada Kurtz is a gentle, smiling lady, very much in love with Van Heusen over the years, always present in Jim's manage. Ralph Harris sums up the general attitude: "I know Ada was important but I don't know what to say because I never did understand the relationship. All I know is that Ada was there

414

whether there were other girls around or not."
Another friend says that "She was in love with Jim
– everyone knows that. And she was a great,
great moral help and support. She was totally
dedicated to him." And another: "Of course, Ada
was around a lot of the time. She was a
companion, I guess. Jim always needed a mother
around, you know, and maybe Ada was a mother
figure. She was always there to rub the back of his
neck if he had a headache and generally take care
of him.

Man cannot live by booze and broads alone, it
would appear.

TWENTY-NINE

Original manuscript for All The Way
Photo courtesy of Jimmy Van Heusen collection,
Frederick and Jean Williams Archives, Cazenovia College

All the Way

Booze and broads were the lifeblood of comic Joe E. Lewis, the topic of the 1957 biopic, *The Joker Is Wild*, the next Sinatra film project.   Lewis (like the actor portraying him) certainly lived his life "All the Way," and there could be no more appropriate title for a theme song. The story of the introduction of "All the Way" to Sinatra by Cahn and Van Heusen has been told by Sammy Cahn on several occasions. At a rare early morning meeting with Sinatra (a famously late riser), the team was accompanied by Cahn's social secretary. In usual fashion, Cahn sang while Van Heusen accompanied at the piano. As they reached the dramatic conclusion, Sinatra looked at them, and with no discernible reaction, entreated the two to have breakfast with him. In tears, Cahn's secretary said how could Sinatra not like it? Cahn replied that he did love it. When asked why, Cahn told her because Sinatra loves all his songs. This, of course, was generally true, but Sinatra certainly found it in himself to turn down at least two Cahn/Van Heusen tunes – "Come Waltz With Me" and "Cathy." Nevertheless, this demonstrates the unspoken yet fierce confidence both artist and songwriting team had in each other.

The song, of course, was a classic, winning Van Heusen and Cahn their second Academy Award. Indeed, the 30th Academy Awards presentation was something of the "Cahn and Van Heusen" show, as, in addition to winning the top prize in their field, they also wrote a wonderful number for Kirk Douglas and Burt Lancaster to sing and dance to – "It's Nice Not to Be Nominated." It was the highlight of the show, and is proof that all Oscar musical numbers need not be soul-annihilatingly awful.

The film was nowhere near as successful as the song, and Van Heusen somewhat ruefully claimed that if the film had chosen "All the Way" as its title, the film would have earned greater success. For obvious reasons, this author believes this contention has merit. Sinatra's recording of "All the Way" with Nelson Riddle's arrangement is one of the finest recordings in the Sinatra canon. So impressive was Sinatra's recording that few vocalists even attempted to cover it during Sinatra's lifetime. On the sheer force of Sinatra's recording, alone, "All the Way" became a part of the American songbook. The song has been covered most recently by Barry Manilow, Michael Feinstein, Celine Dion, and Harry Connick, Jr., each performing the song in a ballad-style, true to the original Sinatra recording (Manilow and Feinstein recorded it for their own Sinatra tribute albums). Feinstein has actually recorded the song twice – once by itself and once paired wonderfully with "All My Tomorrows." That contemporary artists are choosing to record this song is encouraging. "All the Way" is a singularly great song and deserves to be sung and interpreted anew. Like most Van Heusen songs, that concept is much easier said than done. "All the Way" is a challenging song to perform, requiring an elastic vocal range. Right from the start, in the second and third measures, Van Heusen writes the devilishly tricky 10th interval to introduce the song title. And while the "showstopper" ending featured on most recordings is a deviation from the published score – Van Heusen chose to end the song with a low "Eb" – the omnipresence of the Sinatra recording in the musical consciousness of the public would leave audiences disappointed if an artist did not match Sinatra's climactic high note.[19]

To this point, Van Heusen had been asked to write songs for television shows, movies, musical theater and as "singles," i.e. a song written for no occasion in particular. Of course, since his advent in Hollywood, Van Heusen had written precious few "singles," and those were written primarily in the year or so between his collaboration with Burke and Cahn. Now, Van Heusen and Cahn were called upon by Sinatra to write songs that incorporated the elements of the stage/screen and singles. They were to write the opening and closing songs for Sinatra's upcoming concept album celebrating the joys of travel. These songs had to tell a certain story, as in a theater production, but not be so narrow as to need the context of the show to be understood and enjoyed. They could stand on their own, but are more fully appreciated when heard in the context of the whole album. It was a tall order from a demanding customer. The result – the wonderful bookends of "Come Fly With Me" and "It's Nice to Go

---

[19]   Once again, Feinstein, ever a font of musical originality, avoids the ending by segueing from the penultimate phrase to the conclusion of "All My Tomorrows," where he concludes on a marvelously high falsetto.

Trav'ling" for the album *Come Fly With Me*. The former would serve as an unofficial opening concert number for Sinatra for decades, and was the ultimate invitation to the swinging lifestyle. Van Heusen's melody found a great home in Billy May's exciting arrangement. Once again, though, Van Heusen is demanding (and ironic). An anthem to relaxing, taking to the skies and jetting off to Acapulco Bay is anything but easy-going. Octave leaps punctuate the melody with difficult chromatics thrown in for good measure. When Sinatra reaches the end of this marathon session, it is not surprising that he seems a bit out of breath, rather than casually strolling into his cabana in "llama land." The closing song of the album, "It's Nice to Go Trav'ling" is a much less frenetic number, befitting our (somewhat tired) hero's return home from a world adventure. The lyric coolly extols the virtues of the United States – without seeming overly jingoistic – and contains an endorsement of our great nation that might make our politicians blush, but I am sure made Van Heusen swell with pride.

"You will find the maiden and the gay muchachas are rare/ But they can't compare with that sexy line/ That parades each day at Sunset and Vine." History has shown, that he would know.

THIRTY

Only The Lonely original manuscript
Courtesy of Van Heusen Photo Archives

Only The Lonely

1958 was an extraordinarily busy year for the team. They would contribute songs for three films – Paris *Holiday, Indiscreet,* and *Some Came Running. Paris Holiday* was a Bob without Bing comedy featuring French comedian Fernandez, Anita Ekberg and Martha Hyer. They wrote the title song, which was heard only over the opening credits. Also written for the film was a proposed duet between Hope and Hyer called "Nothing in Common." It was dropped from the film, but fortunately was given new life when Sinatra and Keely Smith recorded it for Capitol.[20] Their contribution of the title song to the Cary Grant-Ingrid Bergman masterpiece, *Indiscreet* has Van Heusen making one of his rare forays into 3/4 time. It is a complex, haunting melody darting from major to minor

---

[20]   At the same recording date, Sinatra also recorded two other Cahn-Van Heusen swingers – "How Are Ya Fixed for Love" (also a duet with Smith) and "Same Old Song and Dance."

with the same smoothness and unpredictability as the plot of the film for which it was written. The song suffers, though, from Cahn's unfortunate placement of the preposition "of" at the melodic climax of the song.

Their third film song is one of their finest. "To Love and Be Loved" (from the film *Some Came Running*) flirts between relative major and minor keys to maintain a tension that is finally and beautifully resolved in the final measures, with the singer exclaiming, "to be sheltered and safe from the storm, to be cozy and ever so warm, and for always to love and be loved by you." Will Friedwald in his Grammy-winning liner notes to the Sinatra box set *The Complete Capitol Singles* describes the melody as "semi-classical," and as usual, Friedwald is right on the money. This is Van Heusen writing more as a serious film composer than as a popular songwriter. His broad melody seems to occupy the entirety of the large screen on which it was heard, knowing that it would fill a theater as opposed to the living room of a listener. Like the film for which it was written, the James Jones drama *Some Came Running*, Van Heusen deftly walks the line between intensity and melodrama. Sinatra made two recordings of the song, both with the same Nelson Riddle arrangement, but with the vital difference of Sinatra's singing the final measures an octave higher than written. While not a particularly popular song, it nonetheless earned the team their third Academy Award nomination, ultimately bowing to "Gigi."

Of the next Sinatra album, Frank Sinatra, Jr. said it should be available "by prescription only" because it was "death." The album cover with Nicholas Volpe's painting of Sinatra as Pagliacci is one of the more enduring images of the Sinatra legacy and popular music in general. According to at least one author, Sinatra himself considered it his favorite album. It is the darkest and most beautiful manifestation of the "torch song." This atmosphere is created by the brilliant and innovative orchestrations of Nelson Riddle, a palate of the finest ballads ever written, and the richest singing Sinatra had recorded to date, a crescendo reached from his previous ballad albums – In *the Wee Small Hours*, *Close to You*, and *Where are You*. It can fairly be considered Sinatra's masterpiece. It is *Only the Lonely*.

For this album, Cahn and Van Heusen had two important roles. They composed the vital title song to the album, and they were asked to write the liner notes for the album – the only songwriters afforded that honor. In those liner notes, they give a glimpse both into the creative process of writing "Only the Lonely" and their unique understanding of the artist for whom they were writing:

> For the lyricist and composer attempting to write a song of loneliness for Frank Sinatra, it becomes the challenge of matching words with notes. Lonely words for equally lonely notes.
> The Frank Sinatra that we know and have known (and hardly know) is an artist with as many forms and patterns as can be found in a child's kaleidoscopticon. "Come Fly With Me" is one Sinatra. "All the Way" is another Sinatra. A Sinatra singing a hymn of loneliness could very well be the real Sinatra...First, came the title, "Only the Lonely." Then came the melody.
> Van Heusen: The lyric came very hard. Session after session without the glimmer of a line. Sammy is as facile a man with words as there is in our business, and I thought changing the melody here and there might be helpful. He wouldn't permit me to change a note.
> Cahn: I believe this to be one of the best melodies Jimmy ever composed. While I usually refuse to write a lyric that "comes hard," I'm delighted now that the melody is exactly as I first heard it
> Here then, is Frank Sinatra in "Only the Lonely." We have written many songs for Frank, his

reaction is never over-enthusiastic. It is always the most imperceptible nod. We hope that you will give this album the same imperceptible nod, because where Sinatra is concerned we have come to know it means, "It's a gasser."

A "gasser" might have been a candidate for hall-of-fame understatement, and Cahn and Van Heusen were now the principal providers of the fuel. Three Academy Award nominations in four years, one win, and more projects available to them than ever before (not to mention their cemented status of court composer to the new king), the team was at the top of their game.[21] Each enjoyed power and wealth heretofore unknown to him. The year 1959 would continue their ascent, as they would provide music for Frank Sinatra, Bing Crosby, and Pat Boone, score a movie musical and ultimately win another Academy Award. They would also touch the hem of real power, as they were introduced to a young senator from Massachusetts who would change the course of American political history.

---

[21]   Among the projects considered by Cahn and Van Heusen was a musicalization of the popular novel October Island.

THIRTY-ONE

Jimmy Van Heusen, Bing Crosby, and Sammy Cahn on set
Courtesy of Van Heusen Photo Archives

Say One for Me

By 1959, the era of the film musical had passed. *Gigi* in 1958 was more a throwback than a new beginning. The classics of the Freed Unit were well in the past. There would be successful adaptations of Broadway musicals yet to come, but the original Hollywood musical, for all intents and purposes, was gone. The 1959 film, *Say One for Me*, with Bing Crosby, Debbie Reynolds, and Robert Wagner, was more a film with several songs written for it than a true film musical. Van Heusen and Cahn wrote eight songs for the film, which required the most output from them for a single production than ever before. The film itself could be considered a third installment of Crosby's "Fr. Chuck" character, with the Groaner playing a pastor of a church that caters to the Hollywood set. The team gave Crosby two outstanding songs that certainly should have lived past the run of the less-than-successful film. The first was a "Look to Your Heart" – version of a Christmas song titled "The Secret of Christmas." It is a profound melody and meaningful lyric that would be a welcome respite from the saccharine chestnuts we are served during the Yuletide season. Cahn writes: "The little gift you send on Christmas day/Won't bring back the friends you've turned away/So may I suggest the secret of Christmas, is not the things you do at Christmas time/But the Christmas things you do, all year through." The second song, "I Couldn't Care Less," does not strive for any meaning deeper than a fellow carrying a torch. Cahn bows to the Crosby rule of never saying "I love you" – which, in this pastoral context, is quite out of place, and Van Heusen writes an exquisite melody, giving a seemingly gently wistful melody a deeper dramatic tone with a jump of a seventh on the climactic phrase, "It's a cold and dreary *world* I guess." It is another example of the subtlety in craftsmanship that Van Heusen displayed when at the top of his game that serves as yet another reminder of why he was such an impressive songwriter.

In addition to this output for Crosby, Van Heusen and Cahn also contributed title songs to various other films. This became something of a stock in trade for the pair, as their remarkable felicity of creation (along with, of course, their talent) made them a reliable team for "last minute" creations. These include the title songs for *Holiday for Lovers* and *This Earth is Mine,* with the latter of these suffering the fate of many "title songs." The success of the song is, nearly always, tied to the success of the movie. *This Earth Is Mine* was uniformly panned, and so its title song was forgotten (Don Cornell, who sang the song in the movie, not being a large enough star to give the song life outside of the film). Another pitfall experienced by the movie composer is writing a song whose relevance cannot be understood outside of the context of the film. "This Earth Is Mine" also fits into this category. The film was about the struggles of California winemakers, and its opening song, while trying valiantly to strike some universal appeal among those of us who are not vintners, cannot shake its earthy underpinnings, and thereby remains a song, in essence, about the specific topic of the film. This does not bode for great popular success, and is a principal reason Cahn and Van Heusen insisted upon handsome compensation for these title song projects. Nevertheless, this did little to dull the sting that Van Heusen felt when some very good work went unnoticed. "This Earth Is Mine" is a very nice song, demonstrating Van Heusen's growing ability to write sweeping, almost semi-classical, works for Hollywood melodrama.

The oddest film project the team undertook was providing songs for an adaptation of Jules Verne's *Journey to the Center of the Earth*. This was not to be a musical version of the science fiction novel. Cahn and Van Heusen were asked to write several songs so that the male lead, Pat Boone, could sing. The story does not easily lend itself to musical interludes, so the team focused its efforts on amplifying the romance between Mr. Boone and Arlene Dahl. They wrote three songs for the film: "Twice as Tall," "The Faithful Heart," and an adaptation of Robert Burns' "My Love Is Like a Red Red Rose." While all three were recorded by Mr. Boone for the film (and released commercially), only "My Love is Like a Red Red Rose" made it into the final print.

While neither Van Heusen nor Cahn would admit it publicly, they certainly saved their finest work for Sinatra. The songs written for Sinatra albums and films released in 1959 were no exception. The next installment in the "Come ___ with Me" series was 1959's *Come Dance With Me*. Cahn and Van Heusen were again asked to write the title tune, but also to write an appropriate closing number for the album. "Come

Dance with Me" is a fun, rollicking, swinging number, and it sets the tone perfectly for one of Sinatra's most fun albums. While the opening number practically wrote itself (according to Cahn – a phrase wrought with either understatement or ego), the closing number was something of a challenge. As Cahn stated,

> "We get to the closing song of *Come Dance With Me*, and Van Heusen and I couldn't think of a song about dancing that Irving Berlin hadn't already thought of. He covered all the bases of dancing [in five songs written for Fred Astaire]: 'Cheek to Cheek' (also in Come Dance With Me), 'Change Partners,' (and) 'Let's Face the Music and Dance' (not to mention 'It Only Happens When I Dance With You' and 'You're Easy to Dance With'). Sinatra is used to me coming back the next day with whatever song he asks for. When he doesn't hear from us, he's on the phone: 'Hey, where's that last song?'
>
> "I remember I turn to Van Heusen and said 'Hey, let me ask you a question. Has there ever been a 'Last Dance?' Van Heusen says, 'Gee, I don't know.' We call ASCAP. There's a 'Save the Last Dance for Me' but no 'Last Dance.' Well, we wrote that song as fast as you can speak."

Speed of delivery in no manner detracted from lyrical craftsmanship, as "The Last Dance" is arguably the finest cut on an album full of great numbers. Billy May's brilliant about-face arrangement perfectly complements Van Heusen's lullaby to the stalwart dancer, allowing the listener to reflect and catch his breath after more than a full 30 minutes of hard-swinging Sinatra. It was also a presumed favorite of Sinatra, as it was one of a handful of Capitol recordings that Sinatra would re-record during the Reprise years.

The tone of the second Sinatra album of 1959 could not have been more opposite than *Come Dance With Me*. The almost funereal, Gordon Jenkins-arranged, *No One Cares*. A collection of 12 ballads, it included two Van Heusen selections – the magnificent "Here's That Rainy Day" and the newly-penned title song with Sammy Cahn. "Here's That Rainy Day" was rescued by Sinatra and Van Heusen by this album from the *Carnival in Flanders* Broadway fiasco. The title song was yet another custom written number, and does not seem to have presented the same concern as "The Last Dance." Like "Only the Lonely," it is an important tone setter for the remainder of the album, but these are two very different songs. "Only the Lonely" is a more sweeping, lyrical lament, much in fitting

with that album's selection of songs. "When No One Cares"
takes its cue from the other songs on the album; dirge-like,
small intervalled, more introspective and decidedly darker.

THIRTY-TWO

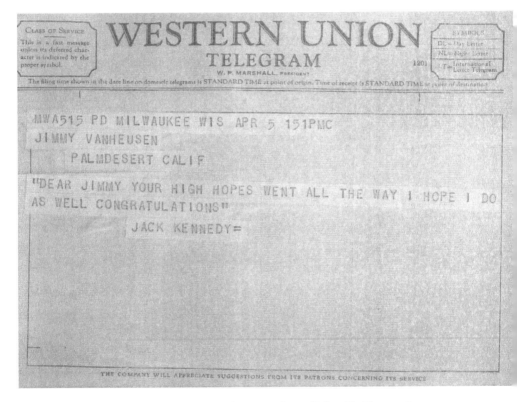

Telegraph to Jimmy Van Heusen from John F. Kennedy.
Photo courtesy Van Heusen Music Archives

High Hopes

It was almost inevitable that they should meet and become friends – the charismatic young Senator from Massachusetts and the king of the entertainment world. Both were at the top of their respective professions. Both were similarly adored. Both wanted what the other had – Sinatra desperately wanted the respect and acceptance of the aristocracy. Kennedy wanted the forbidden scandalous show business life. With the massive gravity of both of those stars, Van Heusen was sure to be drawn into the mix. And, through his work on Frank Capra and Sinatra's 1959 movie, *A Hole in the Head*, Van Heusen was brought into the Kennedy world in a very public way.

The film was a lighthearted tale of the love between a father and a son, and, like most Capra films, the heartstrings were tugged. It would have appeared unnatural for a father/son movie not to include the dispensation of fatherly advice. It would have been even more unnatural for a Sinatra movie not to have this advice dispensed via song. However, as production drew to a close, both Sinatra and Capra noticed this omission and called upon Van Heusen and Cahn to create such a number. Cahn astutely observed that such a song had already been written by Van Heusen, "Swingin' on a Star." Van Heusen assured Cahn it would be something different, and on the very last day of production, with no time to pre-record, Van Heusen played "High Hopes" for Sinatra and his son (played by Eddie Hodges) to sing. The orchestration was added during post-production. Much to Van Heusen's surprise, the song was a runaway hit for Sinatra and ended up winning the Academy Award for Best Song. However, in a striking parallel to "Swingin' on a Star," its success squashed another, perhaps better, song in the film. "Going My Way" was considered by many, including its star Rise Stevens, to be a superior song to "Swingin' on a Star." In "A Hole in the Head." it cannot be doubted that its companion song, "All My Tomorrows," was superior to "High Hopes." It is a tender, lyrical ballad with cleverly optimistic lyrics by Cahn. In those lyrics, Cahn effectively crystallized the message that Capra seemed to convey in all of this films – things might be bad today, but they will get better, and I will be there with you.

The success of "High Hopes" (and perhaps its Academy Award) was helped immeasurably by the star power of Sinatra and the political ascendancy of John F. Kennedy. Sinatra asked Van Heusen and Cahn if they had a song that could be used as a campaign song for Kennedy. Cahn replied that while they might not have a song, they have a title – "High Hopes." The two then went to work on altering the lyrics to fit a Kennedy campaign. The problem that they faced was that the word "Kennedy" did not fit into any of the cadences of the song, and worse, even the great Cahn could not muster a word that rhymed with "Kennedy." After hours of work, with no results, and Van Heusen telling Cahn in so many words, "OK, smart guy, get around this one," Cahn came up with the original idea of spelling Kennedy's name: "K-E-double N-E-D-Y. Jack's the nation's favorite guy. Everyone wants to back Jack. Jack is on the right track. 'Cause he's got High Hopes..." Sinatra recorded the song, and it was an important tool in the Kennedy campaign, establishing him as the favorite of the new, cooler generation, in sharp contrast to Nixon/Eisenhower's staid image.

As if rubbing elbows with Kennedy was not enough, "High Hopes" also introduced Van Heusen and Cahn to another icon of the American political world – Eleanor Roosevelt. Following the death of her husband, Mrs. Roosevelt appeared frequently on television to promote many of her causes. Van Heusen and Cahn suggested to Sinatra that she appear on his next television show to recite the original lyrics to "High Hopes." This would certainly enhance Kennedy's image, and also, perhaps, give an extra push to the commercial and Oscar success of "High Hopes." On February 15, 1960, Mrs. Roosevelt appeared on the Frank Sinatra-Timex show: Here's to the Ladies. Van Heusen recalls:

> Mrs. Roosevelt didn't realize she was reciting John Kennedy's campaign song. Her agent stayed around until after the show when Frank recorded the campaign words to the same tune. He (her agent) didn't say anything, and we often wondered if he was on to our mild trick...By the time Mrs. Roosevelt appeared on the air to recite "High Hopes," the campaign song had already hit the country and most people got the idea that she was plugging the candidate. Later, she endorsed Kennedy on her own so the preview we arranged of her endorsement was all to the good. And then

"High Hopes" won an Academy Award which sort of put gift wrapping on the whole package.

THIRTY-THREE

*Frank Sinatra, Nancy Sinatra, and Jimmy Van Heusen working on
the Frank Sinatra Timex television show.*
Photo courtesy Van Heusen Music Archives
Photographer: Bill Mark

You Never Had It So Good

As grim as the close of the 1940's looked for Van Heusen, that is how sunny things looked for Van Heusen as the 1960's opened. He had won two Academy Awards in three years. His principal patron was on top of the entertainment world, and soon, perhaps, on top of the political world, as well. And, the work was flowing in, seemingly without stop. A 1960 article from the *Los Angeles Examiner* claimed that the team earned $12,500 per song and $60,000 per musical score. The creative output of Van Heusen and Cahn in 1960 was nothing short of herculean. Seven movies, a television political satire for Bob Hope ("Potomac Madness"), and a venture into the world of television production.

Their production work began unassumingly enough – the first appearance of Elvis Presley after his return from the Army. Sinatra's team engineered the coup de gras, garnering the rights to the initial performance on Sinatra's Timex television show. Sammy and Jimmy produced the affair, lining up stars Sammy Davis Jr., Peter Lawford, Joey Bishop and Nancy Sinatra to join "The King." The show produced the largest ratings for any Sinatra television special, and more important, enabled two icons of very different worlds an opportunity to perform together. In matching tuxedos, Sinatra and Presley performed a duet of "Witchcraft" and "Love Me Tender." with each performer singing the hit of the other. Presley appeared awkward next to Sinatra, clearly uncomfortable "swinging" his singing, but performed no less admirably than when Sinatra turned his attention to songs in the rock idiom. There is no sense in determining who "won" this sole meeting of legends, but there is no mistaking who "won" financially – Sinatra, Timex and through their production efforts – Van Heusen and Cahn.

Of the films, the team was now writing for the top stars: *Wake Me When It's Over* (Ernie Kovacs), *Who Was That Lady?* (Tony Curtis, Janet Leigh, Dean Martin), *Surprise Package* (Yul Brynner, Mitzi Gaynor, Noel Coward), and *The World of Suzie Wong* (William Holden). Their five-song effort for the Marilyn Monroe picture *Let's Make Love* was the only bit of life in that ill-fated production. From all accounts, Monroe was not excited to make the picture, and male star Yves Montand was selected only after no fewer than six actors turned down the part. There were numerous script rewrites by Monroe's then-spouse, Arthur Miller, and the film ended up being a montage of cameos of stars trying to teach Montand the arts of comedy and singing. In this latter capacity, Bing Crosby was employed. He sampled for Montand the lovely "Incurably Romantic." This wonderful song has been wrongfully neglected, perhaps a victim of the fate of the picture. There have only been a handful of recordings, with Toni Tenille most recently essaying it in her album *Incurably Romantic*.

Van Heusen and Cahn were also tapped to provide two songs for what might be considered the ultimate Rat Pack movie – *Ocean's Eleven*. Ironically, though, there was no song for Sinatra. For Sammy Davis Jr., they wrote the undervalued "Eee-O Eleven," a swinging, bluesy number. The iconic musical moment of the picture, though, was the Dean Martin standard, "Ain't That a Kick in the Head?" Backed by Red Norvo, Martin's recording has endured as one of the most frequently heard Van Heusen songs in movies, having been featured in no fewer than 23 movies or television programs. It serves as an unofficial Rat Pack/Las Vegas anthem, perfectly synthesizing cool, insouciance, and above all, talent.

Critical success came by way of their work for Bing Crosby in his film, *High Time*, a comedy about a widower returning to college to complete his education. The team wrote two songs for the film, "Nobody's Perfect" and the classic "The Second Time Around." Nominated for an Academy Award, it was recorded, of course, by Crosby, but it was also the first single recorded by Sinatra on his newly formed Reprise label.[22]

The beautiful melody is anchored by a five-note figure, repeating a chromaticism. The figure appears throughout the song—serving as the introduction of the title of the song, closing the bridge (and dramatically reintroducing the 'A' section), and closing the song in a question-answer manner. It is a simple figure, and necessarily so. The song is about finding love again. The sentiment is simple, and the melody needed to suit that feeling: a mature person finding love again, knowing he need not peacock to impress. Van Heusen's

---

22   The "B" side to single was another Van Heusen and Cahn song, "Tina," written for Sinatra's youngest daughter, who was then 12. Van Heusen recalls the commission amusingly: "Many years later, 'Nancy' had other repercussions. When Little Tina got old enough, she said, 'Nancy has her song. Why can't I have mine?' First thing I know the Dago's saying, 'Chesssss-ter' and Tina got her song."

melody fits like a glove. As an aside, the lyric by Cahn always struck me as a bit cold. The character Crosby plays is a widower. One assumes that he loved his wife very much. Why then this lyric: "Makes you think, perhaps, that love, like youth/is wasted on the young?" Are we to think that Crosby's first love was "wasted?" The public did not seem to mind, and the song was a massive hit for Sinatra, earning Cahn and Van Heusen yet another Academy Award nomination. A consecutive Oscar was not to be, though, as the Academy voted to award the top prize to "Never On A Sunday."

THIRTY-FOUR

Bing Crosby's house (center) and Jimmy Van Heusen's house under construction (right) in Palm Springs California.
Photo courtesy of Van Heusen Photo archives.

Betrayed

Van Heusen's labors in 1960 might not have yielded an Oscar, but they, at least in part, yielded a prize much more valuable. Because the Kennedy election became Sinatra's principal cause, it also became the principal cause of his associates – Van Heusen included. He played at countless Democratic fundraisers, campaign appearances and other events associated with the Kennedy campaign. This is not to say that Van Heusen had any great belief in Kennedy's politics (or politics, in general). In fact, this participation in the Kennedy campaign was the only significant political activity in Van Heusen's life. Thus, it would appear that the loyalty was more to Sinatra than to Kennedy. If Van Heusen could help deliver this gift to his friend, it would be worth any number of Oscars, both on a professional and personal level.

When the results were tallied and John F. Kennedy defeated Richard M. Nixon in one of the closest elections in

American history, it fell to Frank Sinatra to coordinate the Pre-Inaugural Gala. It would be fair to say that Sinatra approached this responsibility with the greatest fervor. To him, it was the culmination of his professional career, acceptance at last in the highest strata of American society. The lengths to which Sinatra went to make this event beyond memorable were Gatsbyian in proportion. A sampling of the talent arranged by Sinatra to appear: Leonard Bernstein, Harry Belafonte, Milton Berle, Sir Laurence Olivier, Nat King Cole, Tony Curtis, Janet Leigh, Ella Fitzgerald, Gene Kelly, Frederic March, Ethel Merman, Jimmy Durante, Mahalia Jackson, Peter Lawford, Nelson Riddle, and (of course, Sinatra). When Olivier and Merman plead they had a prior commitment due to ongoing Broadway engagements, Sinatra was not deterred. He closed the shows, refunding ticket prices to disappointed theater-goers. The conclusion of the gala was Van Heusen and Cahn's "Ode to the Inauguration," sung by the entire impressive ensemble.

To all concerned, it appeared that Sinatra was on top of the world. Unfortunately, the hoped-for close union between Sinatra and the Kennedy White House was not to be. Banished due to his alleged ties with organized crime (a principal target of the Robert F. Kennedy-led Department of Justice), Sinatra found himself in an embarrassing predicament. The predicted cache was not available, and face needed to be saved.

At this time, Sinatra and Van Heusen were nearly inseparable, living only minutes apart in practically adjacent Palm Springs compounds. The story of his journey to this newest Palm Springs abode gives more insight into Van Heusen's politics than any work he did for Kennedy or friendship he might have enjoyed with Vice President Spiro T. Agnew. In the late 1950's, Van Heusen resided in the exclusive Thunderbird subdivision of Palm Springs. This was due largely to the request (expectation) of Crosby. However, once Crosby sold his residence, Van Heusen felt free to relocate. To be sure, the moment could not have come sooner, as Van Heusen grew tired of the obvious anti-Semitic sentiment expressed by the executives of the subdivision and the related country club:

> I hear the rumbles from the Jewish members
> (there were never very many) that some
> tremendously important Jewish people have been
> denied membership who applied... Suddenly, the
> thunderbolt struck. All the Jewish members
> resigned en masse. Too many slaps in the face and

obvious discrimination were too evident to be ignored. The group of Jews, joined by some of those who had been turned down for Thunderbird membership, went down the road a piece and built another country club – Tamarisk.

When this happened, I wanted to move, and before long Bing was looking to move. Not for the same reason, however, there was a new real estate development being opened in Palm Desert, and the Thunderbird Heights where our homes were located was getting crowded. The estate sites around us had sold rapidly and homes were beginning to surround us. I wasn't to leave because of the "anti" situation at the club, but Bing "wanted to be alone." Away from the squares, even if they all *were* rich.

The new real estate development was called "Silver Spur," and both he (Crosby) and Phil Silvers were given acreage at a very reasonable figure to induce them to build. Bing gave me three-and-a-half acres. In the meantime, the people running Thunderbird begged the stars who were members and even me, to frequent their dining room and their bar. If I threw a party, the gossip columns printed that fact, and certainly if I hung around Thunderbird, it was assumed that other desirable people would follow. Bing even encouraged me to dine there, and occasionally hosted a dinner party there. I was so irritated at the "anti" aspect of the operation I had to find some way to get even. This I would do by bringing with me almost every time a friend of mine from way back in Syracuse – Murray Wolfe, who's physical appearance was as Jewish as you could get. Furthermore, he was chubby, red cheeked and fat. Arriving for dinner, we would stand in the entrance way of the dining room and in a loud voice I would complain to the man at the door that there was supposed to be bar-b-qued Jew on the menu every Friday night, or whatever night it happened to be. Naturally, all eyes would turn towards the raised voices and would see me standing with the little fat Jew I said should be on the menu. They hated to see me coming, and I inhabited the social rooms no more than I felt necessary to comply with the Groaner's wishes. On one occasion, I managed to get Sinatra to go to the bar with me and join up with Phil Harris' party, but we were so abusive to the people around us that Harris was glad to see us leave.

When the time came to sell my home and it was no longer necessary to be a member of Thunderbird, I thought an elegant letter of resignation was in order. I conveyed my desire to the late and great writer Harry Kurnitz (screenwriter of Errol Flynn epics and Danny Kaye comedies), who naturally detested the club and all the petty principles they lived by, and he prepared my resignation. In this letter to the board of directors of Thunderbird, I said I wished to resign because of the birds that were flying over the golf course. They were Jewish birds and they were dropping Jewish shit on genuinely gentile grounds. These horrifying experiences and sacrilegious sights I could no longer tolerate and requested to be relieved of my social membership. The board of directors played it very straight and mailed me an acknowledging letter accepting my resignation. I had escaped from my second elegant country club that stood for everything I was against.

This episode is telling in its depiction of Van Heusen and politics. Despite his obvious anger at the anti-Semitism he felt was displayed by Thunderbird, he did not resign until Crosby sold his home in the area. He sniped at the edges with his displays at the dining room, but he could not bring himself to a final break until he received the appropriate blessings. There is an unsubstantiated story of Sinatra being so rage-fueled over an encounter with Desi Arnaz that he slashed a print that Norman Rockwell had painted of Van Heusen. When asked why Van Heusen would tolerate such behavior, he was purported to have replied, "Because he sings my songs, that's why. I'm a whore for my music." The exact circumstances of the episode are largely unimportant, as is the exact wording of Van Heusen's reply, but the sentiment is not altogether incorrect. Van Heusen tolerated much from associates, performers, and colleagues so long as they would advance or perpetuate his career. However, it is always important to temper this conclusion with the idea that Van Heusen and Sinatra were close friends, in addition to being musical collaborators. Personal loyalty combined with professional advantage was a combination that was nearly impregnable.

And that friendship would face its greatest test in the very near future.

On the parcel of property given to him by Crosby, Van Heusen constructed a spacious, new, state-of-the-art bachelor pad. It had a commanding view of the desert below, and nearly every amenity that could be desired. The only thing missing for Van Heusen was proper boarding stables for his newly acquired Tennessee Walking horses, which needed to be housed several miles away at nearby Shadow Mountain Stables. Van Heusen even acquired a new toy – a helicopter:

> Quite by accident, I went to an airport nearby in Rancho Mirage called "Desert Airpark," which was a private air strip which had the facilities of a hotel. It had a swimming pool and a restaurant and people would fly in in their own planes and put up at the hotel for weekends. (On) this particular visit, I noticed two helicopters parked on the grass airstrip, one white and the other mauve. Sitting and sunning nearby were the pilots, Al Bayer (then vice president in charge of sales for Hughes Aircraft) and his secretary, whom he had taught to fly helicopters, (and) who was a tall good-looking blonde named Rosemary Widengee. They were practicing an aerial ballet for two helicopters which they were planning to perform for the forthcoming Paris Airshow. Al took me for a ride and I was enchanted with this new Hughes machine called the 293A. I had had previous rides in rotor craft, but nothing as delightful as this trip. I immediately began to scheme and plan how I could get one of these for my own use. One of the few people who could afford a forty-thousand dollar machine, such as

this, was living only a skip and a jump away, and his name was Frank Sinatra.

After Al had flown me around for a while, I told him to take me to visit FS. I knew at the moment he was sitting outside of his house with quite a few guests among which were Ruby Rubirosa and his wife. I persuaded Al Bayer to land in front of the house of Sinatra which is the seventeenth fairway of Tamarisk Country Club. This we did with great flourish, and surprised the assemblage. Sinatra was also quite surprised to see a helicopter suddenly planted in front of his casa, and I knew it would give him ideas of how handy it would be to own such a machine and have it based in your backyard.

When we landed, I told Bayer to keep it running and I climbed out and walked towards the Italian singer and wiggled my forefinger in the motion that says "come hither." He crouched low as he passed under the main rotor of the machine and took a seat with Bayer. Bayer revved up the whirlybird and made a graceful take-off backwards, a maneuver which thrilled the people watching. Bayer proceeded to give Sinatra a demonstration ride in the helicopter and finally brought him back and deposited him, again with all the grace of a swan, on the seventeenth fairway in front of his house. Sinatra was enchanted, as I was hoping he would be. Within days, he had put in an order for his own specially made helicopter, the 239A model, with his own color scheme, the orange and black motif he's addicted to, and his own choice of upholstery.

Van Heusen soon became an FAA approved helicopter pilot, and he and Sinatra were swooping through the nearby valley, terrorizing and captivating the residents. Sinatra had a helipad constructed on his property, and Van Heusen was personally piloting Sinatra's many guests around for rides. Because the particular model purchased was one of the noisiest helicopters made, Van Heusen suggested to Sinatra that it might be better to use the Desert Airpark for departures, lest the neighbors be offended. According to Van Heusen, Sinatra's response was "The hell with them." The neighbors did, in fact, take exception and eventually took Sinatra to court over the whole incident:

> The upshot of the whole travesty was that Sinatra was ordered to cease and desist from annoying his neighbors and to paint a large X over his heliport. The X, in fly talk, means "closed." The helicopter was kept at other places from then on and the

large white X was painted on the port. However, since there is no law that says you cannot land a helicopter on your own property, every once in a while Sinatra would ask me to get the chopper and make a landing on the heliport, even with the X painted on it. This I did many times, and without fail, the police would come and take my identification, my pilots license number, and ask me if I had just landed the chopper at the heliport. I would always reply in the affirmative, and the police would always nod, and then make their report. I expected to be arrested, but it was explained to me that I had not violated any laws, and they were just checking up on the nuisance and noise situation. To this day, (1969) the heliport stands in all its majesty, and at night all lighted up with the white X prominently displayed.

The wonderful new home that Van Heusen had built was to become the flashpoint for the only real tension in his relationship with Sinatra. Because of the significant contributions Sinatra made to the Kennedy campaign, it was generally assumed that Kennedy would use Sinatra's luxurious home for western visits. Whether or not it would serve as a "Western White House," as Sinatra believed, was another matter. The story of Kennedy's snub of Sinatra has been told numerous times. For Kennedy's initial visit of his presidency to the West Coast, he opted to stay not with Sinatra, but rather with Bing Crosby. Doubling the sting was that Crosby was a Republican. Public statements were made about the security advantages Crosby's home afforded, but it was clear to most that Kennedy was distancing himself from Sinatra due to his purported affiliations with those involved with organized crime. In most accounts of this affair, Robert Kennedy is cast as the villain. (However, as an aside, the roles of hero and villain are somewhat unfair. Politics is blood sport, and the naiveté of people like Sinatra and Van Heusen regarding its rules is always surprising, given the ruthless manner in which they pursued their career goals.) Van Heusen believes the true culprit was not Robert Kennedy, but rather Peter Lawford.

Van Heusen felt that Lawford orchestrated the Kennedy snub as revenge for a Sinatra slight in the mid-1940's, where Sinatra's disenchantment with Lawford's ways (particularly his parsimony), led him to expel him from his social circle and perhaps opportunities for better film roles. Van Heusen wrote, "Lawford, knowing that FS had gone to all the expense and effort to put up the President, and really had his heart set on entertaining him, collared Bobby Kennedy and given him a talk that made the attorney general adamant on the subject. Under Lawford's tutelage and telling of tall tales, Bobby put his foot down. Lawford had gotten his revenge, and it made me sick to my stomach to look at him."

With all due respect, the idea of Peter Lawford dictating to Bobby Kennedy or otherwise telling him things he did not know about prospective hosts for the President is laughable. Lawford might have been the easier target, and certainly it is likely did nothing to lobby for his friend's cause, but he simply did not possess anywhere near the power to wield that manner of influence. And, while the idea of the Sinatra insult was offensive to Van Heusen, the next edict from Washington was terrifying:

> The houses they wanted were Bing Crosby and mine. I said that it was impossible, because I wouldn't be a part of embarrassing Sinatra. I then asked what was wrong with all the other houses I had suggested... The perfect spot, according to the guardians of the great, was the Crosby and Van Heusen houses which were backed up against a mountain range, far away from a main road, and even farther from other houses. It was the perfectly secure arrangement and could be easily

guarded and patrolled, and with no one living nearby, any stranger could be spotted instantly...The other phone calls that came in were pointed in one direction – I would be unpatriotic to deny this compound to our Commander-in-Chief, and that I should obtain the use of the Crosby house on the same patriotic basis. The pressure was deftly applied and before long I found myself making a phone call to Bing Crosby in Mexico. After three days of trying to find him he called me back, and I told him what was up. I said that his casa was needed for the top Democrat in the country who wanted to visit the desert and also use my house. He questioned me about which Democrat and I finally had to say it was the President, and although he was a Republican, he was simply obeying a command from our Commander-in-Chief, and that it was our duty to obey.

He was more than a little reluctant, but (he) finally said he would make a call and give instructions to give me the key and also give orders to some people to clean up the place... I disappeared by taking a trip to New York and was still fuming about the lack of consideration for my friend. When calls came to me from the White House from Lawford, I burned their ears with what I thought of the treatment. I made up my mind that Lawford was a creep that I would have to stop talking to. Whatever he had to say to me, from then on, he communicated through his agent Milt Ebbins.

While I was in New York, and more or less waiting for the Kennedy party to finish with my house, I received a call from the President, who told me he was sitting in front of the pool and having a wonderful time and wanted to say thanks. I replied that I was glad to be of service, but wanted to say, really, *why doesn't someone call Sinatra?* How the whole group could enter the area where their friend Sinatra was well known and waiting and never utter a word to him on the phone or write a note was an effrontery and a slight that I could not fathom or understand. But, I didn't have the guts, and simply said goodbye and proceeded to drink a couple of martinis and reflect on how ungrateful and short-memoried are the politicians.

Within a few days I was back at my house and cleaning out the mess that had been left by the swinging presidential party. It was quite something, and obviously there had been plenty of partying. In one of my bedrooms, my

housekeeper discovered a very expensive custom
made brassiere and a can of Fleet's Enema.
Whichever dame wore this expensive underwear
had a bust that was considerable. I wrapped both
things, the brassiere and the Fleet's Enema, and
sent them to the Lawford's with a note that read,
'Whomever left these things behind has a great
pair of tits but unfortunately can't shit.'

Kennedy would occupy Van Heusen's residence twice
more during his presidency. Van Heusen acquiesced each time,
all the while swallowing hard to permit this potential strain on
his relationship with Sinatra. Of course, Van Heusen had
plenty of cover – it was a presidential command, and Sinatra
certainly respected his patriotism, and more significantly,
Sinatra still respected, admired, and liked the President. It
might have been easier for Sinatra to overlook what occurred
as being a Lawford-led grudge or the machination of Bobby
Kennedy, rather than to assign any guilt to John F. Kennedy.
Such an admission would have been crushing, and an
acknowledgment that the hippest man in the world was played
like a fiddle. By perpetuating the "Lawford-as-villain"
narrative, Van Heusen might have been helping his old friend
save face. As such, the only resistance Van Heusen gave to the

government for the subsequent visits was that Peter Lawford was not permitted in either Crosby's or his home. To this demand, the President agreed without hesitation.

Beyond the usage of the residence, there was little further contact between Van Heusen and the White House – not that he expected (or desired) any. In 1962, Van Heusen was invited to a luncheon in the White House to honor the president of Bolivia. He accepted only after he received express approval from Sinatra, who thought that perhaps Van Heusen's invitation was a pretense to tell him something important, i.e., apologize or otherwise inquire, albeit indirectly, about Sinatra. At the luncheon, Van Heusen was greeted by General Ted Clifton, the President's military aide, who informed Van Heusen that he would be seated with Norman Thomas, a Socialist and a six-time candidate for the presidency. When Mr. Thomas inquired as to why he would be invited to such a function, Van Heusen got no small charge out of surprising him by responding that his presence was requested personally by the president of Bolivia: "He turned and looked at me with eyes that practically said, 'Who the hell is this bum?' But I had been told by General Clifton that in Bolivia, Thomas was a hero." After the luncheon festivities, President Kennedy made his way to Van Heusen, greeted him and asked him about his house, which, at that point had been placed on the market for sale. There were a few further pleasantries, and then he excused himself. Not one word was spoken about Sinatra, and with a feeling of disgust, Van Heusen departed the White House.

Van Heusen's brush with power left a bitter taste in his mouth. His respect for Kennedy diminished greatly and it is certain that he felt the pangs of disappointment when this political idol showed his feet of clay. While Van Heusen's earliest support of Kennedy was through Sinatra, it was clear he felt strongly toward Kennedy in his own right: "I must say that the personality and fantastic likeability of the Senator conquered us all. We were all devoted workers, followers of Sinatra, yes, but ready to climb mountains or whatever if necessary for Jack Kennedy." In any event, in the strange world of Van Heusen and his companions, what would have been the event of a lifetime for most people, was a cause of disillusionment and bitterness. He writes of the end:

All that remained of the Kennedy visits and associations was a telephone, strangely enough. One night some of the staff and some of the Secret

Service were dining in a Palm Springs restaurant and spotted me as I walked by. They were always grateful for the booze and the full larder I provided for each visit and wanted to reciprocate in some way. What can we do for you, they said, and facetiously I remarked, 'Let me have the Hot Line to Moscow.' Later that night I walked in Sinatra's house and he said that the Kennedy staff was looking all over for me and wanted me immediately at my house, on a matter of importance. I rushed up to my house (the President had just left) and there were the guys with three telephone instruments. The actual instrument that was attached to the Hot Line to Moscow was a red, white and blue phone with a picture of the White House in the middle. They had requisitioned it from the Signal Corps as the technicians were ripping out the telephone installations and were making a present of it to me. It was the actual phone that had been connected to the line to Moscow during the visit, and although I was kidding when I had made the crack that I wanted it, when I saw it I accepted it eagerly. I knew what I wanted to do with it. I wanted to give it to Sinatra, and sometime later I did so, and it was installed in a room in his house known as the Kennedy Room, the room where he slept on his visits there.

THIRTY-FIVE

Jimmy Van Heusen and Frank Sinatra.
Courtesy of Getty Images

Boys' Night Out

The public rift with Kennedy was a significant blow to Sinatra. His publicity team sought to repair any damage to his image by planning a massive worldwide tour, whose principal benefit would be various charities. Sinatra would be presented as a figure belonging not simply to the United States, but to the world. This tour would eventually occur in 1962 and Van Heusen would accompany Sinatra throughout that trip. However, before this august and proper tour, Sinatra had a hankering to enjoy the world "his way." Accompanying him would only be two people – his trusted valet, George Jacobs, and Jimmy Van Heusen. The following are excerpts of Van Heusen's travelogue from that once-in-a-lifetime journey:

> Life was not always the labor of writing, plugging, publishing songs and campaigns of publicity to win the Academy Award if the song was in the picture, sometimes life was just plain fun, frolic,

and foolishness. So it was with Sinatra. He occasionally took off from performing, or punching the press to simply lay himself out in the sun or if he had the wanderlust, he'd travel. How he and I got involved in taking a trip around the world together with only his combination valet, butler, chauffeur, cook – George Jacobs as our companion, I can't recall, but 'round the world we went. Before we departed, I was presented with two packages of one hundred dollar bills around an inch thick each, and was instructed to carry them in my inside pocket. The skinny singer put two similar packages in his inside pockets, and also an airline travel credit card to pay for the tickets.

There had been talk of Sinatra making a tour of certain cities around the world to give concerts, the proceeds of which would remain in that particular country and be used for needy children. This idea had caught his fancy and the year following our slightly crazy encirclement of the globe, he did go around the world and give those very concerts and raised millions for needy children in many more cities and countries than we visited on the first trip as plain and simple drunks. Perhaps this was an exploratory trip to set up the later one... although I don't think the later trip was definitely set in his mind at the time. Our odyssey was limited to laughs, and lots of liquor. In any event, we found ourselves at the Los Angeles airport one evening being bid farewell by a small group, one of which was a disc jockey by the name of Johnny Grant. We were to go directly to Tokyo, if I remember correctly, because I know we didn't stop at the Hawaiian Islands or Alaska.

Arrangements had been made for us by a woman friend of Shirley MacLaine's called Kay Kamori, who was a newspaperwoman in Tokyo and was more or less the Louella Parsons of Japan with hundreds of syndicated columns to her credit, and she wrote for the movie dan magazines, as well. Shirley said she would be invaluable to us and would show us Japan as no one else would see it. Also, a friend of Sinatra's was alerted who was an American-born Japanese, but who lived and worked in Tokyo, and his name was Jimmy Fugasaki.

As it turned out, we needed no one and spent almost every evening in a night club in Tokyo called Mama Cherry's, which had dozens and dozens of tall pretty Japanese girls who would come and drink with you, dance with you, and after the ball was over, for enough money, go home with you.

We arrived in Tokyo with somewhat of a letdown, caused by the wearing off of the whiskey, and sitting up all night, and getting practically no sleep. Foggy though we were, the mass of details and handling of customs was no chore because we let George do all the work. He took the work out of the whole trip and this permitted the two of us to concentrate on being drunk and disorderly. Sure enough, out of the crowd came a face, and a figure dressed in the legitimate Japanese fashion, that bowed almost to the ground several times and said welcome.

It was Shirley McLaine's friend, Kay Kamori, and she spoke pretty good English. She was making enthusiastic gestures and laying out verbal plans for our every minute in Tokyo. First of all, we should go to a typical Japanese restaurant for lunch, and she had the perfect place for us. After customs and very little crowding for autographs from Sinatra, we were on our way in a taxicab to the hotel, the Imperial, and after checking in, on our way again to this, as she said, typical Japanese dining place. The quarters of the Imperial, needless to say, were lavish and were double suites, the second one being for George. At the restaurant, we were met by other people, and at first I thought it was a causal encounter, but gradually it dawned on me that my Italian friend was being taken advantage of. To begin with, there was a cameraman with several cameras, and a lone broad, Japanese style, not terribly attractive but obviously involved in show business or the movie business and merely there waiting to pose with Frank Sinatra. After many shots with her all sorts of people, and the raw fish luncheon over without my throwing up, Sinatra was asked to take an inspection of the gardens. We hadn't walked far when we came upon a typical set-up that any photographer would make when he is taking some important color shot. There was a white sheet suspended from poles in the middle of the garden and the girl stood in front of it and beckoned to Frank.

He now knew that whole afternoon was a bunch of bullshit and we were being used for the movie rags Kay Kamori worked for, and with a little questioning, I discovered that this little bit in front of the sheet was for the front cover of one of them. F.S., instead of belting a couple of the idiots, was smiling and laughing at the thought that we had been such suckers. He carried it off good-naturedly, although I was steaming, until we returned to the hotel, and then naturally, we both decided that whenever the broad in the kimono called, Kay Kamori, that is, we would not respond. She had had us once, but we would not be suckers for the rest of the trip. I used to have to speak to her on the phone the thousands of times she called and gave all sorts of ridiculous excuses for his unavailability. I don't believe she really thought he welcomed all that posing and photographing. Perhaps in the intervening years, something dawned on her. The adventure continued with other places around the world. After about two weeks of interesting wandering about Hong Kong, we got on a Pan American airplane bound for Beirut, Lebanon, with a stop and change of planes in Bangkok. I had a series of persuasive talks with Frank that resulted in our over-flying India. It was warm and I knew the smell and heat of Bombay or any other Indian city would be unbearable. Furthermore, I hated the idea of watching people die in the streets.

The trip to Bangkok was a rough and extremely bumpy one, and although I got on the aircraft drunk and proceeded to fall asleep the whole trip, Sinatra was terrified. Evidently, the gyrations that the plane was making were extreme, and many people were visibly frightened and throwing up, and before we arrived, Sinatra was punching me and waking me up. He said that if we ever arrived in Bangkok, he would not go an inch further with these pilots or on this airline because the flight thus far had been extremely dangerous.

So, when we finally landed in Bangkok, he refused to board the next aircraft which was to take us to Beirut. He insisted that I go to the Pan Am flight offices there and look at the weather maps and have a talk with the new crew, and tell them that we were not going on the next leg of the trip. With some difficulty, I found a room that had three weather maps on the wall and some idiot standing guard. It was hot, smelly, and giant bugs were everywhere, and I was recovering from being quite loaded. Very sickishly, I read the weather maps and it was obvious that the pilots of the first flight had skirted a very bad and rough weather front. Perhaps the pilots had dates with girls in Bangkok that night and didn't want to waste the time to go around that big blob of bad weather that was apparent on the map. They could have avoided the rough murderous weather by going out and around it and it was obvious as I read the maps. They chose to fly the edge of it, and after an hour went by and there were no signs of the star getting aboard the new flight, the Pan American head personnel came looking for us. He stated flatly that it was too dangerous to fly and would not get back in the plane under any circumstances.

Since we had no visa for Thailand or Bangkok, we presented quite a problem to the bewildered Pan Am employees. They couldn't leave us there, and he consistently refused to get into the airplane. The continuing flight was held up for two or three hours and they wound up begging Mr. Sinatra to go aboard. I joined in trying to persuade him and pointed to the weather map and showed him how our next leg could be taken without suffering any turbulence if the new crew stayed far away from the bad weather front. Finally, the whole crew of the new flight got off from their places in the cockpit and walked into the terminal and put on a plea with the superstar. They promised they would not get into any of the weather we had experienced on the first leg and conceded that the pilot of the first leg was in a terrible hurry to fly so near to that big mass of bad weather. Frank said they should be fired and everyone agreed. With lots and lots of promises for a perfectly smooth flight on the part of the new crew, Mr. Sinatra finally relented and slowly strolled up the ramp of the new airplane, and soon we were airborne.

It was quite a scene in the airport at Bangkok and the Pan American people were completely bewildered, and of course, I didn't help things too much by buying a large curved sword and hanging it around my neck and sometimes waving it in the breeze. I was still slightly stoned, and the experience on the ground drove me to further libation to keep my courage up.

We arrived in Beirut, Lebanon, and the days there were spent on the beach and with some people who constantly wanted to give Sinatra parties and show him off to their friends. We managed to duck the boring business mostly and it was pleasant. Finally, we were escorted to the airport by about twenty people for our departure from Lebanon. As we were strolling down the fairly large hallway to the airline counter, I noticed a swarthy gent from the news stand wiggling his finger at me. Why would he pick me out of all those twenty people I don't know. Probably because I look like what I am, a square from Syracuse. Anyways, when it was obvious that the man was motioning to me and me only, I walked over to this counter as the others went to the airline check-in. What did the man want? He said, 'Do you want to buy some dirty books?' I couldn't resist it. I started to read and of course they were the filthiest and I would up buying about eight.

Our trip around the world was made in just a few very large jumps and the next leg of our journey was to Frankfurt and to West Berlin. Previously, when we had seen William Holden in the States, he had told us that he would be making a picture in West Berlin by the time we went around the globe, and we promised to visit him. The picture was called *The Counterfeit Traitor* and the location was West Berlin. At the moment of our arrival and the first thing we did upon our arrival in West Berlin was to seek out the set of the picture and our friend Holden. We found them working in the street somewhere and our presence stopped shooting and made the director and producers, Perlberg and Seaton, slightly miffed. Holden was delighted and took us into his dressing room, which was a trailer, and served us dry martinis. He had them made up in a giant coffee urn and whenever he needed a bracer he just turned a spigot. We later found out that he arrived in the morning about eight AM for shooting and was turning the spigot for his martinis from morning until late afternoon. He must have been half-stoned most of the time but he never fluffed a line in a scene and always knew the script and also everybody else's lines also. This certainly shows that some people can do and still drink.

Every night during our stay in West Berlin we had dinner with our friend Holden, and if we didn't visit a hook-shop, which I would always request, we would wind up in a little night club that was built like a Pullman railway car...that is, long and narrow. There we would have our nightcaps, and on weekends there was a little music combo playing for the guests. The first visit was a slightly drunk one, and as Sinatra and I heard the sounds from the combo, we both decided that the bass player was the most out of tune. The singer suggested that I have a conference with him and perhaps give him enough money to persuade him to go home. This I did, and within minutes the bass player put his bass fiddle aside and waltzed out of the joint. Now we were listening to a piano player, drummer and clarinet player. Sinatra suggested that the drummer should go next. I walked over to him and made a deal for him to quit for the night, and although he departed very soon afterwards, the quality of the music didn't improve. Sinatra told me to get rid of the clarinet player, and after this was accomplished, the pianist was playing alone. Of course, our friends were laughing it up as they saw the orchestra diminish. Last, but not least, and probably the most awful of the group was the piano player, and so I bought him off, and he departed. The management didn't quite know why these people were departing so suddenly and maybe he was never told. In any event, since there was now no music at all, I wound up playing and everybody was happy.

At my behest, and because I thought we should see the hooker side of West Berlin, the people connected with the picture came up with the address of the best whorehouse in the area. Naturally, after dinner one night, the producer, Holden, Sinatra and I were knocking on the door of the elite establishment. It was located on the fourth floor of what looked like a swanky apartment building, and when we got inside, I spotted a hat rack and because I always wear a hat (my bald head gets cold), [and] I hung up my straw hat. It was June and the straw hat was not uncalled for. There in the middle of the main room, probably a living room, rested my hat, and since I was the only one of the boys imbibing of the beauties, almost immediately I disappeared with three of them into a large bedroom with a giant size bed. While in the midst of my pleasures I heard the shouts and commotion of a near riot in the adjoining room, and it was such a sounding ruckus that all my dames ceased operations and put their clothes on. They rushed out of the bedroom, in a hell of a hurry, to see what was happening and why all the screaming, and I followed with my pants half on and carrying my shirt and coat. I was in complete disarray as I reached the adjoining room to spot the spectacle of my straw hat ablaze on the hat rack. What had happened was that Sinatra was lighting his cigarette with his cigarette lighter while walking past the hat rack and could not resist the urge to also set fire to my sombrero. The resulting fire scared the hell out of the madam and all of the surrounding hookers, and they called the police and fire department. Although a couple of pans full of water extinguished the conflagration, the wrath of the assembled sirens could not be quelled. I never did get completely dressed and only a miracle and fast talking kept us from being arrested. I was more worried about being assaulted by a big bunch of brawny broads than anything else, as I trailed my great pals out of the place. We also had to pay for what was a lot of undelivered merchandise.

When it came time for us to continue our wanderings and take off for London, a change in plans took place because of a telephone call. For some reason or another FS talked to Sammy Davis, Jr., in London and told him of our impending arrival and he leaked the fact to the press. Some other kind soul in London called and said that the press was lying in wait for us, and ready to drive the master crazy by dogging his footsteps. The London press was at that time pretty rough on Sinatra and we had planned to sneak in silently, but now that Davis had opened his mouth and exposed us, we immediately changed our plans and embarked for New York. I regretted not making it to dear old Blighty and cutting short our journey, but under the circumstances, it was the only sensible thing to do. We bid goodbye to all the people connected with the picture Holden was making, and their relief at the news of our impending departure was visible on their faces. We had disrupted the whole movie by keeping the star out all night, and the producer had actually begged me quietly to please leave town. He tried to bribe me with all sorts of promises because Holden was showing up with circles under the bags of his eyes. He was on time, but the cameraman was having trouble photographing around the signs of dissipation and lack of sleep. They were delighted with our departure.

Thus ended our trip around the world. Very large jumps on each leg of the airline map but nevertheless around the globe in much less than eighty days. Closer to a month and a week.

THIRTY-SIX

Jimmy Van Heusen and Sammy Cahn
Photo Courtesy Van Heusen Photo Archives

Where Love Has Gone

The shots that ended the life of President John F. Kennedy in late November, 1963, can fairly be said to have ended the dominance of Frank Sinatra and his music as a trendsetter of American popular culture. The generation that had fought the Second World War was entering its early '40's, and its children were now entering adolescence. Rebellion was natural. Their innocence, purchased with the blood of their parents' generation, was shattered with the assassination of their president. It would further be eroded by the escalating conflict in Vietnam, and ultimately vanish into full-fledged cynicism with the assassinations of Robert F. Kennedy and Martin Luther King, Jr., and the scandals of the Nixon administration. Sinatra's music would be seen as a relic of another time, and its proponents would be marginalized by the changing cultural mores, epitomized by the emergence of rock and roll. Van Heusen weathered one such sea of change in the immediate postwar '40's by embracing Sinatra. There would be no such lifeline in the mid to late '60's. It would be unfair to say that Sinatra and Van Heusen did not have triumphs following the Kennedy assassination. A fourth Academy Award and three more nominations would be earned by Van Heusen. Sinatra would record landmark albums such as *The Concert Sinatra*, *September of My Years,* and two collaborations with Antonio Carlos Jobim. The popular magic, however, was gone.

There were signs that, even before the death of Kennedy, that the ring-a-ding-ding era was ending. Despite his playboy persona, Kennedy was a serious person, elected as a rejection of the Eisenhower-era mundanity. While Sinatra and his associates would be identified with and support the social causes of the day, his music and the popularity of his insouciance were fading. The 1962 song "The Look of Love" is somewhat emblematic of the team's starting to misjudge the popular consciousness. Written as a swinging tune for a Sinatra single, it served its purpose. However, in 1967, Burt Bacharach and Hal David wrote a tune with the same name that was immensely popular. Mark Steyn wrote that Sammy Cahn felt the Bacharach/David effort was superior, or at least had taken more from the concept of "The Look of Love." People wanted to see "the look of love in your eyes" rather than a "fat man eating dinner."

That same year also saw a similar misfire. Ten years earlier, the Hope/Crosby/Paramount team released arguably the weakest entry of the "Road" series – *Road to Bali*. The team looked tired, and the music was decidedly uninspired. (There is the brief respite of "To See You Is To Love You.") The series appeared to have run its course, and to be sure, had been in decline. Apparently rejuvenated, Hope and Crosby decided to have one last run at the genre in 1962 with *The Road to Hong Kong*. There were, of course, some differences. There would no longer be the distinctive Paramount logo introducing the film. This version would be released by United Artists – ergo, the slight title change from "Road to" to "*The* Road to." Burke, of course, would be replaced by Cahn. Crosby, apparently, did not want to involve Dorothy Lamour in the project, due to her age, but Hope insisted upon her participation. Apparently, the idea of a 59-year-old Crosby pitching to a 29-year-old Joan Collins was not too far beyond the realm of possibility. The film is filled with self-deprecating humor, references to previous films and the standard tearing down of the "fourth wall." There are also cameos aplenty – David Niven, Peter Sellers, Sinatra, and Martin. However, it was apparent that the formula had lost its spark. An online consumer review of the film puts it aptly, saying that the film was made as a thank you to the audience, a more fitting conclusion to the series than *Road to Bali*.

For his part, Sammy Cahn did an exceptional job of writing lyrics in his style, but it bowed sufficiently to Burke. Even the titles harken back to those halcyon days of the early 1940s: "The Road to Hong Kong," "Warmer Than a Whisper," "Let's Not Be Sensible," and "Teamwork." Van Heusen's songs were well-suited to the occasion, but lacked a certain spark. "Let's Not Be Sensible" was a serviceable romantic number, and "Warmer Than a Whisper" is certainly the most complex number given to Lamour to sing – in many ways, breaking one of his own cardinal rules for writing for Crosby movies! The nuanced melody might have been better served in Crosby's hands, but that is not certain. The melody meanders, and unlike other such Van Heusen melodies, does not ever appear to find its way. "Teamwork" and "Road to Hong Kong" were, necessarily, recycled from previous efforts.

In a chilling portent, 1962 was the first year since 1956 that the team did not earn an Academy Award nomination.[23]

---

[23]   That year, Van Heusen and Cahn also wrote the title song to the film "Boys Night Out." Patti Page had a Billboard hit with the number, and Sinatra recorded a humdinger of an arrangement of it in 1962. Sinatra also recorded the 1962 Van Heusen/Cahn number, "California," extolling the virtues of the Golden State. It is one of Van Heusen's prettiest melodies, and its inclusion in recent Sinatra folios has given the song much-deserved exposure.

THIRTY-SEVEN

Four Oscars and an Emmy

Courtesy of Van Heusen Photo Archives

Call Me Irresponsible

In 1963, Van Heusen and Cahn contributed songs to four motion pictures. A Debbie Reynolds' vehicle, *My Six Loves* – not as raunchy as the title might imply – featured "It's a Darn Good Thing." Van Heusen and Cahn also wrote the catchy, swinging title song for the Jack Lemmon sexscapade *Under the Yum Yum Tree*. For Sinatra, the team wrote the title song for *Come Blow Your Horn*. All three of these songs were arguably the same, with the finest of the efforts reserved for Sinatra. More alarming, it seemed that the team was moving into a period of a creative slump. Producers asked for a title song, the team got together, pressed a button, and a "Cahn and Van Heusen" song appeared. It was no coincidence that their landmark effort from 1963 was, in fact, not written that year, but several years earlier – and almost never heard at all.

It was 1956. Van Heusen and Cahn were at the start of their collaboration, each probably still better identified with their previous collaborator than with each other. Cahn received a telephone call from his agent that he and Van Heusen were requested to provide songs for a new picture to star Fred Astaire. The film was *Papa's Delicate Condition*. Following their review of the script, Cahn noticed that the word "irresponsible" crept up throughout it. The character was irresponsible, his actions were irresponsible, and so forth. As Van Heusen began exposing the tune, Cahn noted the title, "Call Me Irresponsible," and the song was written that same evening. Cahn's recollection of the writing of the song in an interview for a Syracuse paper in 1986 is a testament to Van Heusen's ability to create seemingly out of thin air:

> I came over to his house and he was lying on the couch. I used to call him the great couch composer. I said, 'What do you think about this for a song, and I threw out some words: 'Call me irresponsible, call me unreliable, throw in undependable too...' He thought about it for a minute; then he got up and went over to the piano and tapped out that tune.

The next day the team auditioned the song for Astaire, who declared it one of the best songs he had ever heard. This, of course, is no small praise, given the past composers who plied their wares for Astaire – men with names like Kern, Berlin and Gershwin. And, even though Astaire would not perform the song on-screen, his imprint is unmistakable. Van Heusen's melody practically is choreography. Written in cut time, the two half-notes opening the refrain call to mind Astaire gliding across the floor. (Note a similar rhythmic figure in "Cheek to Cheek.") The chromatic figure following could easily frame Astaire's impossibly smooth footwork. Cahn's lyrics, while perhaps a bit wordy, were perfect for the conversational Astaire style. Van Heusen's melody, though, is incredibly complex and difficult to sing. It is by far the most sophisticated use of chromaticism Van Heusen attempted, and it demands full attention from the singer, lest he wonder off into a strange and distant key signature. The song is a multi-dimensional structure, but it could not have been constructed any other way.

Astaire would hear another song by Van Heusen and Cahn. Cahn would humbly describe it as the ultimate Astaire song. It is hard to argue the point. "Walking Happy" was supposed to depict the walk one enjoys after having just the right amount of alcohol. Like "Call Me Irresponsible," it is difficult not to imagine the song without picturing it choreographed for Astaire. The melody is jaunty and locomotive. It struts without being pretentious, and it is graceful without being effete.

Unfortunately for Cahn, Van Heusen (and to a lesser extent, Astaire), the 1956 project was abandoned. The movie concept was resurrected in 1962, but the movie would star not Astaire, but Jackie Gleason. Worse, all of the songs were eliminated. This sent Cahn into near apoplexy, as the work that they produced for the original concept was top rate, and to be sure, some degree ahead of what the team was currently writing. At a meeting with the studio heads, Van Heusen and Cahn (but mainly Cahn) convinced the studio to retain "Call Me Irresponsible" and "Walking Happy." In the end, though, only "Call Me Irresponsible" would remain. The studio felt that "Walking Happy" slowed the action of the film. The movie was a critical and box office disappointment, with its only bright spot being "Call Me Irresponsible." Both Sinatra and Jack Jones had hit recordings of the song, and it was nominated for an Academy Award for Best Original Song in 1963. Neither Cahn nor Van Heusen gave it much chance of winning, as it was against "More," the runaway hit from the

Italian documentary *Mondo Cane*. Van Heusen approvingly referred to "More" as an "epidemic." But, when the envelope was opened, the names of Jimmy Van Heusen and Sammy Cahn were heard for a third time together – it would be the fourth award for each man. Cahn did not attend the ceremony, sending his daughter in his stead. Van Heusen, according to Cahn, was handling things in his usual manner – with a flask, away from the crowd. After calling Cahn and being told by Cahn to get back into the theater, he walked to the stage with Laurie Cahn. Ms. Cahn sweetly and succinctly told the audience, "Thank you for my father." Never one to miss a moment, Van Heusen then thanked his father, Arthur Babcock. He then walked off into the evening. It would be the last time either man would ascend the Academy Awards stage as an award winner.

THIRTY-EIGHT

Q: What comes first, the music or the lyrics?
A: The Phone Call.
Photo Courtesy Van Heusen Photo Archives

Style

Work continued apace for the team. They were the "grand old men" of the movies, and were the first choice of producers for title songs or other musical contributions to the films. The quality was still fading. *Honeymoon Hotel* and *The Pleasure Seekers* each had multiple contributions, but the only number remotely recommendable is "Love is Oh So Easy" from *Honeymoon Hotel*. There were still flashes of greatness. "Where Love Has Gone" was written as a title song. It finds Van Heusen returning to the form of "All the Way" and "To Love and Be Loved." The melody is wonderfully textured, full of dramatic intervals, purposefully guided. It was rightfully awarded an Oscar nomination in 1964.

The year 1964 would mark another end for the team – the end of their cinematic relationship with Frank Sinatra. Sinatra was producing a movie "updating" the Robin Hood legend to 1920's Chicago, *Robin and the 7 Hoods*. It would provide the Rat Pack with one last hurrah, as roles were immediately found for Sammy Davis, Jr., and Dean Martin. In a clear sign that the sting of the Kennedy fiasco was not yet behind Sinatra, Peter Lawford, originally cast, was replaced by Bing Crosby. However, even had Kennedy made Sinatra the Secretary of State, it would have been the correct casting call. Naturally, Sinatra turned to Van Heusen and Cahn to create a full musical score, as it was apparent that this was to be a full-blown movie musical. Original movie musicals were something of a rarity in the mid-1960's, as Hollywood turned its finances to proven successes on Broadway. Here, of course, the debate can be joined as to whether movies starring Elvis or the Beatles can fairly be considered musicals. If so, they are a decidedly different animal than "classic" Hollywood musicals, such as *Gigi*, *Seven Brides for Seven Brothers*, or *Singing in the Rain*. *Robin and the 7 Hoods* was to be a bow to the latter, less seen production.

As both Cahn and Van Heusen knew, writing a musical was much more demanding than contributing songs to a movie, even songs used within the movie, as opposed to title songs. Mark Steyn wrote of their effort, "This could have been their *Guys and Dolls*, but by this stage in their careers, neither man was interested in working that hard. So instead they turned in a better score than most movie musicals could boast back then, and left it at that."

Given the state of movie musicals at the time, that is truly damning with faint praise. However, the assessment is a bit unfair, given Van Heusen's less than stellar history writing for the stage, or even those films where he contributed numerous (more than 5) songs. He has uniformly shown himself incapable of constructing a uniformly solid score. There can be moments of greatness ("Here's That Rainy Day," "Darn That Dream,") but the remainder fails to live up to even the hint of the promise of those numbers. With that in mind, the score for *Robin and the 7 Hoods* exceeds all of the more substantive musical work Van Heusen had written.

The musical centerpiece of the film was "My Kind of Town (Chicago Is)." Introduced by a conversational, yet lyrical, verse, the song is propelled by the potential energy Van Heusen creates in the use of half notes with fermata immediately before the chorus and the use of a dotted half note to introduce each line, "My-y-y kind of town, Chicago is/"My-y-y kind of town, Chicago is." Then again, at the end of the first A section "Smile at you, and, each..." However, there is something unsatisfying about all of that energy being resolved in the four note patter, "Chicago, is." And, so, the song ends with an explosive coda, extolling all of the virtues of the town – "The Wrigley Building, Chicago Is/ The Union Stockyards, Chicago Is/Chicago is one town that won't let you down." Finally satisfied, Van Heusen ends it with one last burst of whole notes, shouting to the world "IT'S MY KIND OF TOWN." It is a brilliant moment in the film, exceeded only by those live performances of Sinatra, swinging the traditional Riddle arrangement, and, in a neat meshing of the two Chicago songs that defined his career, adding a coda incorporating the end of Fred Fisher's "Chicago" to later performances of the song.

The remainder of the songs in the film does not match "My Kind of Town", but that is an unfair bar. However, unlike Van Heusen's previous instances of contributions of numerous songs to a production, these songs are uniformly of superior quality. "Style" is a wonderful vehicle for Dean, Frank, and Bing. It is a cocky, fun number that provides the soundtrack for one of the most memorable sequences in the film. "Mr. Booze" is similarly good-natured fun. I doubt Norman Vincent Peale would have approved, but at least Van Heusen finally got around to writing a hymn. The Dean Martin number "Any Man Who Loves His Mother" and Sammy Davis' "Bang! Bang!" continue the action, without any appreciable decline in quality.

"Don't' Be A Do-Badder," while not one of the strongest songs in the film, demonstrates why only Van Heusen could have written the music for an original musical starring Bing and Frank. "Don't Be a Do-Badder" is a quintessential Crosby number – an exhortative tale to youngsters. It could not be "High Hopes" for Crosby, any more than "High Hopes" could be written as "Swinging on a Star" for Sinatra. Each singer demanded (and was entitled to) his own non-derivative style of composing, and only Van Heusen could provide that. "Don't Be a Do-Badder" was a uniquely Crosby song, in a film produced and starring Frank Sinatra.

It is no surprise in this retelling of Robin Hood that Sinatra is Robin Hood, or "Robbo." And, since this is Robin Hood, there must be a Maid Marian. That role is ably filled by Barbara Rush. Something, though, is missing. We have Sinatra putting his own unique spin on one of the great romantic heroes. We have one of the great couples of literature. We have Cahn and Van Heusen. What this film does not have is a love song. The blame for that does not lie at the feet of Cahn and Van Heusen. They wrote the charming "I Like to Lead When I Dance" for Sinatra to sing to Barbara Rush. It was ultimately recorded by Sinatra for the film (and released as a single), but it was cut from the film. Van Heusen crafts a trademark subtle melody, steeped in chromatic and harmonic nuance. It is a difficult song to sing, demanding exacting attention to detail. Cahn's lyric, while not his best, makes great use of the title, with its deeper message obscured by the disarmingly smooth Van Heusen melody and Cahn's wordsmithing. Leading the dance is code for being in charge. Was this a veiled shout to the men of the United States, who were slowly becoming embroiled in the emasculating counterculture of the 1960s? Was this one last shout from the men of Eisenhower's America?

In the end, *Robin and the 7 Hoods* was not *Guys and Dolls*. It was, though, a fun way for the Rat Pack to ride into the sunset.

THIRTY-NINE

Jimmy Van Heusen kicking back on a flight
Courtesy Van Heusen Music Photo Archives

September of My Years

There are opportunities in popular music where composers are able to perfectly capture a singer's personality. It is not a question solely of talent or familiarity. The timing is essential. The moment is vital. By 1965, it was clear that the era of ring-a-ding-ding was over. Van Heusen was 52; Sinatra about to turn 50. Their music was slowly, but inevitably replaced from the pop charts by rock. Moreover, the Beatles were starting to demonstrate the musical ingenuity that would catapult them to stratospheric heights. No more could rock be considered "cretinous goon" music. The Sinatra movies, such as they were, no longer captured the imagination.

The simple fact was they were getting older. However, instead of running from the inevitable or otherwise engaging in demeaning antics, Sinatra embraced the possibilities of maturity with his landmark album, *September of My Years*. It was by far Sinatra's deepest philosophical album, providing a measured look at the joys and sorrows of aging. The last (and heretofore, only) album Sinatra had a title song composed for was *Ring-A-Ding-Ding*.[24] Sinatra again turned to Cahn and Van Heusen for the title song of the "coming of age" album. Van Heusen complied with "September of My Years." It was brilliant. The conversational, yet lyrical melody, perfectly framed Cahn's nature-inspired lyric. There was no climactic crescendo. There was no big-note ending. It was a purposeful, reflective song. Here was a song that had Sinatra gladly accepting maturity, it was not something to be feared or resented. Age was to be approached while "smiling gently." By doing so, Sinatra was telling his generation it was okay to grow old, and for many, his was the tacit approval that was needed, and another generation moved to accept the responsibilities of middle age and senior citizenry. Sinatra recorded "September of My Years," and he would frequently perform it. The concert mainstay of the album, though, was the folk song, "It Was a Very Good Year."

---

24   Van Heusen and Cahn were commissioned to write a title song to All Alone, a collection of waltzes. Not surprisingly, they created "Come Waltz With Me." Sinatra recorded it, but decided not to use it as the title song, nor, in fact, to release it at all. Steve Lawrence would give it some life with his recording, but it was decidedly not their best effort.

This is unfortunate, as it had the tendency to overshadow other brilliant original songs on the album. One such was Cahn and Van Heusen's, "It Gets Lonely Early." This is not the same loneliness as in "Only the Lonely." This is the loneliness brought by the empty nest. Once again, there is acceptance and joy, with the past not full of regret but "truly wonderful." Both Cahn and Van Heusen numbers were written with verses, and for once, Sinatra recorded them. However, these verses were not mere throwaway introductions, but vital mood setting devices, without which, the song would lose some degree of meaning and depth. "September of My Years" opens with the singer realizing he has reached the near mid-point of his life – September – too quickly. He wonders where the springs and winters of his lifetime have gone. The verse in "It Gets Lonely Early" introduces us to the family man, without his family.

"September of My Years" would mark the last time Van Heusen would pen a concept album song for Sinatra. In fact, the team would write only two more songs specifically for Sinatra – "When Somebody Loves You" and "I Wouldn't Trade Christmas," and both have been mercifully forgotten.

FORTY

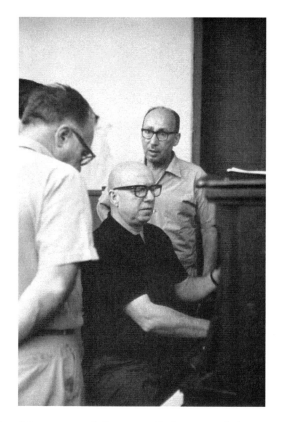

Jimmy Van Heusen and Sammy Cahn practicing songs for the Broadway show Skyscraper.
Photo Courtesy Van Heusen Photo Archives

Ev'rybody Has the Right to be Wrong

Confronted with a change in musical culture, Van Heusen and Cahn turned their attentions east to New York, Broadway to be exact. There were several aborted attempts: the team was slated to score the 1960 Lucille Ball show *Wildcat*, but due to legal entanglements, that task went to Cy Coleman and Carolyn Leigh. They also wanted to write a musical based on the British stories involving the gentleman thief, "Raffles." That too, however, did not come to fruition. Not for any lack of interest, but during the early 1960's, Van Heusen was too busy – writing film songs, traveling the world, campaigning for JFK, bedding beautiful women, and gallivanting with Sinatra. The money was rolling in, and it seemed Van Heusen had his finger solidly on the pulse of American musical culture.

Seemingly overnight, things changed. However, the popular usurpation of rock over jazz/swing was both gradual and inevitable. The bobby soxers were now the CEO's, and

Van Heusen's music was the preference of the establishment. It was a transition Van Heusen was neither prepared nor equipped to weather. For a musician trained in the art of subtlety, there was little refuge in the late 1960's. Rock had put music on a race to the bottom where shock value rather than innovation was prized. Who needed the subtlety of a raised eyebrow or double entendre when it now was permissible for you to simply tell a girl you wanted to have sex. Instead of defending its turf, Van Heusen's style of music retreated. What was considered the great American songbook would fall from popular consciousness, and an entire generation would be raised associating the finest music America has produced with corny routines on the Lawrence Welk Show.

The one venue where subtlety and craft survived in music during this time, and arguably to the present, was Broadway. The Great White Way sitting as a modern-day Constantinople, futilely struggling against the barbarian tide, preserving a noble musical legacy, so, eastward, Van Heusen fled.

Van Heusen and Cahn were under contract with the legendary Cy Feuer (*Guys and Dolls*) and Earnest H. Martin to produce two musicals for release in 1965 and 1966. Van

Heusen had a significant backlog of material and considered the idea of a musical not to be daunting, and in fact, a pleasant change of pace. It remained the one medium he could not conquer. This time, it would seem, there would be no excuses. Unlike 1939, the musical was fully developed and audiences were used to sophisticated music. Cahn was certainly mentally and physically healthy, unlike Burke. And, for once, the team had the time to concentrate on the effort.

However, things appeared to have been confused well before the team even signed their contract. The producers never seemed to have a clear idea as to what type of show they wanted to create. They had first developed a plot surrounding a woman who refused to sell her historic brownstone building to developers hoping to erect a skyscraper in its location. In fact, the Feuer and Martin had announced in 1957 that they were going to create a musical based on this premise. But, nothing happened. In 1959, they announced a musicalization of the Elmer Rice play *Dream Girl*, which tells the story of a "female Walter Mitty" taken to "occasional flights of fancy." Once again, though, nothing came of this project.

Despite Feuer and Martin's affinity for these stories, it was a third idea that resulted in the first Broadway show for which Van Heusen and Cahn would provide a score – a musicalization of the Roger Brighouse play, *Hobson's Choice*. It was to be called, *Walking Happy*," and would feature many of the songs written for, but discarded from *Papa's Delicate Condition* in 1956. Van Heusen and Cahn completed their score rather quickly, but to be fair, they had a bit of a head start, in addition to their recycled songs for *Papa's Delicate Condition*. As early as 1960, the team was crafting songs for a musicalization of *Hobson's Choice*, only the hope was for it to star Frank Sinatra in a Paramount production.

The score was prepared, and the producers had landed Mary Martin to star. When Ms. Martin decided not to pursue the role, the decision was made to halt production of *Walking Happy* and move forward with another concept. This would combine the stories of the holdout property owner and the dream girl. The show would be called *Skyscraper*, and it, rather than *Walking Happy*, would be the first release of the new creative group, though the score for *Skyscraper* was written after they had completed the score for *Walking Happy*.

It was to be an unconventional experience, to say the least, and certainly one befitting the bizarre and portentous events surrounding the creation of this new creative team.

The plot of *Skyscraper* had to be tweaked to permit a love story. Georgina, the property owner, would be wooed by the architect tasked with attempting to change her mind to permit construction of the skyscraper. The two would, of course, be opposites – flaky woman versus practical man.

The casting of Georgina would be vital, and the show was very fortunate to have landed Julie Harris, who, at that time, was one of the biggest stars on Broadway. However, she was not a singer. That turned out to be rather convenient, because the material she was given to perform barely qualified as songs. Peter Marshall, cast as the architect, was given infinitely better material with which to work. That might have been deliberate, but it certainly does little to help audiences connect with the lead character, when you have given the choice numbers to the supporting cast.

Marshall and Van Heusen were already friends at the time of the production. Marshall had been in California since the mid-1950's when he was working at the legendary Palm Springs nightspot, the Chi Chi Club. Marshall availed himself of the famous Van Heusen hospitality throughout his time. Like most, Marshall recalled that Van Heusen's home was open to everybody and was fully stocked with food, booze, clothes, and women. A frequent guest in those times was Van Heusen's old friend Polly Adler, described by Marshall as a "sweet little yenta." It was apparently no contest that Marshall would be the male lead in Van Heusen's return to Broadway.

The score for *Skyscraper* was anchored by two exceptional songs that have justifiably survived the duration of the show – "Ev'rybody's Got the Right to Be Wrong" and "I Only Miss Her When I Think of Her." A hidden gem from the show was "More Than One Way," a song of near operatic drama by Van Heusen. It loses its effectiveness, though, outside the context of the show, and also suffers from some forced rhymes, namely "My hands are on the handle bars."

The show endured labor pains throughout the process, but especially during its tryout in Detroit at the Fisher Theatre. Sammy Cahn recalled, "We were trying it out at the Fisher Theatre in Detroit, and one night we went to the traditional hotel room and co-producer Ernie Martin, who is succinct, said, " We have no show." He also said the first thing we should do was get a new "book." Peter Stone, who had written the book, is really a considerable talent, as well as a good soldier – if I ever go into the trenches again I want to go with

Peter. He locked himself in a room and wrote a different act every two days of the run."

A portion of the problem was that they had a non-singing leading lady. Van Heusen had worked with this particular obstacle when he wrote for Dorothy Lamour, but Julie Harris, as talented as an actress as she was, compared unfavorably to Ms. Lamour. Moreover, the music that Van Heusen wrote was not simple fare and required considerable skill to carry it off – a live performance was unforgiving to even the most-seasoned singer. Compounding this issue was that Ms. Harris did not have a particularly strong voice. Given the limitations of amplification equipment at that time, a rather unique and perhaps bawdy solution was crafted. A full microphone was inserted in Ms. Harris' shirt. Given the phallic nature of the device, Marshall, Van Heusen, and certainly some other cohorts, christened it the "dildo mike."

Marshall and Van Heusen got along well during the show, not only because of their similar personalities, but also because Marshall worked diligently on the show and offered suggestions that served to highlight the strongest numbers that Van Heusen wrote. When it was clear that Ms. Harris was having difficulty with "Ev'rybody Has The Right to Be Wrong,"

Marshall suggested that he sing the song, with Ms. Harris' character providing a brief reprise. Van Heusen mockingly derided Marshall's suggestions saying, "You little shit. You have the two best songs in the show (I'll Only Miss Her When I Think of Her" and "More Than One Way"), now you want the other?" But, Van Heusen, as well as the rest of the team, knew that Marshall was correct. To use a baseball analogy, you need to put your strongest hitters in the best position to knock in runs.

Marshall's instincts extended beyond the music in the show. He tells the story of a piano player and singer at a bar located near the Fisher Theatre in Detroit. He told Van Heusen that there was a great group of guys who had come up with a fantastic song that Van Heusen needed to hear. Never one to miss a bar date, Van Heusen and Cahn went over, heard the song, deemed it "workmanlike" and left. Marshall said that the songwriters would have given the song away, well, for a song. But not that night. They did eventually sell it, though, and we know it today as "For Once in My Life" – a standard by any definition and a long time concert staple of Sinatra.

Cahn wrote, "At the end of three weeks, we came to New York, where the consensus was: we have a first act."

However, there was a problem – the role of the shifty accountant, Roger Summerhill, originally performed by Victor Spinelli, was recast at the very last minute to star Charles Nelson Reilly. He was cast with practically no rehearsal time, entering the show only days before opening night. His performance caused a significant problem for Van Heusen. Namely, he found it so hysterical that his laughter from the wings could be heard onstage and was disturbing the players.

Not every last minute tweak was a success. Van Heusen and Cahn wrote, "Haute Couture" for the preview performance, and it was a showstopper. Unfortunately, the performer forgot the lyrics. A special rehearsal was held for the song, but once again, during the preview, the lyrics were forgotten. It was worked back into the show for later performances, but to the show's detriment, the number was not included in opening night.

Skyscraper ran for 248 performances, from November 13, 1965, to November 11, 1966. The show was nominated for Best Musical, Best Director (Cy Feuer), Best Choreography (Michael Kidd), Best Scenic Design (Robert Randolph), and Best Actress (Julie Harris). Of these nominations, the last is certainly the most ironic, especially given the opinion of Sammy Cahn of

Ms. Harris' performance. He was plainly averse to her casting, and in fact, attempted to avoid hearing her singing altogether. A neat trick, to be sure, in a musical. He wrote, "Each time she sang, I couldn't help it – I left the theater. (Usually in the theater when the book (script) is playing, the song men leave the theater, and when the song takes over, the book author leaves. Julie Harris reversed tradition."

There are many reasons why *Skyscraper* was not the success a Van Heusen/Cahn musical was supposed to be. Ms. Harris' performance was nowhere near the top of the list. There were better shows running on Broadway at that time. It was a banner year for Broadway in 1964, with the premieres of *Hello, Dolly!, Funny Girl,* and *Fiddler on the Roof* – all of which were still running when *Skyscraper* opened. In addition, also released in 1965 was *Man of La Mancha.* There was the fact that the musical focused on a corporation's desire to alter the traditional landscape of New York, when the people of New York were mobilizing to preserve its architectural landmarks. However, when a musical fails, it is, more often than not, that the score simply did not satisfy. And such is the case with *Skyscraper.* Despite the inclusion of some very nice songs, the score was simply not high caliber. There was a vast chasm between the outstanding selections from the score and the other numbers. Van Heusen's songs lacked charm, they meandered; many of them simply had no discernible melody. In his review of the re-release of the *Skyscraper* cast album, Steven Suskin put its aptly when he wrote, "Van Heusen and Cahn seem to have consciously written typical pop songs and then added unrelated mini-songs at the top. Not verses, which should naturally lead into the refrain, but separate sets of music and lyrics that attempt to link the song that follows to the scene that preceded it." The song "Opposites" typifies the dashed expectations of this first Broadway musical. This semi-duet between Marshall and Harris should have been cast in the mold of the Crosby/Hope numbers from the "Road" pictures, and to be sure, the audience was expecting it. It never came. In its stead came a wordy Cahn lyric that seemed to have been written merely to rhyme "dinner" with "Yul Brynner" and a Van Heusen melody that is devoid of charm. At some point, the audience understood that, despite their hopes, Hope and Crosby were not going to be strolling on stage. Those days, it would appear, were over.

Cahn described *Skyscraper* as "a devastating experience – which nearly separated some of us from our senses." That might be a bit of an overstatement, considering the score, but it did yield two bona fide standards. However, it was a very public swing and a miss, or at least, not the extra base hit everyone expected. Suskin offers a darker take: "Perhaps the worst year ever for Broadway musicals was 1965. (Up until 1965, that is.)...*Skyscraper* wasn't the worst, but it was pretty far down on the list."

FORTY-ONE

An announcement for the musical, Walking Happy
Image Courtesy of Van Heusen Photo Archives

Walking Happy

Martin and Feuer followed up *Skyscraper* almost immediately with *Walking Happy*. *Skyscraper* closed on November 11, 1966. Barely waiting for the body to cool, *Walking Happy* opened on November 26, 1966.

Mary Martin's decision not to star in *Walking Happy* led the producers to delay production of *Walking* Happy until Ms. Martin could be persuaded to accept the part. This never occurred. As such, the producers were compelled to find a suitable replacement for Ms. Martin. To that end, they turned to Louise Troy, an established Broadway actress but not particularly offering much star power. She was nominated for Best Featured Actress in a Musical in 1963 for *Tovarich* and in 1964 for *High Spirits*. Also starring, in his first appearance in the United States, was the dynamic Norman Wisdom, a comedy film star in the United Kingdom whose career in 1966 was starting to wane. Both were capable and competent performers, but not particularly able to draw crowds. To the extent there was a star, it would be the team of Cahn and Van Heusen. However, would this show suffer from a *Skyscraper* "hangover?"

Walking Happy opened to near unanimous positive reviews. The critics were uniform in their praise of Norman Wisdom. Van Heusen and Cahn's score was infinitely superior to *Skyscraper*, to the point where one wonders if the men wrote the two shows. Considering the show was largely written a decade previously, the observation is not altogether unreasonable. Nevertheless, the show closed after only 161 performances.

Why?

Again, as strong as *Walking Happy* was, it was facing *Man of La Mancha, Hello, Dolly!, Funny Girl, Fiddler on the Roof,* and now, released in 1966, *Mame, Sweet Charity,* and *Cabaret.* Indeed, it was in comparison to *Cabaret* that *Walking Happy* seemed to suffer, not because the score was significantly better, but because *Cabaret* was an edgier, racier, more modern musical. *Walking Happy* was a pleasant nostalgic journey, while *Cabaret* was cutting edge. Ten years prior, perhaps, *Walking Happy* would have been a blockbuster. In 1966, however, it appeared to be additional evidence that Van Heusen and Cahn were out of touch.

It might have been fitting that the show was about a cobbler, given the score was cobbled together from songs from various sources. Whatever its source, *Walking Happy* was the most consistent large score that Van Heusen ever composed for the stage. It comes closest to fulfilling the expectations that an audience should have for the composer of his stature. The score is charming, melodic, daring and contains songs that should rightly be considered standards. It is unfortunate that, with the possible exception of the title song, the entirety of the lot has been forgotten.

Of particular note is "What Makes It Happen," a lovely ballad. Worthy companions to this number are "If I Be Your Best Chance," "Where Was I," and "I'll Make a Man of the Man." Within the rhythm numbers, "Walking Happy" is ably joined by "Just Use Your Noggin" and "How D'Ya Talk to A Girl?" To be sure, these songs were intimately connected to the plot, and without its context, lost their impact. What is important is that the score for *Walking Happy* cannot fairly be considered the reason for the show's failure.

Despite multiple Tony nominations (including a second for Van Heusen and Cahn), a failure it was. And, such as it was, it was the last major project of Van Heusen's career. The Van Heusen/Cahn team would labor through two more years, during which they wrote catchy title songs for two Julie Andrews projects – *Thoroughly Modern Millie* (1967) and *Star* (1968), both of which earned Academy Award nominations. "Thoroughly Modern Millie" was one final flash of originality from Van Heusen, as he successfully produced a fusion of classic swing pop with the music of the Roaring '20's. They also contributed six original songs to a 1967 animated musical version of *Jack and the Beanstalk*, and original songs to a 1968 television production of *The Legend of Robin Hood*. Slowly, but surely, though, the phone stopped ringing. The times had changed, and Van Heusen, at least, saw no reason to tarnish his legacy by writing in popular idioms that he did not fully grasp nor with which he could identify. The Van Heusen/Cahn era, therefore, ended in 1969 with their meager contributions to the Zero Mostel oater, *The Great Bank Robbery*.

FORTY-TWO

Bobbe Brock and Jimmy Van Heusen at their Yucca Valley Ranch
Courtesy of Van Heusen Photo Archives

The Tender Trap

For Van Heusen, though, his hard-living lifestyle was beginning to take a toll on his body. By 1967, he had been ordered by his doctor to stop drinking completely, lest he suffer complete liver failure. It was a directive that he reluctantly and imperfectly obeyed. A long time sufferer of back pain, Van Heusen underwent an experimental disc fusion surgery in the 1966. The surgery was not successful, and worse, due to possible negligence, Van Heusen's pain increased dramatically following the surgery. His mobility was limited, and his lifestyle significantly curtailed.

The recuperative period had a much darker effect on Van Heusen. Because of the pain he endured, his physicians proscribed pain killers. Without the palliative effect of his beloved booze, Van Heusen became more and more dependent on the painkillers. There is even some indication that the painkillers were "supplemented" by mood-altering medications such as Ritalin. The effect on Van Heusen was disastrous. He became withdrawn, paranoid and increasingly isolated from his friends and colleagues, essentially retreating to his Yucca Valley ranch.

It was out of this relative chaos that Van Heusen found the saving grace of his life. Already something of a fixture in the Palm Springs social set, Bobbe Brock was a woman who was well acquainted with the world that Van Heusen inhabited. She was born Josephine Brock in 1901 in Memphis, Tennessee, the middle sister of Kathlyn and Eunice Brock. The girls decided to form a singing group – "The Brock Sisters" – and traveled to Broadway in the early 1920's. They were cast in Irving Berlin's *Music Box Revue of 1921*. It was at Berlin's suggestion that the ladies renamed themselves "The Brox Sisters." First name changes were also in order: Kathlyn became "Patricia," Eunice became "Lorayne," and following a brief time as "Dagmar," Josephine became "Bobbe." The sisters became a favorite of Berlin, and were featured in his 1923 and 1924 revues. This led to additional roles in other Broadway revues, including those featuring the Marx Brothers. They were offered recording contracts with Brunswick and Victor, and their records were best-sellers. They were popular stars on

Broadway, and like many other such stars, they were poached by Hollywood with the advent of the talking picture. In 1928, the sisters made a number of Vitaphone short subjects. In 1929, they starred in their first full-length feature film, *Revue of Revues*, during which they, along with several others, performed "Singin' in the Rain." Appearances would follow in 1930 with *The King of Jazz* – featuring Paul Whiteman and The Rhythm Boys (including a young Bing Crosby) – and *Spring is Here*. The latter would be their last appearance in a film. The group disbanded in the early '30's, in no small part due to Bobbe's marriage to William Perlberg, the group's agent. Perlberg would eventually become one of the most powerful producers in Hollywood, adding his name to such motion pictures as *The Country Girl*, *Miracle on 34th Street*, *Song of Bernadette*, *State Fair*, and *The Bridges at Toko-Ri*. Bobbe and "Bill," as he was known to friends, remained married until his death in 1968.

Bobbe was a striking blonde, exactly the type of woman whom any man, but especially Van Heusen, would be attracted. It is unclear as to how they specifically met, but it would be fair to assume that their social circles, even during Van Heusen's relative solitude, often intersected. They bonded over their love of music and horses, and given the recent death of her husband, a desire for mutual companionship. She was some 12 years his senior, and offered a sense of grounding that previous women were unable to do, or perhaps, Van Heusen was unwilling to accept. More important, she had lived the Hollywood lifestyle (as both participant and spouse), and presumably had her fill of it. At that time, Van Heusen was similarly finished with the same things, although it is not altogether clear that it was his choice. Medical issues were plaguing him, he was unable to drink, and the tide of popular culture was against him.

It was fortunate, though, that for the first time in his life, he really did not have the need to work. He had substantial income from the royalties from his music. He was not in debt, and he had savings. It was time, at last, to enjoy the wealth he had worked so hard to amass. Of course, all of that was threatened by the self-destructive path he was currently traveling.

It is not an exaggeration to say that Bobbe saved Jimmy's life. She moved in with him, weaned him from the painkillers and nursed him back to health. He slowly reappeared on the Palm Springs set, but Bobbe knew that continued exposure to Hollywood and the temptations therein could be deadly for Jimmy. A photo of Jimmy and Bobbe taken in 1969 in Palm Springs shows a gaunt Van Heusen, worlds away from the vibrant, healthy man of just two years ago. All through his life Jimmy was in tune with his body. Sammy Cahn recalled him as a "walking Merck manual," having diagnosed himself with a hernia and self-medicating through injections of Vitamin B-12. And so, now, he knew what he needed. He and Bobbe were married in 1969.

Bobbe was astute enough to know that the lure of Hollywood, the well-meaning temptations of his friends, and Jimmy's general disposition to please all people would inevitably lead to problems and hinder his recovery. They needed to move. She took Jimmy east, very near to where it all began in upstate New York, to the bucolic community of Brant Lake. They left their Yucca Valley ranches, transported their prized horses across country and began a quiet new life. Jimmy was still Jimmy, though, and he acquired his Brant Lake property in true Van Heusen style. Upon taking a boat ride on their first day in Brant Lake, Jimmy saw a piece of property he liked. He bought it the same day.

From thereon, Van Heusen lived a very quiet life in upstate New York with Bobbe. He was so unassuming that very few of the townspeople knew that a man of his celebrity was in their midst. On those rare occasions where they would entertain, Van Heusen would play the piano, offering people a glimpse of his former life. Still, though, it was Bobbe who offered the entree into Brant Lake society, so much so, that when Sinatra offered Van Heusen nearly 40 tickets to his show in Saratoga in 1975 to open the Saratoga Performing Arts Center, it was Bobbe who needed to round up the audience!

While Jimmy and Bobbe were comfortable, they had fallen far from the economic status they had once enjoyed. Jimmy, generous to a fault, would give – not loan – money to anyone who asked. His home, furnishings, food and booze were free to anyone who asked. He lacked any real financial sense, and made a number of foolish investment choices. Compounding the stress, royalties diminished due to the decline in the popularity of his music. Most significant, though, both Bobbe and he were unable to sell their rather large Yucca Valley ranches. The mortgages proved to be crippling. The party was over.

FORTY-THREE

Van Heusen relaxing in Yucca Valley, California
Photo courtesy of Van Heusen Photo Archives

It Gets Lonely Early

Unlike many of his contemporaries, Van Heusen accepted the marginalization of his music and the decline of his celebrity with indifference. While he certainly did not like rock music, he did not resent the success that those musicians and performers enjoyed. In particular, he thought highly of the music of the Beatles, Kris Kristofferson, Barry Manilow, and Carole Bayer Sager. In a 1981 interview, Van Heusen expressed hope that he could work with Sager on a Broadway musical.

When pressed, though, the one artist with whom he wanted to make one last charge at Broadway was Johnny Mercer. It was with Mercer that Van Heusen wrote his last song – the 1974 Frank Sinatra saloon song, "Empty Tables." The melody has been described as "boozy," with all the requisite implications of melancholy, wistfulness and tedium. It was, however, a fitting end to Van Heusen's songwriting career and his creative association with Sinatra. What better way to bow out than with a song about a bar as metaphor for life and love.

Van Heusen would continue to write songs throughout his retirement. These ranged from spirituals with lyrics by Bobbe to countless unnamed melodies that still remain unpublished in the Van Heusen archives. There was one last, incomplete assignment from Sinatra, though – a request for three songs for an upcoming "suicide album." Van Heusen was to write them with the great Yip Harburg, but only one was finished. The title was "Love Being What It Is." Harburg fell ill and died in 1981 before completing any other lyrics. Given the timing of Harburg's death and the characterization of the project as a "suicide album" by Van Heusen, it is almost certain that the Sinatra album was *She Shot Me Down*.

It was a lovely song, making one regret that the two could not have worked together more. Van Heusen's melody is fresh. There is the hint of transition into a different style of songwriting, not quite as deliberately harmonically complex, more bucolic, and the almost simplistic Harburg's lyric bears repeating:

Nature doesn't work discreetly
Blossoms bloom as sweetly
Tho our love is done.
And she points out rather neatly
That it's all begun and won
Or lost in fun.
Might have been a different tale
But love's a breeze
And I'm a sail.
And who am I to dare to question my lot
Love being what it is.
How can I blame the waning moon,
The rose that withers all too soon
If love must fade well then it's part of the plot
Love being what it is.
Since, you wandered by,
Like, a firefly
Love was mine to know
And if not love
At least the glow
If tears could talk and words could weep
If splintered hearts could only sleep
Perhaps I could forget the way you forgot
Love being what it is.

It would have been nice to have had Sinatra record it.

Even during the height of his career, the name "Van Heusen" never merited the level of recognition that a composer of his stature deserved. During his retirement, as his popular songs faded from the airwaves, his name vanished to near obscurity. Among the musically literate, though, his place was secure, and it was always the appreciation of musicians that Van Heusen treasured. As such, of all his awards, it is his election in 1971 to the Songwriters Hall of Fame that Van Heusen prized the most. Membership was voted on by his peers, fellow songwriters and musicians. It was of great pride to him that he was selected in the first class, following its founding.

It could be considered Van Heusen's last public shining hour took place in his hometown of Syracuse, New York in 1986. The Civic Center's Crouse-Hinds Theater was filled to its 1,848 capacity, for an all-star tribute to Van Heusen called "High Hopes." It was hosted by Tony Randall, and featured performances by Tony Bennett, Margaret Whiting, Jack Jones, Maxine Sullivan and Sammy Cahn. Telegrams of congratulations poured in from President Ronald Reagan, Frank Sinatra, Irving Berlin, Bob Hope and Hal David. At the end of the three-hour festivity, Van Heusen took to the piano to perform "High Hopes" with the performers. Overcome with emotion, he told the audience, "It's hard to find the right words to thank you for this wonderful evening. It means even more to me that it happened in my hometown."

During that final celebration, Jimmy was accompanied by Sammy for all public interviews. This physical proximity belied a secret carefully hidden throughout their profitable professional association: the two did not like each other personally. Jimmy did not care for Sammy's constant self-promotion (even of the material Van Heusen composed). As we have learned, Van Heusen shunned the spotlight, hated awards shows and was most comfortable in the background. His previous collaborators shared this aversion. For Van Heusen, the performer was the star, and the composers were satellites upon whom the star reflected its light.

Of course, Sammy and Jimmy had dramatically different concepts of social life. Sammy was a family man while Van Heusen was the perpetual bachelor. This carefree lifestyle certainly helped him solidify his relationship with Sinatra, freeing him to partake in late nights and shenanigans Cahn was unable to (and perhaps unwilling to) participate in. Ever protective of his status as "Sinatra's lyricist," Sammy no doubt saw Van Heusen's close friendship with Sinatra as a threat, or at least a mild irritant.

Ultimately, though, it may have been the manner in which Van Heusen exited the scene that miffed his former partner. Cahn came from very humble beginnings and worked very hard to achieve both professional and financial success. Knowing the fickle nature of the business, he had seen – and was seeing – numerous stars marginalized by the rapidly changing concept of popular music. Van Heusen, even though his career was impacted by physical ailments, essentially stopped composing in the late 1960's, leaving Cahn without a partner. Cahn was seemingly deserted by a second long-time collaborator, and there appeared to be no suitable replacement candidates anywhere on the horizon. Indeed, until his death in 1993, Cahn did not work with a steady partner.[25]

Cahn never visited Van Heusen following his retirement, despite spending a great deal of time on the East Coast, including starring in a 1974 Broadway show featuring his lyrics (many of which were set to Van Heusen's music),

---

[25] He did return to work with old partner Jule Styne for the 1970 Broadway musical *Look to the Lillies*, for which he wrote the lovely, eminently Cahn-esque, "I, Yes Me, That's Who."

Words and Music. The show featured ribald, sometimes apocryphal tales, of the creation of songs, and it highlighted the brilliant but boisterous qualities of Van Heusen. Indeed, there was still gold to be panned from the "team," and there was no productive use in casting the light of truth on the personal nature of their relationship.

So, without the soothing (financial) balm of songwriting to salve an underlying dislike, absence permitted the heart to grow less fond. On discussing Van Heusen with a friend of Van Heusen, Cahn purportedly inquired of the friend as to why Van Heusen "never liked him." Without waiting for an answer, Cahn, to paraphrase, said "Van Heusen never liked Sammy Cahn because he wanted to be Sammy Cahn." The friend reportedly responded that the preceding statement was exactly why Van Heusen did not like Cahn. Van Heusen would sooner have watched his soul leave his body than to ever make such an egocentric remark. It is not unfair to assume that Van Heusen heard (and might have been subjected to) his fair share of those comments throughout their professional relationship.

Even the sight of an infirm, wheelchair-bound Van Heusen receiving his hometown tribute did nothing to heal the old wounds. Outside the spotlight, Cahn was very cold to Van Heusen, seemingly resenting Van Heusen's lack of mobility. For his part, Van Heusen found speaking difficult, and could only easily communicate by use of facial expressions due to a recent stroke. However, any doubts about his feelings are dispelled by Barbara Sinatra's recollection of her and Frank's visit to Van Heusen on his deathbed. In her book, *Lady Blue Eyes*, Mrs. Sinatra wrote, "When Frank and I went to visit Jimmy toward the end, he was lying on a couch and could barely manage a facial expression because of paralysis. Frank (knowing of the team's feelings for each other) leaned forward and said, 'Sammy Cahn's here Jim. He wants to see you.' Well, Jimmy's face twisted into a grimace then like you wouldn't believe. Bless his heart."

The purpose of these anecdotes is not to scandalize the public perception of this great songwriting team. In fact, it is quite the opposite. If anything, this speaks to the highest degree of professionalism and integrity each man brought to his art. They both knew they were presented with a special and unique opportunity to create music for the finest exponent of American popular song. The songs they wrote were evidence that the two were destined to create together. Only

Sammy Cahn could write the lyrics to "All the Way." Only Jimmy Van Heusen could give voice to "September of My Years." As recipients of their genius, we, the listening public, owe both men a debt of gratitude that they did not permit petty personal differences to undermine the greater good of their art. Would that others would be so selfless.

FORTY-FOUR

Jimmy Van Heusen's marker located in the Sinatra Family Burial Plot in Desert Memorial Park located at Cathedral City, California.
Courtesy of Van Heusen Photo Archives

The Last Dance

Jimmy and Bobbe returned to live predominantly in Palm Springs in 1986. They had always maintained residences on both coasts (including a Manhattan apartment), but they decided that the time had come to move westward. They were not in California long when Jimmy suffered a second, more serious stroke, rendering him essentially incapacitated. He was unable to move without great assistance, but, fittingly, his principal means of communicating was through the piano, which he retained his ability to play. Never was that more poignantly displayed as when Brook Babcock and his father Don (Jimmy's nephew) visited Jimmy in California in 1987. Brook recalled Bobbe bringing Jimmy out to greet Don and him, and while unable to speak, played the piano for a brief time. For the entire three hour visit, Jimmy sat there in silence, occasionally playing a tune. Only when Don and Brook rose to leave did Jimmy muster the ability to say, "Goodbye." It was the last time either man would see Jimmy alive, and it would bring tears to their eyes.

In his time of greatest need (physically and financially), in swooped Frank Sinatra. Sinatra made sure that during this time all of Jimmy's expenses would be paid, that his friend would want for nothing. And when Jimmy died on February 7, 1990, with Bobbe by his side, Sinatra paid for the funeral and burial, and he delivered the eulogy at the intimate service. Van Heusen is interred in the Sinatra family burial plot, with the simple inscription on his grave marker, "Swinging on a Star."

I am sure he is.